COLLAPSE

To Larry and Linda — With love! Medora

COLLAPSE

DREAMING ANOTHER WORLD

Medora Woods

Wise Ink Creative Publishing

ISBN 13: 978-1-63489-186-8

Printed in the United States of America
First Printing: 2019
23 22 21 20 19   5 4 3 2 1

Cover design by Dan Pitts
Interior design by Patrick Maloney

Wise Ink Creative Publishing replaces every tree used in printing their books by planting thousands of trees every year in reforestation programs. Learn more at wiseink.com.

Content reproduced with permission from:

Chiron Publications. 400 Linden Avenue. Wilmette, IL.

Psychological Perspectives. Taylor and Francis Group, LLC. 325 Chestnut Street. Philadelphia, PA.

Quadrant: Journal of the C. G. Jung Foundation for Analytical Psychology. XXIX:2. (1999) Pp. 37-52.

In the words of my dearest *maśke*, Rosalie Little Thunder,
Siçangu Lakota, teacher, scholar, artist, warrior, and friend:

You belong to the collective.
Don't go wandering off or you will perish.

CONTENTS

PREFACE

My relationship to the story I tell in this book began in the early 1990s when I was training to become a Jungian psychoanalyst. A decade before, I had left my life as a lawyer working in a bank trust department and eventually found my way into Jungian analysis. If feminism took me into the very male worlds of law, banking, and business, it also carried me beyond those worlds into a fascination with feminist psychology and eventually to the most urgent of all questions: How have we come to the point where the global society we have collectively created threatens itself and all of us with collapse?

I went into Jungian analysis in the mid-1980s believing a story about myself and my life. That story emerged from memory and family mythology. It was also powerfully influenced by everything I had unconsciously absorbed as a woman growing up in Euro-American culture in a very particular place and time. I gradually became aware of that story through a meandering, nonlinear analytic process which lasted more than a decade.

In this book, I offer my perspective on the origins of what I call Western consciousness as another meandering, nonlinear story, one I followed for over two decades until it reached the point where it was ready to tell. Just as my experience of analysis wandered around unconscious personal, family, and cultural stories so that I might start to see them clearly and do my best to let them go, this book wanders around unconscious stories I believe we in Western society must make conscious in order to become aware of the part they play in creating our unsustainable world.

One particular story, an ancient Babylonian creation myth, offers an image I see underlying our culture's destructive dissociation from the earth, our fellow creatures, and each other. It is the story of the Hero who kills and dismembers the Mother-of-all and creates the world out of her pieces. If a culture's myths are also its collective dreams, I believe Western culture's dream of the heroic individual and his creations has come to the end of its usefulness. It is time to dream another dream.

I went into analysis to recover from childhood trauma. I didn't understand that at the time; I only knew that I had experienced a collapse of meaning and couldn't find my way forward. In the same way, I imagine that the images of that ancient Babylonian creation myth underlie a pervasive unhealed trauma: for the earth, for our fellow creatures, for our communities, and for those of us who live in that story. We are experiencing a collective collapse of meaning.

I make no claims for the story I tell: that it is true or correct, or that it definitively answers the imperative questions so many are asking in these perilous times. It is only my personal meditation on those questions. There are many stories about the challenges we face as a global society and how humans might meet them, individually and collectively. I am grateful that the tellers of these stories share them with the rest of us. I listen to as many as I can and weave them into my understanding of the larger shared story in which we now live.

I am also grateful beyond words for my experiences of working with indigenous colleagues, writers, and friends. I learned from them that there are ancient stories which can lead us to a deep understanding of the fundamental interconnection and interdependence of all life. The story I tell in this book is not their story; that story is not mine to tell. But their stories opened my eyes to my own.

Western consciousness dreamed our unsustainable global society into being. We are now dreaming its end. There will be no way through that story until we are willing to face it squarely and look unflinchingly at the world we have created. We have everything we need to dream another world. We need only the desire.

COLLAPSE: THE BRIDGE

On August 1, 2007, shortly before six thirty in the evening of a very hot day, I was at the computer in the study of my house in the quiet, leafy suburban neighborhood where I live, just outside the city of Minneapolis. As I half listened to our local public radio station, something unusual about the sound of the announcer's voice tugged at my attention. He sounded breathless, dramatic. Something about a bridge . . .

I walked into the kitchen and turned on the television. I was immediately disoriented. What on earth was I looking at? There were cars, buses, and trucks hurled in all directions, some at impossible angles, huge slabs of roadway fractured and upended with cars perched precariously on their sloping sides and broken edges. A truck in flames sat dangerously close to a tilted school bus; perhaps it was the school bus. The raw places from September 11 and Hurricane Katrina opened up. I burst into tears and wept on and off for the rest of the evening.

As I wept, I didn't know that dozens of people who lived on the shore of the river had rushed to the site. Without care for their own safety, they began rescuing people. Some on the broken bridge miraculously walked away from smashed vehicles with only scratches and went immediately to help others. As it turned out, the backed-up rush-hour traffic made it difficult for first responders to get quickly to the scene. The volunteers made the crucial difference between the tragedy of thirteen deaths and the potential for many, many more. They jumped into swift water to help struggling people out of the almost ninety vehicles that had been thrown into the river. They climbed the jumbled slabs of concrete to help dazed and injured people out of cars and trucks. In the school bus, a young camp counselor with extraordinary presence of mind helped lead all the children away from the burning truck and off the bridge to safety.

A friend bicycled to the 10th Avenue bridge, parallel to the I-35W bridge and just downriver, reaching it only forty-five minutes after the collapse. He later told me that by the time he arrived, the "rescue" part of the search-and-rescue effort was over. The grim search remained. The community watched sadly for the three agonizing weeks required for divers from all over the country to brave murky water and jagged wreckage and force the river to give up our dead. The removal of each body from the river was marked by prayerful silence among those at the scene. The nearby 10th Avenue bridge was closed to traffic and onlookers until everyone missing had been found. When the search operations were done, the *Minneapolis Star Tribune* reported that all those who had perished in the river—Peter, Sadiya, Hana, Vera, Richard, Christine, Scott, and Greg—had been recovered and united with their families.

Later that fall, editors of a local magazine reflected on the tragedy, linking the collapse victims to the demographic community we were in the summer of 2007:

Official explanations would have to wait for at least a year, we were told. Meantime we could only shake our heads at the perverse improbability of the disaster and, per Minnesotans' stoic tradition, remind ourselves that it could have been worse. Given the fact that more than 100 vehicles (including construction equipment) were on the span when its center buckled and the heavy sections both north and south gave way and fell, there could easily have been, according to authorities, 14, 40, or 140 dead. . . . So many of the parts of the local "demographic" circa 2007 seemed to have suffered a loss.

Their ages ranged from twenty-two months to sixty years. Seven were male, six were female. There were students, professional people, and what we used to call blue collar workers. There were lifelong Twin Citians, foreign-born, and an undocumented immigrant. There were married men and women, fathers and mothers, singles, and divorcees. There were residents of the inner city, major suburbs, and towns on the periphery of the greater Twin Cities. Familiar northern European

surnames—Hausmann, Engebretsen, and Holmes—shared the list
of the dead with a Native American name, Blackhawk, and not-so-
familiar names from around the world: Sacorafas (Greece), Sahal (So-
malia), Chit (Cambodia), Trinidad-Mena (Mexico)
    At 6:05 on August 1, they all shared the bridge.

Of all the stories of people who perished, one haunts me. Sadiya
and Hana Sahal were mother and daughter. Sadiya was barely in
her twenties and was pregnant. Hana was almost two, the only
child to die. As I remember their photo on the *Minneapolis Star
Tribune* website, it was of a serenely beautiful, brown-skinned
woman in pale blue, traditional Muslim dress, head modestly
covered by a hijab, holding a laughing naked toddler on her lap.
Madonna and Child for the twenty-first century. Only we—the collective, institutional "we" that had built and cared for that bridge—
had failed them, and they were dead. Any one of us could have
been on that bridge.

I was stunned and foggy for days. I couldn't stop thinking about
what it might have been like, sitting in stalled traffic at the end of a
too-hot summer day, annoyed at the delay, perhaps, thinking of ordinary things, when suddenly, brutally, the known world vanishes
and I, my vehicle, and the pavement itself drop sixty feet through
space—crashing to earth or plunging into dark, rushing water, as
everyone and everything on the bridge falls with an enormous
rumble and shudder, falls into pure and terrible chaos. So many in
the community drove on that huge bridge. It is on my son's regular
route to and from work. I kept thinking about Persephone inno-
cently picking flowers in a field as the earth opens up with a roar
and Hades and his chariot rush out of the darkness to snatch her,
wrenching her away from her mother and carrying her off to rule
over the Land of the Dead.

On September 10 I went to see the collapse site. The 10th Avenue
bridge had recently reopened to pedestrians, bicycles, and cars.
I saw no sign of damaged vehicles, in or out of the river, or of any
debris other than huge pieces of broken bridge. One of the two

sections that had fallen into the river was gone, and the other was almost gone, nothing left but a skeleton of green metal floating on dark water. A third collapsed section on the east bank of the river was being broken up with jackhammers. Their faraway sound floated up through the stillness. Giant machines carted smashed wreckage away. An official-looking boat or raft with a canopy rested quietly just downriver of the bridge remains.

It was a perfect Minnesotan early fall day. Perhaps like the beginning of September 11 in New York City, almost exactly six years before. The air was exceptionally clear, the edges of everything especially sharp. Clouds like dark-bottomed cotton balls clustered in intense blue sky above tall downtown buildings upriver, almost close enough to touch. My jacket was too warm in the afternoon sun, but the breeze from the river was cool. During the weeks the 10th Avenue bridge had been closed, the city had made ample room for pedestrians and bicycles on the collapse side. Chain-link fence had been installed above the railing. Sturdy concrete barriers separated us from heavy traffic moving at a funereal pace, faces staring toward the collapsed bridge. I was touched by the thoughtfulness of the city bureaucracy in making space for us, despite the detriment to traffic.

The bridge that Monday afternoon wasn't a mournful place, but it wasn't a cheerful tourist place either. Dozens of people walked about and stood at the railing, some staring sadly or quietly at the river, some talking in hushed voices, some taking photos. I walked three-quarters of the way across in order to get a full view and then slowly, very slowly, walked back. I felt compelled to stop and look, time after time. It seemed as if others there felt what I felt, something much greater and more mysterious than the work below. I needed to stand very still as I stared, not exactly at the collapse site but in that direction, sensing presence beneath the human activity. I didn't want to leave. The workers, the broken bridge, the clouds, the city, the river, the onlookers: we floated in timelessness.

Some days later, again in the *Minneapolis Star Tribune*, I came across an arresting thought from William Morrish, director of the Design Center for American Urban Landscape at the University of Minnesota. He said that the bridge collapse, like Katrina, changed the collapse site from secular to sacred because of the loss of life. Exactly. The collapse site was now sacred space. But I wondered if it were not the other way around. That it wasn't the loss of life that created sacred space, but that an explosive irruption of the sacred had broken through the veil between worlds, destroying the bridge, killing thirteen people and wounding almost a hundred and fifty more, profoundly altering daily life in a large Midwestern city. The sacred lingered at the site; power beyond words.

Hurricane Katrina devastated a city described as the soul of this country, where the Mississippi River meets the Gulf of Mexico. The I-35w bridge collapsed into that same river in the city nearest its headwaters, a river central to American history, mythology, and economic life, a plumb line of moving water dropped through the middle of the country.

How could these events not be connected?

Toward the end of September, I had lunch with a former colleague. Almost as an afterthought, just as we were about to leave, he told this story: It was after midnight on August 2. He and his wife were asleep below deck on a small boat on which they and two other couples were sailing the Adriatic Sea. The boat was moored just off the town of Lumbarda on the eastern side of an island off Croatia.

Suddenly, both of them were jolted awake by violent rocking, exactly like the rocking they had felt the night before during a fierce storm. Going up to the deck to find the source of the disturbance, they were surprised to find the harbor perfectly calm. They returned to their cabin, puzzled, wondering if they'd both been dreaming about the previous night's storm, as odd as that coincidence might be. The next day, renting motor scooters in a hotel lobby, they heard a radio announcer mention Minneapolis, St. Paul, and the Mississippi River in a news report that was otherwise in Croatian. Curious, my friend and his wife went to a nearby internet café, where they learned what had happened.

It was a while before they realized that they had been shaken awake just as a giant bridge collapsed on the other side of the world.

I was not the only one in my community who felt sacred space at the site of the bridge collapse. I read more than one description of it in the days that followed. As the catastrophe penetrated community consciousness—first of the onlookers, next of the first responders, later of the entire community—I felt a palpable sense of connection in a deep collective grief. That sense of connection persisted in a myriad of ways, small and large, individual and communal, throughout the aftermath of the collapse and the rebuilding of the bridge. On the one-year anniversary of the collapse, precisely at 6:05 p.m., local television stations silently broadcast photos of those who had perished. I watched, standing silently in my kitchen, the same place I had been the year before. The city held a ceremony down by the river and announced plans for a small memorial park near the spot of the collapse.

The bridge collapse site rapidly became a construction site. I visited it again on a cold, sunny early-spring day. Now there were signs describing exactly what we, the onlookers, were seeing in the jumble of cranes and construction equipment that was creating a much more imposing bridge in record speed, dwarfing the collapsed bridge which had once seemed so massive and brutally broken. I remember being there and some of what I saw, but it is not etched into my memory the way the first visit is.

The sense of the sacred was gone.

There had been a design contest for the new bridge, and the four final proposals were widely circulated. Drawings of the proposed bridges were published, and members of the community weighed in on them and the eventual choice. I was pleased that one of the requirements, besides sturdiness and redundancy, was that the river be visible to drivers on the bridge. In all the times I had driven across the bridge that collapsed, I had not known that I was on a bridge.

On the late September day in 2008 when the rebuilt bridge opened at 5:00 a.m., a caravan of cars lined up to go across for the first time since that terrible August day when the bridge went down. A friend, one of those early-morning people to drive across the bridge, told me he had been pulled there for reasons he couldn't articulate—reasons of the heart, not the head.

The collapse of the Interstate-35W bridge seized me and would not let me go. With a vague sense that I might someday write about it, I methodically printed out all the stories I could find about the collapse and the aftermath in the *Minneapolis Star Tribune* and other publications, putting them in a pile in a cabinet in my study. It was a large pile, as stories about the survivors, the replacement bridge, and the legal questions continued to engage the community for almost two years. The newspaper was one of the important ways in which the community came together around the tragedy, with stories, photos, letters from readers, opinion columns, blogs, and videos illuminating our shared trauma from many perspectives.

I bought an image of the empty collapsed bridge from a local photographer. It had won a prize at the Minnesota State Fair slightly more than a year after the collapse. The image shows the broken bridge and—beyond it, up the river—the city, underneath a strip of pale, slightly clouded, dawn sky. The city is lit with warm, pink light from the rising sun on a late August morning a few weeks after the collapse, the broken bridge dark in just-before-dawn shadow. Framed, it is more than four feet long and takes up one wall of my study. For two years it reminded me that the collapsed bridge was waiting. It took me those two years to start to understand what it wanted from me. I believe what it wanted is this, what you are now reading.

What is going on in this brand-new century? A giant freeway bridge collapses into a great American river. Jet airplanes fly into towering buildings, turning them into massive skyscrapers of smoke and fire and death. Our government makes wars that bring chaos and death to millions of people we don't even know—and to our own. Waves of water destroy a cherished American city. Japan is devastated by a tsunami, damaging a nuclear power plant that is releasing the worst of all toxins, radioactivity, into the sea, creating wreckage that, as I write, still washes up on our west coast. An earthquake destroys the city of Port-au-Prince, the human infrastructure and built infrastructure of a small island nation shattered beyond imagining. Dead migrant children wash up on the beaches of the Mediterranean Sea. Record droughts, storms, and fires plague large swaths of the planet, burning the rain forests of our Pacific Northwest. Ten-thousand-year-old glaciers melt and begin to disappear. As I begin this writing, the worst economic meltdown in generations, perhaps ever in our nation's history, persists. What story are these events telling us? Why now?

These events, in their inhuman magnitude and devastation, are apocalyptic. An apocalypse (Greek: *Apokálypsis*; "lifting of the veil" or "revelation") is a disclosure of something hidden from the majority of humankind in an era dominated by falsehood and misconception. The veil being lifted is the *calypsos*, derived from the Greek *kalupto* or *kalypto*, meaning to cover, to veil, to hide, or to conceal. In John's apocalypse, the <u>Book of Revelation</u>, he refers to the "unveiling" or "revelation" of <u>Jesus Christ</u> as the <u>Messiah</u>. To evoke the idea of apocalypse is to summon an image of the end of the world.

While there are all too real, flesh-and-blood consequences of these apocalyptic events, these events are also our collective dream. This collective dream, these terrifying images—what do they tell me about the dreamer? What in our times so desperately needs to be revealed? Where must we strip away the veil of lies and unconsciousness about the world we have created? And who is that dreamer but all of us, the human community?

Humanity dreamed this world into being. Are we are now dreaming its end?

I search for a way to understand these times other than the end-time language that tenses my body and shuts down my heart. When I fear the End of the World, I am caught in the illusion of linear time and the archetype of Apocalypse. Even if my body lives in linear time, my soul does not and the soul of the world does not.

These times may also be the beginning of a world yet to be. As storyteller Michael Meade says about the great ongoing round of human existence:

> People have always feared The End. Fear of the end of the world has been there from the very beginning of it. The End has been repeatedly predicted and religiously expected, yet has never arrived. Sometimes the greatest safety comes from going to where the fear seems to originate. Facing The End may be the best way to begin again. Amidst the roaring of the threatened and troubled world, surprising ways to begin it all again may wait to be found.

Or, as writer and activist Rebecca Solnit puts it, "Again and again, far stranger things happen than the end of the world."

There is wisdom in the depths of our fear, our feelings of terrible vulnerability in a world careening out of control. The empty, broken bridge in the just-before-dawn light speaks to me of two worlds. There is a bridge that needs to be (re)built, a bridge between the world coming to an end and a world yet to be, a bridge between the society we've become and the society we so desperately need. Just as almost everyone in the city drove over the seemingly indestructible bridge, just as it could have been any one of us, any one of the people we love, the image of the broken bridge forcibly reminds me that everyone and everything is connected to everyone and everything else. Just as the dawn light in the photo pushes back the darkness, the bridge photo speaks a wordless truth; we are between worlds, the old one in shadow and the new one barely dawning. There are many, many stories about the nature of those worlds, where we've been and where we are going. This is mine.

DISCOVERING WESTERN CONSCIOUSNESS

In the spring of 1997, I graduated from the psychoanalytic training program of the Inter-Regional Society of Jungian Analysts. As part of my training, I was required to write a thesis. I was fascinated by the question of how our collective cultural life creates and molds the way each of us sees the world. In particular, I was drawn to explore what I think of as Western consciousness, that way of seeing and organizing the world which originated on the shores of the Mediterranean almost five thousand years ago and which came to the lands Euro-Americans inhabit over five hundred years ago. I let my unanswered questions and the interest they sparked in me guide my reading and thinking.

I was drawn to writings by indigenous people, those who call themselves "indigenous" because their ancestors inhabited a particular land for millennia and because they often understand themselves to be the original inhabitants of that land. Those writings were windows onto other worlds, their worlds. Imagining myself into their worlds opened me up to an outsider's perspective on my culture. I began to see how little I had understood about our history with the millions of peoples who were here when the European settlers came, whose ancestors had lived for millennia on the lands we now think of as the North American continent. I learned another name for the North American continent, their name. As poet Gary Snyder says about that name:

> Turtle Island—the old/new name for the continent, based on many creation myths of the people who have been living here for millennia, and reapplied by some of them to "North America" in recent years. . . . A name: that we may see ourselves more accurately on this continent of watersheds and life-communities—plant zones,

physiographic provinces, culture areas; following natural boundaries. The "U.S.A" and its states and counties are arbitrary . . .
impositions on what is really here.

Shortly after I graduated, I met an indigenous international activist and began my travels in the actual Indian Country, as opposed to the one I'd been reading about and imagining. Other
Indian people and organizations dropped into my life, and a few
years later I left the world of Jungian analysts and my clinical practice in order to work as an activist and experience that other world
more deeply and personally. I was drawn to something I couldn't
articulate then and probably don't understand completely even
now.

I knew that if I were to let what I learned there inform and inhabit
what I think and write, that it would be wrong of me to take something from Indian Country and give nothing back. That would be
repeating, in a small way, the five-hundred-year relationship between the European settlers, who my Indian activist friends sometimes call "invaders" and "colonizers," and the original and still-in-
digenous inhabitants of this land.

I see now that I needed to go deeply into a world in the shadow of
my Euro-American culture in order to learn something about that
world and my own, about the cultural other and myself. I didn't
just go physically into that world; I went into an unknown part of
my psyche, my personal part of the cultural unknown, in order to
illuminate both at the same time. How do I ever sort out what's just
me, what's out there, and what's something shared by all of us in
contemporary Euro-American life? How do I draw a line between
the inner world of experience, memory, and imagination and the
outer world, which I imagine is just what it is? How do I differenti-
ate between the world of each of us as individuals and the world of
all of us as a collective?

I can't draw those lines. I realize now that for decades I've been
exploring the ways in which each of our minds—influenced more
than we can ever know by our culture, our time in history, our

place in geography and our language—creates vastly different worlds. Each of us creates our own. These worlds exist side by side, mostly invisible to each other, jostling and interpenetrating, sometimes in collisions we are not even aware of.

When my older grandson was small, he created an imaginary planet. As he said to me then, everybody has their own planet. He was so right. For a long time, I've attempted the near impossible, trying to penetrate those other worlds and learn about them from the inside, always from within my own world, peering out through lenses my life history and cultural context have created.

With that understanding, I write about wandering in Indian Country and the questions I was pursuing there about the nature of dominant Western culture and consciousness and everything that lies outside them. As I pursued those questions, the answers gradually wove a story about the world that may be coming to an end, about the possibility of renewal, the story I am now attempting to tell. Everything I say is colored by the fact that I am a Euro-American woman with Eastern European Jewish, German, and Irish ancestors, some who arrived on this continent before the Revolutionary War and some who arrived at the beginning of the last century. I was born at the beginning of World War II. I grew up in the hilly, wooded suburbs of New York City, in a family with particular rules, expectations, and taboos. I have been educated in the institutions of my culture. I carry in my very being a perspective I will never see clearly. Expecting anything else would be like expecting a fish to understand that it is in water.

I will inevitably blur the lines between inner and outer to tell this story. The Indian Country I explore is both "in here" and "out there" and what I call "the dominant Western consciousness" is both Euro-American consciousness and my own. I have tried and failed to write something abstract and theoretical, objective and impersonal, about my research into our shared consciousness and what I imagine lies beyond it. I can't write about the nature of Euro-American consciousness and not write about my own. My

mind is both the tool I use to explore and the object of my explo-
ration. As someone said at a long-ago gathering of women in New
Mexico: "I dip my paintbrush in the river I paint."

The myth of scientific objectivity says there is a bright line between my inner world of thoughts, feelings, fantasies, memories,
images, and dreams and the world beyond my skin. One is subjective and the other is objective. I can manipulate objects in the
outer world; all too often the inner world manipulates me. But
the two are separate, says the Cartesian myth. In one I can make
measurements, perform experiments, and get results. In the other
I can't.

Scientific objectivity is a useful myth. It has allowed human culture to achieve technological miracles that were unimaginable
fifty years ago, never mind to my ancestors. My childhood self who
loved to read and write could not have imagined writing with a research tool that corrects my spelling and allows me to look up a
word like "hegemony" without opening a book. Nor could I have
imagined reading a book on a small tablet on my lap and sending
it back into the invisible "cloud" when I'm done with it. The difficulty comes when I identify with the myth of scientific objectivity
and imagine that it explains everything. Then I imagine that what
cannot be perceived by my physical senses, measured, or manipulated, doesn't exist.

Although work on the frontiers of theoretical physics and mathematics has been challenging the hegemony of that myth since
early in the twentieth century, it is astonishing how little that scientific understanding has unsettled my everyday certainties. It is
hard to accept that the world I experience is not just exactly what
it seems. When quantum mechanics takes me beyond the visible
world, I become Alice, exploring the topsy-turvy world behind the
looking glass. To use just one well-worn example, in the quantum
world, light is neither a particle nor a wave. Its state at any moment
depends on the experiment used to measure it. Recent ideas about
dark matter and dark energy tell me that most of the universe is

invisible to my senses and to science's most sophisticated measuring instruments. I inhabit and understand an infinitesimally small piece of that universe.

In the early twentieth century, as physicists and mathematicians described the strange worlds which underlie the world apparent to my senses, psychological pioneers, starting with Sigmund Freud and C. G. Jung, called attention to the importance of what lies below the surface of conscious awareness, challenging ideas about the sensing and measuring mind itself. They threw out assumptions of objectivity and certainty and focused on what they called "the unconscious," that invisible inner filmmaker which creates and projects a story onto my experiences, a story into which I fit everything I experience and call it "reality."

These men are my ancestors. However I may agree or disagree with them in particular ways, they and those they inspired have allowed me to question everything about how I see the world, to wonder what unconscious inner story creates what I imagine exists outside me, to wonder how the shared unconscious inner stories of Western culture create what we collectively imagine exists. The shared inner stories of the Western way of seeing the world dream the lived world into being. The nightmares of the twentieth century have become the apocalyptic visions and events of the twenty-first.

The ancient Hermetic saying "as above; so below" continues on to say "as within; so without." If we think of the horrific events of this new century as a collective dream, they are a desperately urgent wake-up call for the dreamer. Jung said that dreams speak about all that lies beyond ordinary consciousness, particularly what Jung called "the shadow": everything I reject about who I am, everything my mind pushes out of awareness. I am capable of everything that humans have ever been, the best and the worst. Much of my potential lies out of my awareness because I resist knowing that I act every day in ways I'd be ashamed to admit or knowing that I am capable of so much more than I have ever imagined.

Our Euro-American cultural heritage also drives certain potentials for good or evil out of collective awareness, as well as the parts of our history that don't conform to cherished beliefs about who we are as a culture or as a nation. I know from years of working to bring my own unconscious stories to light that searching for what is out of awareness, using the very awareness that is choosing not to see certain truths about itself, is tricky business.

There is no easy path to the psychological realities contained in the deepest part of my shadow. I can look for clues, for subtle, easy-to-miss hints. I can listen for marginalized and rejected voices speaking from the fringes of my consciousness and my culture. I can notice what upsets me and arouses my defensiveness and judgment. And I can pay attention to my visions and dreams. From my experience, as a Jungian analyst and someone who had years of Jungian analysis, I know it can be dangerous not to listen to dreams. Jung said that what we do not handle psychologically in the inner world we will experience in the outer world as fate. What I imagine as outside me—difficult bosses, infuriating friends, accidents and illness, situations that are not of my choosing—are just parts of me knocking on my psychic doors, insisting on being let in.

It is often painful and, at best, disorienting to let those parts of me in. There are good reasons why I have kept them at bay. But finally accepting, even loving, myself as a deeply imperfect human being, capable of everything I have despised and envied in others, is the doorway to a fully lived life. At some point along the way, I arrived at a strange combination of belief in my personal agency, ability to follow my passions and create my own life, and humility about how little I understand about life and how little I control. I feel more securely grounded in the particular person I am.

Just as individuals have shadow, rejected, and unknown parts of themselves, so do collectives: groups, communities, nations, and cultures. When I describe my experience of the sacred at the site of the collapse of the I-35W bridge, when I imagine that the sacred had irrupted into the everyday world, destroying the bridge and killing thirteen people, when I tell the story of my friends being awakened on a boat in the Adriatic Sea, I am hinting at something hard to articulate in a culture caught up in the myth of scientific objectivity.

If an analytic patient had brought a dream in which the I-35W bridge collapsed, I would have understood that something significant was pressing to become conscious, something that involved much more than a slight shift in awareness to include a neglected part of her personality. The dream would warn us both that an urgently necessary and radical transformation of her most essential psychic structures was demanding her conscious attention, one which would be experienced by my patient, at least initially, as profoundly destructive. The dream would tell me that a transformation of my patient's psychic structures would be necessary if she were to become fully engaged in life. She would be presented with the necessity of a life-changing paradigm shift.

If the collapse of the I-35W bridge is a collective dream, what does it say about the dreamer? The image of the bridge collapse resists rigid, reductive interpretations, humbling me as I touch the irresolvable mystery at its core, that experience of the sacred which compelled my presence to it at the collapse site. At the most obvious level, it is an event, a cataclysmic tragedy beyond words that reminds me how powerless and vulnerable humans truly are and how completely interconnected I am. Any of us, any one of the people we love, could have been on that bridge. I will consider the bridge collapse from a number of angles, letting this tragedy inform me as I ask, What must end if life is to be served? I want to try to find meaning in a terrible event which destroyed the lives of its victims and brought my city to its knees.

VOICES OF THE COMMUNITY

For me and for my community, the unthinkable happened on that steamy August day. An apparently sturdy bridge at the heart of our city fell down. A stunned Senator Amy Klobuchar spoke for the community when she said that in Minnesota bridges shouldn't just fall down. Not only is Minnesota not a "third-world country"—shorthand for someplace far away, where I imagine shoddy construction and inept governance are common—but also Minnesota has seen itself for many years as a solid and effective, good-government state. If something like this could happen in Minnesota, it could happen anywhere.

Our state bard, Garrison Keillor, who was in New York at the time of the collapse, voiced my feelings, not just my shock and sorrow at the loss of the bridge and those who perished, but also my feelings of terrible vulnerability and abandonment, my sense of outrage. If I didn't understand after a hurricane destroyed New Orleans and I saw the horrific aftermath, maybe now I would. We're on our own.

The bridge collapse was front-page news in New York . . . and for three days running. Bridges are not supposed to fall down unless there is an earthquake. People die in violent storms, plane crashes, epidemics, but a person is supposed to be able to drive home on a summer evening and cross a river on a steel truss bridge and not find himself plunging headlong into the abyss. . . .

Minnesota is a state of rivers, the Old Man and his many tributaries, and what is unsettling is the list released by the state showing 36 major bridges even more deficient than the bridge that fell down. . . . The day when we look to big government for solutions to our transportation problems is gone. . . . [I]t's up to us to solve our own problems. . . . Don't expect Minnesota to take care of you.

I was among those who saw in the story of the bridge collapse a tragic commentary about the dilapidated state of the nation's roads and bridges, just one casualty of a concerted focus on the evils of government and taxation for over thirty years, the far-from-benign neglect of almost every aspect of this country's social and physical infrastructure. The assumption has been that the anti-government movement started with President Reagan, who declared government to be "the problem." Or with political activist Grover Norquist, who famously desired to shrink government to the size where it could be drowned in the bathtub. But Reagan, Norquist, and their followers are just the latest manifestation of an individualistic, anti-collective attitude that has always existed in Western culture. It is an attitude which began to dominate this country with the robber barons that made fortunes from industrialization, beginning in the second half of the nineteenth century.

President Eisenhower warned in vain of the dangers of the military-industrial complex. A lifelong Democrat, I never imagined as a child that I would ever agree with President Eisenhower. Our household was fiercely loyal to Adlai Stevenson, the balding, articulate intellectual with the famous hole in his shoe, who was electorally crushed by Eisenhower in the '50s. Twice. But Ike was right. The years since his presidency have seen an unwavering commitment to armament and war as our national treasure has been siphoned off to fill the pockets of weapons manufacturers and the military-industrial establishment.

I learned in high school American History that the governmental and corporate elites realized at the end of World War II that the nation faced a stark question. How was government going to stimulate the economy to produce the jobs necessary to continue the recovery from the Great Depression, when the country had pulled itself out of an economic abyss only by ramping up the all-pervasive war economy of World War II?

I dimly remember the war effort, the white margarine in a plastic bag that was squeezed and kneaded by hand in order to break a little sac of red-orange food coloring and turn the margarine yellow so my family could imagine we were spreading butter on our toast. The bald, irreplaceable tires on our little black Pontiac convertible coupe, one of which went flat and stranded me and my mother on a trip to New England right around V-E day, just before my birthday. The coffee cans of congealed fat from cooked meat that my mother faithfully brought to the butcher behind the counter in the Gristedes grocery store at the center of the little town where I grew up. And my plaintive question (I was told years later) about whether sugar would "ever be free?"

I understand the years of World War II to have been an unprecedented and never-repeated moment of shared mission and shared sacrifice. The war effort had brought the country out of a terrible economic depression, made more protracted by a collective failure to understand the kind of persistent ongoing investment in shared social and built infrastructure which was required. What would take its place?

The country could either invest in a vast war machine—which would require testing from time to time in combat, reducing our stockpile so it would need to be replenished—or invest in our national infrastructure, providing the dual benefit of giving jobs to vast numbers of working people and maintaining the physical and social fabric to hold us all in a viable, healthy community. Those who had the power to make that choice decided to invest in an ever-growing war machine. The war machine required permanent war. A story that began in the middle of the 1940s and dominated political understanding during my childhood and my early adult life justified never-ending war. We were the leaders of a "free world," locked in a permanent struggle against the menace of communism. Community or communism? The similarity of those two words is not an accident, nor was our choice.

The years just after World War II are often understood as

economically vibrant years during which a comfortable middle class was created and supported. The fiercely individualistic ideology of the robber barons had temporarily lost ground to a progressive movement championing community, relationship, and responsibility during President Roosevelt's New Deal, a movement that was in the air I breathed as a child because my parents were part of it, living and working in Washington, DC when I was born in 1941.

I didn't understand when I became a young adult that, though they were continued and strengthened in the latter half of the twentieth century, the social innovations of the Depression years— Social Security, unemployment insurance, strict bank regulation to prevent self-dealing and self-interest, eventually Medicare— were from their very inception targets of those who saw no reason why their wealth should go to support the innumerable others who had caused their own economic misery by being shiftless, lazy, and undeserving. Once the country shifted rightward, once Reaganomics took hold, I was angry and sad when I realized that the New Deal had been the aberration, that the dominant political culture of the latter part of the twentieth century would come to be selfish, hard-hearted, and mean-spirited.

Even my beloved adopted state eventually succumbed to that culture. When my husband and I moved to Minnesota in the early 1960s, we were very involved in the politics of the Democratic-Farmer-Labor party, the DFL. The political wars between Republicans and Democrats were hard fought, but, whichever party held the statehouse or the governor's mansion, a commitment to education, infrastructure, and social programs was assumed, even if we had different ideas about how best to achieve our shared goals. We tinkered with the existing structures around the margins.

At some point, those shared assumptions vanished, both in Minnesota and the rest of the country. Now, the understanding that we have a moral, and practical, obligation to care for and support all our citizens has all but disappeared. The prevailing refrain among those who increasingly dominate the political discourse is "no new taxes." The man who was governor of the state when the bridge collapsed twice vetoed an increase in the gas tax to repair our crumbling roads and bridges, the connecting links among us. As I observe our increasingly raucous and polarized political discourse, I don't feel a shared sense of how interconnected we all are, how poverty and neglect in one part of our community diminish us all.

In the autumn of the year the rebuilt bridge was opened, Thomas Fisher, now a professor of architecture and director of the Metropolitan Design Center at the University of Minnesota, wrote a piece in a local magazine about the shifting balance between public and private investment.

> When it comes to bridges, it has been the best of times and the worst of times. Minneapolis, the site of the first bridge over the Mississippi, now has two other firsts along the river: the building of the Guthrie Theater's "endless bridge," the longest occupied cantilever in the country; and the collapse of the I-35 bridge, the largest such collapse in the U.S. not caused by wind or earthquakes.
>
> . . . Those two bridges reflect . . . a shifting view of the good life. Although Congress funded the interstate highway system in the 1950's largely for national security reasons, that system also facilitated suburban sprawl. . . . Some 50 years later, Congress' decision seems more like a well-intentioned idea gone awry, given the highways' part in the abandonment of our cities and the pollution of our air. Like the I-35W bridge, the hopes of the interstate highway system seem to lie like ruins in the river of our dreams.
>
> . . . The interstate highway system represents one of the largest public investments ever made in this country to facilitate peoples' withdrawal from the public.
>
> . . . Whatever the ultimate cause of the I-35W bridge collapse, no one doubts the effect of deferred maintenance on its demise, a reflection of the public sector's underinvestment in infrastructure repair, to the tune of trillions of dollars. Meanwhile, the federal government has been cutting taxes to spur private investment, which has helped fund the philanthropy to build structures like the Guthrie Theater.

Fisher's piece trails off without fully exploring the implications of what he is saying. He doesn't mention that the crisscrossing of America by the interstate highway system was less a response to a public opportunity or a "well-intentioned idea" than a response to pressure from oil, gasoline, and automobile interests, that, even in Minnesota, mass transit was destroyed as the community ripped up and paved over perfectly useful streetcar lines and people became dependent on their automobiles. The federal government has not been "cutting taxes to spur private investment"; it has been cutting taxes to alleviate the "tax burden" on the corporations and well-off individuals who donate to political campaigns. I see the idea of "spurring private investment" as a convenient cover for selfishness.

Fisher briefly mentions two important developments in the evolution of the relationship between public and private choices in the latter half of the twentieth century and moving into the twenty-first, choices with far-reaching implications—implications I learned about when, in the late 1970s, I was on a committee for Citizens League, a Twin Cities public policy group, studying transportation in the metropolitan area. When the streetcar lines were ripped up, a piece of our shared social fabric went with them. Until that point, Minneapolis's neighborhoods had developed in tandem with the streetcar system; where the streetcars ran, so did housing and small businesses. When that link was severed and the freeways were built (destroying vibrant city neighborhoods in both Minneapolis and St. Paul), the central cities began to die.

The idea that transportation is a public good, that everyone in the community must be served, died with them. Freeway development in my community flung residents farther and farther out from the central city, allowing them to live out a fantasy that their fortunes were no longer inextricably interconnected with those they left behind, increasingly the poor and people of color. Individualism, whether the individual choice to drive alone from work to home or to disconnect home life and the education of children from life in the city, supported by decisions at the community level about where and to whom resources would be made available, increasingly frayed the social cohesion created by the policies of the New Deal or the sense of shared sacrifice many, like my parents, felt during World War II.

Fisher's piece seems ambivalent about the movement of our society away from a system in which elected officials make decisions about spending public dollars in ways that support a decent quality of life for everyone in the community and toward a system in which individuals at the top of the financial hierarchy make decisions about what's good for the rest of us. I wonder if philanthropists will be motivated to change the system that has been so generous to them. On my first visit to the new Guthrie Theatre, I noticed the name of a CEO of a local health insurance giant attached to a performance space. He had recently been investigated by the Securities and Exchange Commission for possible violations of securities law in relation to the dating of stock options. The Minnesota attorney general joined a shareholder lawsuit against the CEO's company raising the same question. Perhaps his contributions to the rest of us come out a wash.

The Twin Cities, where I have lived for most of my adult life, has been home to a vibrant and committed philanthropic community whose members have been extremely generous in their personal and financial support of its arts and educational institutions, very few of whom would ever be caught in self-dealing behavior. In an ideal world, public and private decisions would work side by side, complement, complete, and support each other. An absence of generous philanthropic decisions would terribly impoverish our shared community life. An absence of public decisions for the common good would destroy it.

In the months after the collapse, the *Minneapolis Star Tribune* reported all the factors that cascaded into that awful moment, dooming the bridge and thirteen of the people on it. The bridge was carrying twice as many cars as it was designed to carry. The gusset plates that held the beams in place were not designed properly for a bridge carrying that load, perhaps not even for the bridge as it was originally built. Bridge inspectors had been put off by the difficulty of getting to hard-to-reach places under the bridge covered in pigeon guano, so cracks in the gusset plates had gone unnoticed.

The repair work on the bridge that August day was eventually determined to have been the fatal blow. The surface of the bridge had been absorbing more and more of the stress that should have been handled by the underdesigned gusset plates. That surface was being removed in order to replace it. Heavy equipment and construction materials overloaded the bridge. The day had been especially hot, and traffic was stalled rather than moving quickly over the bridge.

The gusset plates gave way.

Eventually, the legal complicity of all the players was settled by lawsuits and the question that so obsessed me and the community for months after the collapse was answered: the construction company doing work on the bridge was found to be primarily at fault. As a lawyer, I appreciate the difficulty of sorting out many competing factors and arriving at a legal conclusion, but I also know that a legal resolution cannot perfectly answer a question implicating the judgment and actions of many people. If my community is unwilling to adequately fund infrastructure construction and repair, I am, to some degree, responsible. All parts of my city's freeway infrastructure are critical to its functioning, but the particular nexus this bridge has become is one of the most critical, a vital link that was brutally severed.

As systems theorists say, the system is perfectly designed to do what it does. The system was perfectly designed to achieve the collapse that happened that August day. If the community doesn't like the results, we need to look at the system and how it functions, not point fingers at one another or attempt to fix blame on any particular actor, although that is currently the only way that victims can be compensated for their loss.

All institutions and structures are created by fallible human beings. None of them will ever be perfect or perfectly safe. All of us—those involved in designing, building, and maintaining the bridge, those involved in the reconstruction effort taking place at the time of the collapse, and those who failed to insist that we have a communal obligation to adequately fund government programs ensuring the safety of the bridge—failed to imagine that the bridge could fall down.

We were wrong.

So, from one perspective, a dream about the i-35w bridge collapse would be about systemic failure. The imaginary patient who comes into my office with that dream has been warned that a critical part of her psychic infrastructure is in danger; something central about how she thinks about herself, how she views the world, is failing to serve life, her life, life as a whole. She is being asked to imagine her world in a radically different way.

If the dreamer is the community, the society, or the culture, the circumstances surrounding the collapse point to a radically disconnected society. Siçangu Lakota teacher and activist Rosalie Little Thunder taught what she called a "cultural map" of traditional Lakota lifeways, concentric circles describing ever-widening spheres of relationship and responsibility. Her circles began with the individual self and extended out to the Universe. When did ideas of community, relationship, and responsibility become un-American ideas condemned by right-wing TV pundits? Why?

As I move further into the symbolism of the dream, I ask, What is a bridge? A bridge connects two sides of a divide. So much of the current political discourse is dominated by polarities: red state/ blue state, liberal/conservative, individual/community . . . From a spiritual perspective, life in the material world always involves twoness; from the One comes Two and then the Many, the ten thousand things of the Tao de Ching. The embodied world always involves polarities: male/female, light/dark, day/night, and right/wrong. Yang and Yin.

It is easy to get caught in them, to take sides. Yet life in the material world of space-time is always ambiguous; one side of a polarity always implies the other, needs the other in order to exist. Yang and Yin are in an ongoing condition of perpetual oscillation, each containing the seed of the other. If I release my certainty about right and wrong, I must live with the ambiguity of direct experience. The Lakota say *takuskanskan*. Everything that moves is sacred; everything that is sacred moves.

The idea that direct experience is fundamentally ambiguous is the tension underlying the statement I made earlier about sacred space at the collapse site. How could an event that destroyed a critical piece of my city's infrastructure, killed thirteen people, and wounded so many others be a manifestation of the sacred? For me, the idea that it was thirteen tragic deaths that created sacred space at the collapse site pulls something fundamentally mysterious into the limited realm of human understanding. In a polarized, material world, the collapse of the bridge was an evil and someone must be held responsible. In an ambiguous, symbolic world, the collapse of the bridge points to something greater and more mysterious, the meaning of the collective dream the I-35w bridge became at 6:05 p.m. on August 1, 2007.

If I am to tease out some of the deeper possibilities of that dream, I will begin with Euro-American collective shadow because our national shadow is all that we have collectively chosen not to see, the veil of unconsciousness and illusion that invited an apocalyptic event. The dream tells me that something hidden in our national collective shadow urgently presses toward collective awareness. I begin with shadow because Euro-American shadow, like all individual and collective shadow, is a moral problem. All humans in the binary world of modern Western consciousness have shadow. In our world, unconsciousness is the necessary counterpart to consciousness. If I refuse to acknowledge and accept as much of my shadow as I humanly can, I am refusing to look squarely at the truth that I often cause suffering to myself and others.

Becoming conscious does not end suffering. It transforms neurotic suffering into real suffering. When I cause suffering to others, I have a moral responsibility to understand how I am injuring them and, to the best of my ability, stop. I have a responsibility to acknowledge to others that I have harmed them. I have a responsibility to experience the real suffering that for moral people always accompanies learning about the ways they have caused harm to another. What is true about my personal shadow is also true about my, and our, Euro-American cultural shadow.

EURO-AMERICAN CULTURAL SHADOW

One particularly dark part of our shared Euro-American cultural shadow is our history with the indigenous peoples who for millennia inhabited this land. From the perspective of my indigenous activist friends, the European invaders and their descendants exploited this land, seizing its resources to build the country of their dreams, violently pushing aside and killing its inhabitants, and then dropping the knowledge of that history into the shadow of our culture, where it has largely disappeared from everyday discussion.

Another dark chapter is our history with the African peoples who were brought to this country in chains and the fetid bellies of boats to be an indispensable part of the labor force that created the wealth of the country; the wealth that, in large part, neither they nor their indigenous brothers and sisters share. I can't ignore the Euro-American history with the African peoples, but my story has taken me into the particular part of the Euro-American cultural shadow inhabited by the native peoples of the Americas. I will not explore the African holocaust here, although I believe that much of what I have to say about Euro-American consciousness is equally relevant to that history and present-day reality.

I believe my personal and collective Euro-American ancestors seized the land of the original inhabitants of the Americas and traded other human beings as slaves because of the nature of the consciousness of their European ancestors. That consciousness, the inner world of the colonists and their descendants, has created the outer world of our history and our present-day society. It has created a world in which, again and again, the interests of individuals are imagined to be directly opposed to the needs of the community. First that consciousness creates the polarity between individual and community, and then it chooses one side of the polarity, pushing the community and its needs into the shadow. It creates a world in which a few wealthy, self-interested people control far too much of the world's benefits and resources, to the detriment of the rest of us and to the detriment of the earth.

The destructive impact of that consciousness must come to an end if the human species and our plant and animal relatives are to survive in any coherent way on the amazing, beautiful planet that is our home. What I am calling "Western consciousness" has pushed much of what it means to be human into Western cultural shadow. It is that limited awareness to which the apocalyptic events of this new century now come as disruptive and disturbing dreams.

I single out Euro-American consciousness and the history of North America because they are my consciousness and history as well as the consciousness and history of my personal and cultural ancestors. There are other kinds of consciousness that have had similar results in other parts of the world. There appears to be, still, a different orientation to the polarity between individual and community in some Eastern, or Asian, cultures, even if to a large extent the kind of consciousness I examine is coming to dominate those societies. An anthropologist whose work I will explore has called the two forms of awareness I am discussing "preconquest" and "postconquest" consciousness, and those words may come as close as any to telling the story I wish to tell.

Indian Country is mostly invisible in the world of Euro-Americans, but the world of Euro-Americans is all too visible in Indian Country. I was radicalized by my travels in Indian Country, and I can understand why many Euro-Americans resist seeing the country through an outsider's eyes. When I tried to describe what I was experiencing there to some of my good-hearted friends who are non-Indian, I was sometimes shocked at their reactions.

Much of it was defensive, pushing away what I was saying and minimizing its significance. What I was saying was old news, well-worn ground; why should anybody care about it now? I could not find language to penetrate those defenses. I felt unheard and invisible, often angry. My experience of invisibility mirrored the experience of those whose world I was attempting to describe. At those moments I was caught in the shadow of Euro-American culture along with them. The indigenous peoples of Turtle Island have long been unseen and unheard. Invisible. To see them and to deeply understand our history with them requires an awakening.

In 2005, I returned to my Jungian analytic training institute and presented a paper in which I tried to explain to my colleagues where I'd been. Here's a slightly revised version of what I said then:

I believe I am not being disrespectful when I use the term "Indian Country," as it is the term Native Peoples themselves use for a territory that seems to be both an actual place and a state of mind. "Indian" and "Native American" are among the names we have given to the First Peoples of Turtle Island, the indigenous name for this land we call the North American continent. These are not the names they have given themselves. Their real names often translate as some variant of "the people." Hundreds of communities of First Peoples, speaking well over a hundred languages, still exist within US borders, each with distinctive lifeways.

Where are your people from? Who are your people? These are among the first questions I often hear asked of a stranger in Indian Country. The answer locates the speaker in a web of relationships—with the land; with human, plant, and animal relatives; and with the ancestors and the unborn, whether or not the speaker is still living on the land where their ancestors' bones are buried. Hearing these questions always reminds me that I have walked across an invisible border into another country in the midst of my own. I think about the questions so often asked by Euro-Americans who don't know each other: What do you do? Where do you work?

Some years ago, at a powwow on the Rosebud Reservation, I

bought a T-shirt with an outline of the continental US and just the words "Indian Country" inside it. Over time, I have imagined levels of meaning in that image. It says that five hundred years ago, all of what we now call the continental United States was inhabited by indigenous peoples whose territory has been almost entirely taken from them. It gently mocks the artificial outline of the continental US, drawn by agreement among or conflict between European nation-states and without consultation with the indigenous peoples who lived and still live in communities severed by that line. And, finally, it speaks of the invisibility of the twenty-first-century First Peoples of Turtle Island.

Indian Country is everywhere and nowhere. The land my country occupies was once inhabited by many millions of indigenous peoples, and millions are here still. Many of their creation stories tell of the emergence of their people onto the land. Where did those peoples go? The First Peoples and our history with them have been almost completely erased from our cultural memory and our day-to-day perceptions. That invisibility tells us we are in shadow territory, the place where we collectively stuff everything we'd prefer not to see about who we are as a nation.

When I first walked into Indian Country in the late '90s, I began to realize that even in situations where Indians might be visible to us, they are not. Discussions of "minorities" or "people of color" seldom included so-called Native Americans. I understood for the first time that the little told of our relationship in my American History textbooks was told only from the Euro-American perspective. I understood that sometimes I'd unconsciously fallen into a projection that rendered real Indians invisible: the image of the mystical, eco-sensitive Indian and the accompanying attempt to appropriate Indian "spirituality" to fill a pervasive void in the Euro-American psyche.

On a midwinter weekend in January of 2010, I was a guest at a gathering of project affiliates of the Seventh Generation Fund for Indian Development. We were at the Sausalito Headlands for the

Arts on the coast of northern California, a collection of nonde-script, pale-yellow, one- and two-story, wooden-frame buildings that appear suddenly beside the narrow two-lane road that winds toward the coast through the spare hills of the headlands to the shore. It had the barebones shabbiness of a place tended by people who love it despite fading support, worn like the hills that cradle it.

Their website explains:

> The Marin Headlands was originally home to the Native American Coastal Miwok, who lived seasonally here for thousands of years. In the 18th century, Spanish and Mexican ranchers occupied the land, eventually giving way to Portuguese immigrant dairy farm-ers. In the 1890s, the first military installations were built to pre-vent hostile ships from entering San Francisco Bay. The Fort Barry buildings were erected from 1907 to 1913 and served as an active military center until 1950.

Now the anonymous buildings housed a few nonprofits, their presence announced with modest signs. Pale wintery sun greeted me for a few hours when I arrived on the first day and early in the second, triggering memories of that particular light from my days as a small child in Berkeley. In my memory, the weather during the rest of the gathering was gray, misty, and sometimes rainy, fog erasing the boundary between sea and sky, just beyond the crash-ing, gray-green waves. Rounded, red hills, covered with low, sparse vegetation, sported military crew cuts, echoing the barracks-like feel of the buildings lined up in rows along the road we walked from meals to meetings and back. The rest of it was the sea, winter waves smashing against rock and beach, a roaring, pulsing pres-ence embracing everything we did there.

Only a few of us—some Seventh Generation Fund staff members and a few funders and friends—at the gathering of well over a hun-dred people were "white." To me, that meant we were in what I had come to know as Indian Country. My Indian Country is anywhere I am with contemporary Indians, at gatherings and meetings, in communities, in person, on the phone, on email, on Facebook, in

movies and videos made by Indians, in newspapers and books . . .
Having spent over a decade wandering in that Indian Country, I
have a sense of what it means to be there, how it feels like another
world, at least to me, an outsider.

Meals at the Sausalito Headlands conference center were served
on a precise schedule. Our group had the dining hall for breakfast
from 7:30 to 8:30 a.m., not a minute earlier or later. Life in Indian
Country is rarely that precise, and I was amused by our marching
orders, a necessity for staff serving meals to several hundred people three times a day, yet also a subtle collision of worlds.

At breakfast one morning I sat with Peter, program director of a
foundation, one of the few other Euro-American allies and friends
of the Seventh Generation Fund. I'd talked with Peter at other
gatherings and remembered him as warm and sympathetic, easy
to talk to. It was a rare and delicious chance to trade experiences
with somebody like me, a Euro-American outsider drawn there for
reasons that we couldn't seem to articulate to our friends, our families, or our colleagues. As we circled around the questions—Why
are we here? What draws us? Why can't we find language for what
we experience?—we settled on something heartfelt and inexplicable: We feel like we're coming home.

What does "coming home" mean? There is sadness, richness,
hope, grief, outrage, and so many thoughts, images, and ideas
bound up in that apparently simple question. I am impelled to write
about that question but not *about* the First Peoples of Turtle Island
because that writing comes from them, not from me. I haven't been
exploring *their* Indian Country for over twenty years; I've been exploring *mine,* the Indian Country of an outsider, a descendant of the
invaders. It is as much about what is missing in me and my Euro-
American culture as it is about something that actually exists in
Indian Country, although what I find in Indian Country sometimes
hooks my longing for something that is missing in my everyday life.

Some years ago I ran across this idea: in indigenous communities, ceremony is a powerful healing tool. It is recognized that the

individual is ill because the community is ill, and often both are healed in the same ceremony. When I first ran across that idea, I had only a dim idea about ceremony and indigenous cultures, and I still don't know a whole lot. However, the idea that the individual is ill because the community is ill arrested me, feeling both stunningly obvious and completely novel, jolting me into a personal paradigm shift. Of course the individual and the community are completely interrelated in sickness and in health! At the time, I was in an analyst training program focusing on only half our illness. If the illness of the community is sending traumatized people to analysts for healing, how could what I was learning be useful in healing the community? What might healing the community look like?

One principle of Jungian analysis with individuals seems particularly relevant to community healing: Analyst and patient work for years to illuminate the patient's shadow. If an authentic life, a life spent unfolding the mystery of one's nature, is the goal, befriending one's shadow is the essential, first, and always-ongoing task. What can't be seen can't be embraced.

I'm aware that some of the material I need to include in my story of discovery may be difficult to accept. I know from my clinical work as an analyst that it is advisable not to bring up the most difficult shadow material in the early weeks and months with a patient. Even if the analyst does bring up shadow material, the patient is not likely to see it because they are not ready. An atmosphere of intimacy and trust needs to be established. Patients need to become accustomed to the process of befriending neglected and rejected parts of themselves and need to learn how much is gained by experiencing the feelings, particularly shame, that often accompany finding out that they are what they despise or envy in others.

I use my personal story of discovery to tell this collective story about beginnings and endings, in part, because during the lifetime which has brought me to this place, I only discovered what I was ready to find.

STORIES

Everybody has a story. I have a story. I weave a story out of my life experience, but my story isn't just my personal story. I weave in elements of my family story, my culture's story, and stories humans have been telling each other since the beginning of human time. Humans have always been fascinated with stories. Long before there was writing, there was story. Story allowed my ancestors to transmit the history and understanding of my people, keeping ancestral knowledge alive down through generations. Shared stories are a vital part of the glue that holds communities together, their communal DNA.

Until I made my personal story conscious and reflected on it, it too often limited my sense of possibility and kept me trapped in unhappy or neurotic scenarios that caused suffering for me and others. Children who are treated insensitively or arbitrarily often internalize a story about not belonging or not being good enough. Severely dysfunctional families create adults with a profoundly damaged sense of who they are. Inevitably, they replicate in the outer world the confusion, chaos, and violence of their inner world. I have seen all too often what happens when severely damaged people become leaders of families, movements, communities, or nations.

Telling my stories to a willing and empathic listener was profoundly healing. My experience of analysis—in my analysis and my work as an analyst of others—is that, over time, dark and painful stories constructed from childhood experiences, family, and cultural heritage can shift, becoming less compelling and less painful, and can be replaced with stories that feature forgiveness and openheartedness instead of trauma, anger, and grief. Unconscious stories are powerful and compelling. Once my stories become conscious, they are still sometimes powerful, but I have learned to distance myself and recognize a particular story when it arises, becoming more able simply to live life as it comes. I exchange the neurotic pain caused by staying stuck in my stories for the real pain and joy of being alive and conscious on planet earth. I become free just to be ordinary.

I found the same freedom when I stopped being unconsciously compelled by the stories of contemporary Western culture. I began to distinguish how story functions in indigenous cultures and how stories function in contemporary Western culture. As I understand it, life in traditional indigenous communities was and is knit together by what some contemporary indigenous peoples refer to as "lifeways." "Lifeways" are all the aspects of indigenous life that weave the community together, aspects I had once seen as separate and unrelated. They include story, language, ceremony, prayer, art, food, plant and animal medicines, everyday life, and the interrelationship among the community, the spirits, the ancestors, the plants and animals, the land, and the children as yet unborn. It has been close to impossible for me to imagine the role of story in that experience. Here are the words of Abenaki storyteller Joseph Bruchac:

> As a storyteller, I've long been aware of the dual purpose of stories in American Indian life—that stories are designed to both entertain and teach. As I've grown older, I've also learned that our stories frequently (if not always) have a third purpose. That purpose is to heal. We human beings are not just body and mind. We are also spirit and emotion. There are few things which speak as clearly as stories speak to the needed balance between all four of those components which make up human life. Stories have great power.

Stories still have great power, but in the contemporary Euro-American world they often have a fragmenting effect, as they unify those who belong to the many splinter groups that exist within the whole. Here is how Bruchac describes stories as they can too often be used in my world:

> I have also learned that stories may have the power to destroy. If told wrongly, if told with evil intent, stories can confuse the minds and the spirits of those who hear them. They can lead the listener away from balance and into the twisting paths of anger. . . . Stories in which those from other cultures are portrayed as evil and dangerous have been used to convince people that those others are less than human and must be eliminated. . . . Ethnic caricatures and sexist "humor" are further examples of the way certain stories can debase and lessen the humanity of others. In a very real sense, stories can be used to kill both the spirit and the body.

Stories are used to justify cruel and inhuman policies in relation to immigrants from south of our border, Muslims, and anyone who might be labeled a "terrorist." More subtle stories about Native Americans and other peoples of color support the ongoing racism which is alive and well in the Trump-era United States. Dehumanizing language and stories whipped up anger and hostility toward the Obama administration, much as they did during the Bush administration. The rhetoric can be completely divorced from reality, as when President Bush was accused of wearing some kind of brain-stimulating device under his clothing or President Obama was accused of being a "secret Muslim" and lying about his birthplace. The central story, that the President is illegitimate and does not deserve the office, is the same.

The dehumanizing effect of these stories goes well beyond their targets. They dehumanize those who believe them and live in a state of perpetual anger and fear. These stories are most attractive to those who left childhood with a profoundly damaged sense of who they are as a result of being abused psychologically, physically, and spiritually by those who were supposed to love and protect them. Profoundly wounded people use stories as an opiate and a psychological defense with which to diminish the childhood pain that haunts them. Belonging to a group that hates and dehumanizes others can provide someone who has been treated inhumanely with an otherwise elusive sense of a coherent self.

Liberation came when I freed myself from my stories and the stories my Euro-American culture imposed on me, stories that kept me from being able to accept the essential ambiguity of direct experience. I have spent many years exploring the ways in which my personal and family stories have been interwoven with the collective story, exploring just what that collective story is and how it causes profound suffering, individually and collectively.

I'm old enough to see how an earlier version of me lived in thrall to those stories until I was able to make them conscious. From that vantage point, I see that I was asleep for a very long time, wandering through the world, closed off from all that was around me, held in a cocoon of assumptions about myself and the world. My sleepwalking was related, first, to particular features of my personality and the ways I reacted to my family stories in early life. It was also related to living through a particular time in which women woke up to a very different understanding of themselves and their place in the culture. Like the heroine of the fairy tale Briar Rose, I slept in a castle covered in the vines, branches, and thorns of rose bushes, waiting. Waking up happened slowly, one paradigm-shattering moment at a time.

I was born at the beginning of the 1940s, the first of four children. My parents lived with first me and, later, my younger brother in a white wooden duplex in the Georgetown section of Washington, DC. It was wartime. I think of it as New Deal Washington because my parents and so many of their friends from that time were inspired by President Roosevelt and the ideals his administration expressed. My father worked as a lawyer for the US Maritime Commission, and my mother was a librarian for the Bureau of Labor Statistics.

We moved for a short time to Berkeley, California, toward the end of the war, and then to northern Westchester County, a bedroom exurb of New York City. My mother stopped working "outside the home" after "the war" ended and, like many suburban women of the '40s and '50s, did volunteer work for the rest of her life. Two more children, a sister and another brother, were born after my family moved to Westchester. My father took the train, the Harlem Division of the Hudson River Railroad, to Manhattan every day, where he practiced law in small firms with ever-changing names. The trains he rode were filled with suited businessmen and a few businesswomen, who, for a few hours every morning, poured through the impressive spaces of Grand Central Station, returning in the evening in a reverse migration.

I don't suppose anybody's childhood seems remarkable to them. Like any child, I was absorbing the stories of my family and my culture, learning the rules and assuming that they were simply the rules. How it is. There were glimpses of other realities. I remember riding the train between Grand Central Station in Manhattan and the Chappaqua station at night, staring into lighted rooms of apartment buildings in Harlem and the Bronx—blue, yellow, and green rooms flickering by—wondering what it might be like to live in one of them. Going to the Midwest for college was my first chance to see my childhood from the outside, but even that did not dislodge my stories, as many of my classmates at Carleton College came from similar places in a very white middle- to upper-middle-class world. Although, I remember my astonishment and horror at finding out that a classmate thought that Senator Joseph McCarthy was a hero, when in my world he was a villain who had destroyed the lives of some of my parents' friends. How could we have such different stories?

In my family, we read the *New Yorker*, a habit I have continued, and that was my world, the world created by storytellers like Cheever and Updike. I was surrounded by woods in the foothills of the Taconic Mountains. Narrow, winding roads followed Indian trails that eventually became colonial pathways and roads. The Indians were imaginary because, as far as we were concerned, they were all gone, nothing left but the names: Katonah, Taconic,

Chappaqua. Those names didn't evoke thoughts of Indians in me, although I remember finding a rock in the woods near our house with mysterious painted markings that we children imagined had been put there by Indians and that I now suspect had been put there by my father for us to find and make stories about.

I spent much of my early childhood in the woods and fields around our first house on a steep road in Pleasantville, in the hills on the eastern side of the stream that is the beginning of the Saw Mill River, part of the Hudson River Valley watershed. In the summer, we were shooed out the door to play and weren't expected back until a gong sounded for lunch or supper. I took books outside to read in the dappled shade of leaves on grass. It was many years before I could wake to the sound of rain in the middle of the night and not worry that I had left a book outside. It was a beautiful place to be a child, and it nourished me in ways I didn't understand until much later. I did not have a way to articulate the shadow side of that life until long after I left.

It didn't strike me as odd that I lived in a community where so many of the fathers took the train to work in the morning and returned at night. We lived in two different houses during my childhood, one on each side of the Saw Mill River Valley. We could hear the train running at the bottom of the valley, next to the parkway and the little river. On darkening, humid summer afternoons, just before rain, it sounded like the train ran through our yard. The mournful sound of a train whistle, the distant church bells from the stone tower of the Episcopal Church in downtown Chappaqua on Sunday mornings, and the metallic screech of the blue jay are among the sounds that most evoke memories of my childhood.

The train punctuated our days, an alarm clock for the adults. The busy wives, who needed to be in the line of cars at the little station to pick up their husbands, were warned by the whistle of the approaching train if they were late. Even the children knew the morning and early evening train schedules by heart. Tardy morning commuters who heard that sound knew to the minute, as they drove hurriedly toward the station, whether they were going to miss the train. Woe to the child hitching a ride with my father who caused him to miss the 7:39. Then, with my father at the wheel muttering dark curses, we raced down the parkway to the station in North White Plains, making up just enough time to catch the train there.

The mothers I knew took care of children, played tennis when the children grew old enough to be in school (or when they put their children in the care of nannies), decorated the house, did volunteer work, threw dinner parties, and greeted their returning husbands with dinner on the stove and a cold pitcher of martinis or a bottle of sherry or scotch. We didn't have a TV until I began junior high school, but when it arrived, it reflected that image of reality back to me. So did the advertisements in the glossy magazines that everybody read: *Life, Look, Time,* and the *Saturday Evening Post.*

The part of northern Westchester County where I grew up wasn't exactly *Leave It to Beaver.* Many of the houses were bigger and farther apart, the roads more winding, the neighborhoods hillier and leafier and the men's jobs more high-powered and high-stressed: lawyers, advertising executives, and magazine editors. Unlike Ward Cleaver, my father was likely to have called my mother to say that he wouldn't be home in time for dinner with "the children," so the four of us would eat early supper in the dinette, a small room between the kitchen and the dining room into which a square wooden table with a white top barely fit, and were put to bed before my father came home. Years later, as a young mother at home with two very small children, when those same phone calls came from my lawyer husband at the end of long, gray winter afternoons, I understood how sad and abandoned my mother might have felt.

It's hard to tease out with accuracy what I actually knew as a child and what I later came to understand about that world. For years, the head of my bed was up against a door which was on one side of a small passageway between my parents' bedroom and bathroom. I couldn't hear what was said, but I often fell asleep to the sound of murmuring voices in the next room. Based on my sense of them from that proximity, I don't think they fought much, certainly not in front of us. I remember my mother occasionally letting out an exasperated "*Da*-vid!" and then falling silent, sometimes for a long time.

But I knew, in some part of me, that despite that apparently idyllic life, my mother was not happy. Her mother, my grandmother, had raised four children, one of them crippled by polio. In the early part of the twentieth century, my grandmother maintained her family and the family fruit-growing business in rural Dade County during the long stretches of time when my grandfather was away, supervising construction of the railroad bridges he designed to link the Florida Keys to the mainland. My mother had been an English teacher in Florida and then a working woman in Washington, DC before she married my father at the end of her twenties. It was wartime, and women all over the country worked "outside the home," largely because of the war effort. Her working stopped with the end of the war, and my family was a part of a national movement, a suburban diaspora, headed out from the city to find breathing room and space. I didn't reflect until many years later on the overwhelming "whiteness" of those suburbs or wonder how or why that might have come about.

I thought of my mother as shackled to the steering wheel, doing errands, ferrying children, depositing and picking up my father at the Chappaqua train station at the end of each day, at least until we bought a second car. The focus of her volunteer work was the Democratic party of northern Westchester, in those days a losing proposition. I now imagine that she put her exceptional organizational skills and common sense in service to the party, only to have men make most of the important decisions.

I don't want to diminish the importance of what my mother did, what the mothers of my friends did, or what many women still do. Holding up their half of the sky by nurturing children and doing the unsung work of holding the community together, women's work is essential. When families no longer worked as an economic unit, when men's work and women's work went in different directions, the work women did and still do had less intrinsic value, partly because it was unpaid and partly because it was done by women. Other Western societies have found ways to value that work by giving government support to those who bear and nurture children, but ours has been slow to reach that point.

Some women still affirmatively choose that work and the economic dependency that goes with it. But that choice was missing in my childhood world. If my mother were a young woman now, I imagine she would still have children, but she might have shaped her life differently; it might have looked more like mine or my daughter's. As it was, I felt her subliminal message to me: *You will grow up and have some kind of job you love before you have children, at which point you will stop working in the world outside your home. You will love your children dearly, but you will feel that something essential is missing.*

For a female child of the '40s and '50s, the range of possibilities for "some kind of job" was extremely narrow. Even though our family pediatrician was a woman and two of my parents' female friends were lawyers, I never imagined I would be a doctor or a lawyer. When I told a second-grade classmate that I wanted to be a doctor, he told me that girls didn't become doctors and I believed him, even though I knew from my own experience it wasn't true. I had no vision for what I might become after leaving school.

The summer I was sixteen, I took the train into the city to go to secretarial school just off Times Square in order to learn how to type and do other kinds of office work, taking classes in the mornings and working in the afternoons for shoestring businesses in various parts of Manhattan. This experience was to give me typing and shorthand skills, a necessity for a young lady entering the world. Nevertheless, I had already decided to be an English teacher. Of all the things I did as a child, I loved reading the most, and it was the only future I could even barely imagine. My mother had been an English teacher in rural Florida before she went to Washington. I think she did her best to dissuade me, although her choice may have come from a similar place in her, as she told me about eagerly awaiting the latest issue of *St. Nicholas Magazine* for children. I imagine her rushing off to read it, lying on pine needle-covered red dirt under the trees of the then-remote part of Dade County where she grew up.

In all fairness, I don't remember that my parents ever explicitly articulated limited ambitions for me and my sister. I think if either my sister or I had insisted that we wanted to pursue law or medicine, they would have supported us. My mother had come to adulthood when horizons were beginning to open up for women, and she always let me know how much she valued those years when she was on her own working a job she loved. Some years ago, I found a photo of her taken during that time; it is one of the most beautiful photos of my mother I have. I see the bright face of a young woman in love with life and possibility, just a slightly sad, faraway expression in her eyes.

My parents were opposed to my early marriage, at twenty, when I was still in college, but they and my husband's parents gave us just enough financial support, which I know was often difficult for both families, so that I could stay in school and finish my college degree while my husband was in law school. However, the pressure of what Betty Friedan later called the "feminine mystique," along with growing up surrounded by women who, willingly or unwillingly, became housewives, was too much for me. I made choices that it took me many years to see were also the choices of many of the middle- to upper-middle-class women who came of age when I did. The personal and the collective were intertwined.

Long after college, I read about a study that looked at the incidence of depression among young women in college. The study connected that depression to their unconscious realization that their postsecondary education was probably going to be pointless. That study finally made sense of my memories of lying on a dorm-room bed covered with clothes and books, taking long and frequent naps, to the amusement and annoyance of my freshman-year roommates.

I dimly remember my mother telling me that I would go to college in order to be an educated mother for my children. Now, I wonder if she meant my sons. Many families in northern Westchester, including mine, sent their sons away to private day and boarding schools to give them a rigorous academic foundation and enhance their chances of getting into an Ivy League college. While there were bright students of both genders in my high school, the girls dominated the class academically in a high school still considered to be one of the best in the country, because few families in that suburb sent their bright girls to private school.

The unspoken message was that I would go to college to find a suitable husband to father those children I would intelligently mother. My own version of that depression was, as clinicians say, "overdetermined." There was ample reason for it besides having internalized such limited cultural expectations, but the personal and cultural reasons for it are impossible to separate. My illness and the illness of the culture were completely interrelated. I was an undisciplined student, excelling in classes I liked and doing poorly in classes I didn't. I took as many English courses as I could, majoring in English because I loved to read.

I did what I was supposed to do, however. I fell in love, leaving college a year early to marry and finish my education in Boston, getting a teaching degree while my husband was at law school. When he was done, we moved to the Twin Cities, where his family was.

That decision was, in large part, mine. Chappaqua is the home-town of Horace Greeley, newspaperman and founder of the *New York Tribune*. I grew up with a greenish, life-sized statue of him just beyond the railroad station and the parkway, arm outstretched, saying, "Go West, young man, go West." If we went "west" to live in Minneapolis, we would not live in the suburbs, and I imagined that I could escape my mother's suburban fate.

I had concluded at some point during my childhood that I didn't have enough self-esteem to live on the East Coast. I liked Minneapolis and the Midwest. They seemed livable and comfortable, without the edges and competitiveness of life in New York or Boston. No difficult decisions about whether "the city" or "the country" would be the best place to raise children. My experience of my mother's frustrations and my sense of her as trapped in the suburbs left me determined to avoid them.

However, during the 1960s, I was well on the way to recreating my mother's suburban fate in the pleasant, elm-filled city of Minneapolis. At some barely conscious level, I'd fallen in love with a bright, ambitious man in part because I could tell that he was going to be successful—if I weren't to have my own dreams of success in the world, at least I could be part of his. I taught English in high school for three years and then left teaching to have children. In those days, the mid-1960s, visibly pregnant women were not allowed to teach. I also remember that women teachers—and many of us were women—were expected to wear heels because the principal liked the way they made our legs look.

My mother died while I was teaching. I was in my early twenties. She was a smoker, and the official reason was metastasized cancer, which had ended up in her lungs. But I knew that her children, the center of her world, had left home one by one, and I had left that part of the country for good. I sensed tensions between her and my father that might have been laid bare in the empty spaces left by departing children. She made an abortive attempt to re-enter the world, to enroll in Columbia University's School of Journalism. But it was too late.

I know the official diagnosis, but I believe that she died from a broken heart.

I read accounts of the turmoil of the '60s and feel like I was living in a parallel universe. My husband and I were born well before

1946. We were in the pre-baby boom generation, the dutiful, con-
forming children of the '40s and '50s. As I remember, toward the
very end of my time at Carleton College, there were a few student
radicals, but the majority of us were more interested in our studies and social lives. The Vietnam War had barely begun and I was
teaching *Macbeth* in a suburban classroom when the announce-
ment that President Kennedy had been shot came over the PA system.

My parents had been young adults during the Great Depression
and the Second World War. My sense now of the 1950s world in
which I came of age is that families in the newly enlarged middle
class wanted to put the recent horrors behind them and create a
world that was normal and ordinary, at least on the surface, enthusiastically embracing a materialist life that had been impossible for twenty years and out of reach for many before that. It isn't
clear to me now how much of the desire to create that materialist
life was in the zeitgeist and how much was the result of decisions
made in corporate offices to sell a compelling vision of American
life based on consumer satisfaction.

The price of that illusion was conformity and worse, a pervasive image of the American housewife as a passive consumer, cut
off from the world around her and immersed in her life as nurse,
cook, chauffeur, nanny, and decorator—Betty Draper of the TV
series *Mad Men*. Too much of the injustice and inequity of the
world was swept into our national shadow, and reaction was inevitable. Many women couldn't afford the luxury of staying home
with children, but those women were invisible in the world I knew
at that time.

Some of us were slow to wake up to the eruptions of the 1960s. I
certainly was. I wasn't oblivious to what was happening—certainly
not to the civil rights struggle, which I passionately supported. But
I didn't start paying serious attention to the war in Vietnam until
some years after the resistance had begun. My energy was almost
entirely focused on a new life, a new city, being part of a couple,

and buying a house, and then on our son, who was born in the late '60s.

I was trying to become a grown-up.

I remember an intense argument with my father about the protests that erupted at the Chicago Democratic convention in 1968. I defended the protestors as my angry father denounced their assault on his beloved political party. I remember another discussion, which took place on the porch of our house in Chappaqua on a warm summer night. This time the subject was the women's movement, but the person arguing with my father wasn't me; it was Susan, one of my earliest childhood friends. I sat silently during that argument, not exactly sure what it was about, while my father patronized my friend, explaining in a kindly avuncular way that what she was saying was all wrong.

In my memory, three things are closely related. Cleaning out the crawl space off the study of our 1905 wood-frame house in Minneapolis after our daughter was born in 1970, I found papers I had written in one of my favorite college English classes, taught by a professor who had always challenged me to do my best. I read them and realized to my horror that I didn't understand significant parts of them, that I couldn't remember writing those words. Had something happened to my mind? For at least a few months after our daughter was born, I was moderately depressed. And, most important, right around the time my daughter was born, I read Betty Friedan's *The Feminine Mystique*.

RESISTING THE FEMININE MYSTIQUE

I give Betty Friedan and the women's movement credit for starting me in a direction that eventually saved my life. My mother died of cancer early in 1965, just after turning fifty-four, never having come to terms with her depression. I don't want to be simplistic about my mother's depression. As much as I love that photo of her as a young woman in her midtwenties, taken when she was living a life she would later remember with pride and longing, even then the sad, faraway look I knew so intimately was there in her eyes. Later, I learned enough about my family history to make me suspect that I was only the latest in a long line of depressed women reaching back through my maternal lineage. The personal, familial, and cultural origins of that depression are permanently entangled. But how could my mother's sense of being trapped in the life of a suburban housewife not have been part of hers?

As I reread Friedan's book, it's clear that women's lives had begun a very different trajectory in the '30s and early '40s and that the imposition of what she called the feminine mystique had interrupted a natural evolution toward an expanded understanding of women's roles. Here is how Friedan talks about the woman being described in the media of that period:

> The image of woman that emerges from this big, pretty magazine [a typical issue of McCall's in July, 1960] is young and frivolous, almost childlike; fluffy and feminine; passive; gaily content in a world of bedroom and kitchen, sex, babies, and home. The magazine surely does not leave out sex; the only passion, the only pursuit, the only goal a woman is permitted is the pursuit of a man. It is crammed full of food, clothing, cosmetics, furniture, and the

physical bodies of young women, but where is the world of thought and ideas, the life of the mind and spirit?

I imagine that the depression which I believe was implicated in my mother's early death was widespread among those women of her generation who attempted to conform to the story of the feminine mystique. While women became depressed for personal and family reasons, those reasons were entwined with women's marginalization and denigration. Women were ill because the culture was ill, because society denied their aspirations, their sense of autonomy, and their sense of self. They were ill because society denied their humanity.

I remember very little of what I read of Friedan's book then, but reading it was an epiphany. Now I could see why I'd made those choices that I thought had been mine alone, choices that had brought me to a place of depression and emptiness. The possibility of realizing my ambitions in the world beyond my house and beloved children was powerfully liberating. I could reclaim for myself the ambition I'd asked my husband to carry for me.

Awakening was one thing; deciding what to do next was quite another. Not every woman of my generation had identified with the fantasy of the feminine mystique. Some of my women friends from high school began in those years a lifetime of doing work they loved that expressed who they truly were—teaching in college and working in foundations and as editors in publishing houses—but rarely was that work outside the domains where women had historically been allowed.

It now seems that many of those who, like me, allowed themselves tobe taken over by the fantasy of the feminine mystique unconsciously assumed that women were essentially passive, that they were passive in their essence. Everything around me supported that assumption. I passively went along with the assumptions of the feminine mystique. I see now that I had internalized a collective story rather than going the hard and often confusing route of deciding what *I* wanted, what at some deep level would be satisfying to the unique person I was, in a culture which did not support that search. Yet, as Jung said, early adulthood is the time when the urge to become what we imagine the cultural collective wants of us is the strongest. In that sense, there was nothing surprising about my choices.

I don't want to fall into one side of a polarity and denigrate passivity. All human beings are passive from time to time. Passive is simply the other side of active. Not that I understood that then. Nor did I understand that Western culture tends to split off large portions of psychological territory. Those qualities which are unacceptable to the culture are pushed into the cultural shadow, where they can be recognized only as characteristics of the unknown, depersonalized other.

Our cultural relationship to the idea of passivity is a good example of how that splitting works. The words "active" and "passive" simply describe energies that Jung imagined as archetypal, collectively inherited, unconscious ideas, patterns of thought, image, and experience universally present in the human psyche. Active and passive energies are aspects of Yang and Yin, the fundamental energies of life in Chinese philosophy. Light, day, and the Sun express Yang energies; dark, night, and the Moon express Yin energies. Like day and night, Yang and Yin energies alternate in the flow of space and time, each preceding and succeeding the other, each being essential to the other, supporting each other, bringing the other about, as in this rendition of the ancient Taoist symbol:

In the world of archetypal energies, Yang and Yin are associated with masculine and feminine. However, what may or may not be true in what Jung imagined to be the eternal world of archetypal energies is not automatically true in space-time. The archetypal energies of masculine and feminine do not simplistically equate to men and women. Men can be passive and women can be active. Nevertheless, in patriarchal Western societies, these interrelated archetypal energies have been unconsciously split. To some degree, men and the "ruling principle of consciousness"— the worldview, mostly unconscious, that governs individual and collective psychic life—are identified with the Yang energies. Often women and other groups marginalized by the culture carry the Yin energies.

I wrote about the ruling principle of consciousness of Western culture in my thesis for Jungian training, "patriarchal mind" being the way I then described what I am now describing as Western consciousness. Patriarchal mind, I said, embodies largely unconscious values that lead to a tendency to choose one of a pair of opposites over the other, denigrating and discarding the other, which is carried in projection by others who are seen as inferior: i.e. women, people of color, children, and, in general, those who are different. Here is a list of some of those opposites.

light	dark
thinking	feeling
active	passive
objective	subjective
rational	irrational
self/individual	group/other/collective/relationship
Logos	Eros
product	process
spirit	matter
Father	Mother
conscious	unconscious
mind	body
masculine	feminine
order	chaos

If I read each list separately, each of them presents a picture of the way men and women have thought about themselves and each other in Western culture. I can also see clearly which qualities have been valued and which have been marginalized. A pervasive story involving the splitting of human possibilities has been constructed over the last five thousand years, a narrative that has come to dominate my culture.

Splitting of human characteristics into two groups like the ones above has been codified in law and practice, both religious and secular. In my first year of law school at the University of Minnesota, I learned that in early English property law husband and wife were one, and that one was the husband. In that conceptual move, I felt women disappear, just as in the widely stated belief that we each come into the world alone, I feel the Mother disappear.

As feminists have pointed out, women disappear from history. History in Western culture is his-story, not her-story. For both men and women in Western society, the consequences of this conceptual move have been devastating. Yang and Yin were irretrievably split, with men and the dominant culture embodying Yang qualities and women and people of color, along with their subordinate cultures, embodying Yin energies. Each gender has carried half the qualities of being human and has forced the other gender to carry the other half in projection, seeing those qualities in someone else and not in oneself.

That split was strongly in force when Jung developed his theory that what he called the Animus and the Anima were the psychological contrasexual other within each of us, the Anima in men and the Animus in women. His theory was the product of an assumption that men and women are so different that the existence of the stereotypical characteristics of the other gender in their psyches must be the opposite of their core psychology. For example, a gentle, nurturing, feeling man must be expressing his Anima, something other to his basic masculine nature. An intellectual, ambitious woman must be expressing her Animus, something other to her core feminine nature.

Everyone has been psychologically and spiritually impover-
ished by that split. Men have been denied access to their feelings
and their relationship with their bodies, their warmth, their nurturing instincts, and their capacity to be passively present to the
world and other people and to listen intently and take other realities in. Women have been denied their autonomy and freedom of
choice, their ability to express initiative and curiosity in the world,
to step out of the domains of family and relationship to which
they have been confined. We think of ourselves as a democracy,
but half the population, women, were denied the vote until the
twentieth century. Carrying projections of archetypal energies
for each other has vastly complicated relationships between men
and women. When I see repressed and discarded parts of myself
in someone else, it's almost impossible to see them as an ordinary
human being.

When, in 1972, two years after my daughter was born, I decided
to apply to the University of Minnesota law school and become a
lawyer, I saw myself as bold, adventurous, and radical. Now I wonder if I was also acting out of a brand-new collective dream, the
dream of the liberated woman. It seems ironic that I was almost as
passive in adopting this dream as I had been in adopting the first
one.

I had thought briefly about enrolling in graduate school to get
a degree in urban planning. When I explored the coursework required for the newly designed degree, I discovered that a course
in calculus was among the requirements. My heart sank. Given my
lack of interest in math, mastering calculus seemed like a remote
possibility. However, I went to talk about my interest to the dean
of the School of Public Affairs at the University of Minnesota, the
school which offered the degree. I only vaguely remember being
in his office, but I clearly remember the dark, hopeless mood I was
in when I stopped by a friend's house on the way home to report
on the interview.

The Dean said that I had young children at home and should stay home and take care of them.

The idea of going to law school seized me at a nonprofit board meeting where a friend resigned, saying she was going to go to law school. My father, husband, and one of my brothers were lawyers. How natural that I would envision myself stepping into a man's world by entering the same profession as the men I knew most intimately. If I were even considering learning calculus in order to get an urban planning degree, I might as well go to law school, which seemed impossibly difficult to me. Law school would give me a more broadly useful degree when I was done.

Even though the men of my family were lawyers, I had only the dimmest idea what lawyers did. Those were my conscious thoughts while, underneath, I was rejecting my mother's life as a suburban housewife as resoundingly as I possibly could. And I was beginning to live out her never-realized dream, that she could be somebody in the world of men.

Women, said Friedan, were suffering a collective identity crisis. Some of us instinctively went to work in the world outside home and family in deeply satisfying careers that expressed who we were. Others of us went to work in the world of men and attempted to be as much like them as we could, assuming a predetermined identity instead of struggling with our own. Feeling deeply and intimately the shame I had internalized from my culture and my childhood, I repressed it, becoming single-minded and fiercely ambitious in the world of men as an antidote.

Of course, I could not avoid being denigrated in that world, too. My woman's body betrayed me. I found I was most acceptable and least threatening if I adopted men's dress: suits, sport coats, buttoned-down oxford shirts, and feminine versions of men's ties. The image of me and other women running around the corridors of power in our diminutive versions of male suits and ties makes me smile now, but I was completely serious. I had to be.

I suppose I'm being too hard on myself to say that I misunderstood Friedan's message, which was about becoming more fully human, not more like men, but I don't think I was the only woman who understood Friedan and the women's liberation movement that way. Jung's idea that each of us has both a conscious psychology appropriate to our gender and an unconscious, opposing, contrasexual masculine or feminine side may be a psychological artifact of patriarchy and not an immutable aspect of human nature. Even so, for me, the unexpressed part of me was "the masculine," and it's not surprising that I overidentified with that unexpressed part of myself on the road to becoming complete.

Something else happened when I read Friedan's book. I understood for the first time that I could experience a sudden paradigm shift that would sweep my assumptions away and radically change my life. Now I knew that was possible, no matter how unconscious and passive I might have been in taking on another dream. Even while I held firmly to that dream, there was still a part of me that did not invest in it quite as completely as I had in the first one, a part of me that knew that I might not believe in it forever.

There was a part of me that would be prepared to deconstruct that dream, too.

Reading Friedan's book began what I see now has been a forty-year quest to explore the territory outside my cultural awareness, to illuminate the dark territory which is both my cultural shadow and the shadow of my culture. I wasn't conscious that I was on that quest for many years. My initial travels into the world outside cultural norms were exhilarating. My law school classmates in 1973 included a number of women who had been out of college for some time, had pursued other careers, and, often, had married—a number of us with children. "Older women" (I was in my early thirties) were common in the law classes of the early 1970s as many of us responded to the awakening of women in the zeitgeist.

I felt like a pioneer during the '70s and early '80s as women broke down barriers. I suffered the indignities of everyday life in a man's world: sexist jokes and sexual innuendo, being patronized and assumed to be incompetent, being hit on by superiors, being told that I shouldn't leave my children to go to school or work or shouldn't compete with men for jobs. I worried that I would be called that worst of all possible things, "shrill," if I pointed out the unconscious gender bias in the air I breathed. I chafed at not being allowed to enter through the front door of the Minneapolis Club where important meetings were held. But I felt solidarity with other women as we shared those stories and the stories of women's triumphs. We were outsiders to men's culture, but we had each other.

Shattering my cultural assumptions and understanding the ways in which my humanity had been denied had another lifelong benefit. I don't simplistically equate the struggles of other oppressed peoples with the struggles of white, middle-class women, but understanding that I was a member of an oppressed and marginalized group gave me insight into and compassion for the struggles for justice and liberation by others in the cultural shadow. Being allowed conditional entrance into the corridors of power, even if I was not given that power, allowed me to see how that power operated. Fighting injustice was not just an idea; it became lived experience.

It slowly dawned on me that the two domains inhabited by men and women, the world of work and the world of home, were also two cultures. It took me a while to see that I was being held back from achievement in the male world by the assumptions and dictates of mine. As I became a student of the peculiarities of men's culture, I could see that men didn't understand that they had a distinct culture, that men believed it was just how things were. They were right; the dominant culture was, and is, a male culture.

A lawyer in the first law firm where I worked talked with me once about what had happened to the women in his law class. He observed that they hadn't gone to work with any of the prestigious firms which dominated law practice in the city, preferring instead to set up their own small law firms. He wondered why they made those decisions. I took a breath—he was a partner and I was a lowly associate—and gently asked if the fact that none of the big firms would hire women at the time he graduated might have affected their choices.

At the time, the words "man" and "men" were assumed to represent both men and women. It seems a long time ago that someone could say with complete certainty that the word "men" meant people of both genders. I remember that my response—it didn't feel that the word "men" meant *me* when I read it—was dismissed as irrelevant. I began to see the differences between men's and women's culture more clearly as I tried to figure out how to live in the male world. Understanding that acculturated differences in power structures are profound and invisible was helpful later on when it finally came home to me that I also needed to deconstruct my Euro-American "whiteness."

During my time in the culture of men, I saw women who apparently adapted perfectly to that culture. Some Jungians call women who seem identified with an inner male counterpart "Animus possessed," but that description betrays a subtle sexism that exists in Jungian psychology, too. Jungian men, particularly older Jungian men, can be quick to label a woman with a well-developed thinking function, who isn't afraid to use it, "Animus possessed." However, there are women I think of as honorary men because I experience them as identified with their adaptation to the male world and not grounded in a secure sense of themselves as women. I feel sympathy for those women who feel they have to give themselves up in order to survive and prosper in the world of men, even if I often don't feel comfortable around them. And I know that for a number of years I was one of them.

My feminine acculturation was ill-suited for the world of men. Looking back, I can see how my male law school colleagues leapt

into the role of lawyer, taking charge of their work, acting inde-
pendently and autonomously. To my bewilderment, and that of
the lawyers I worked for, I was doing it all wrong. I didn't figure
out for some time what the problem was. It wasn't about being
smart, researching well, and doing what I was asked or being dutiful, obedient, and subservient. It was about taking an assignment
and completing it, without direction from the assigning lawyer,
using my initiative and creativity. The passivity which Friedan
documents in her book as one of the primary characteristics of an
appropriately feminine woman was still my primary mode of operating, an inextricably intertwined mix of personal and cultural
factors.

However, the story of my first few years as a lawyer is about more
than just an eventual awakening to my passivity. There was not a
good fit between me and the first law firm where I worked, something I realized later when I joined another firm, where I was much
happier. I wasn't in the right place and, instead of acting on that
understanding, I fell into a familiar depression, put my head down,
and kept going, passively accepting my unhappiness as just how
things were, how life is. My depression compounded the problems
I was having adjusting to my supervising attorneys' expectations.

Now I see there were signs I was going in the wrong direction. I
remember my first assignment as a law clerk with that firm at the
end of my second year of law school. A construction client had
stumbled on Indian burial remains while excavating a site. There
was a very clear state statute that made it illegal to move the remains and outlined the steps to be taken when remains were ac-
cidentally discovered. The client, however, did not want to stop
construction, and I was asked to research a way around the statute. I was completely opposed to the task and could not do it. I felt
utterly helpless, and I dimly remember that the assignment was
given to another law clerk. In retrospect, I could have understood
that very particular conflict at the moment I entered the world of

lawyers as a message from my future, telling me I was headed in the wrong direction.

I felt helpless a lot during those years. It was tied up with my failure to act out of a sense of myself as a lawyer rather than a student. Toward the end of my time with the first firm, I got it. I started tackling my assignments with initiative and creativity, thinking ahead about what was going to be needed and supplying it before I was asked. Had I been able to do that from the beginning, those first few years in practice might have been very different, even if my sense that I was in the wrong place for me was correct.

LIFE IN THE BANK

I left that firm for another and, in the early '80s, was managing a small legal department housed in the trust department of a large bank headquartered in downtown Minneapolis. I had been recruited by someone I met during my days as a volunteer with the Citizen's League, the Twin Cities public policy group where I had been on a committee studying transportation. Peter was head of the trust department, whose business was investing assets held in the form of trusts for individuals and institutions. He had fired my predecessor as trust counsel, manager of the small legal department advising the trust department, for sexually harassing a woman lawyer in his office. Clearly Peter wanted to shake things up, and hiring a woman for the job must have seemed like the perfect way to do it. If I unconsciously wanted to immerse myself in a hierarchical organization as a learning experience, I couldn't have chosen a better place.

Peter understood the institution well and asked me at our final interview if I wanted to be hired as a vice president. I didn't realize until after I started the job how important it was that he had offered it and that I had said "yes." In the very large banking organization that included the trust department, I was only the third female vice president, while there were dozens of male vice presidents throughout the bank and its parent holding company.

The women vice presidents were extremely visible. As soon as I joined the bank, the other two sought me out, and we instantly became friends. If we went out for lunch together, it seemed that every male banker who passed us in the skyways would joke that we were headed out to plot a women's uprising. We laughed at their paranoia, but there was truth to it. While we weren't planning an uprising, they were right that women in that world were marginalized and that we wanted things to change.

I never met my predecessor, who had held the job for twenty-five years, but I concluded from the things I learned about him after I joined the bank that he'd been pretty self-important. It was clear that he'd made sure that the bankers he worked with understood how legally complicated their operations were and how difficult it would be to do what they wanted. Even though I had been hired by the head of the trust department, I initially reported to the manager of the personal trust division, who reported to Peter. In most business organizations, reporting relationships are an instant indicator of status. Despite my VP title, I was already down a level in the "org chart." Being a woman may have had something to do with my initial placement, but I suspect that I was on probation for other reasons. I don't think it was concerns about my competence but more about taking time to assess how much of a nuisance I was going to be.

Because of the national banking legislation known as Glass-Steagall, there was a strict division—known, unfortunately, as the "Chinese Wall"—between the lending and investment businesses in the bank. Information could not pass from the commercial lending side of the business to the investment side. The law was designed to keep the investment business in the trust department uncontaminated by the lending relationships on the commercial side, to prevent self-dealing by the bank or conflicts of interest in investment decisions. If a banker on the commercial side of the bank was lending to a publicly held company, it would be a conflict of interest for the commercial banker to ask the trust department to invest client assets in that company's stock.

The commercial lending side did not have its own internal legal department but, historically, the trust department had its own small legal department, the office of trust counsel. There was also a legal department in the bank holding company, and one of the city's premier law firms, with offices in the same fourteen-story downtown building, was outside counsel. The trust department worked with a small group of lawyers in that outside law firm who specialized in the laws regulating bank trust departments and the laws of probate, trusts, and estate planning.

I'm not sure being hired for the position of trust counsel was a huge breakthrough for women. As law jobs went then, in-house counsel, working in a legal department inside a business organization, was on the lower end of the status totem pole, just above forming your own small firm. When I applied for the job, I was interviewed by the outside lawyer who supervised his firm's work with the trust department. I remember his small office in our shared building, the window behind him letting in the dim light of a gray, overcast day as I sat meekly in front of his desk. He stated unequivocally that he didn't understand why any lawyer with self-respect would go to work for the bank.

I worked in a tiny office with two other lawyers and a secretary, tucked away on the fourteenth floor of the building, isolated from the much lower floors where the actual business was done. That location may have been related to my predecessor's meddlesome habits. The trust counsel office was vestigial, an organizational appendix. Some years after I left the bank, as concerns about keeping the lending and investment arms of banks separate (unfortunately) diminished and Glass-Steagall was repealed, the office of trust counsel was folded into the bank holding company's legal department and ceased to exist.

My predecessor must have been a nuisance. On Friday afternoons, my friend, the head of the trust department, held a meeting with the four senior vice president department heads who reported to him. The meeting was called the senior trust meeting. It was in two parts, a short, formal part that I, as trust counsel, was invited to attend, and a much longer, informal part, which I was not invited to attend. Peter's personal secretary took minutes during the first part, and we, the two women, would leave the room together at its conclusion. The previous week's minutes were formally approved and stored in tall wooden file cabinets behind her desk. The real business was discussed in the second meeting.

Eventually, I was allowed into the second half of the meeting. At first, I would be asked to stay for a particular reason when Dorothy left the room, and then it was assumed that I understood that I should stay. Nobody ever said it directly. I was just supposed to figure it out, and I could be pretty slow on the uptake when issues of authority were at stake.

Some months after I started, my boss—the manager of the personal trust division—retired, and I officially began to report to Peter. I had been mostly silent in those meetings, as we sat around the large, dark wooden table in the conference room near Peter's office. I had no idea what people were talking about and was terrified of making a mistake or sounding stupid. Perhaps my silence made me appear smarter and more knowledgeable than I was. In any event, I convinced Peter that I wasn't going to be an in-house counsel in the mold of my predecessor. I brought the perspective of a lawyer in private practice. If the client wants something, it is the lawyer's job to figure out how to make it happen, not throw up roadblocks.

Like most people, even those in the worlds of law and business, I had no idea what a trust department did when I took the job, never mind anything about the laws and regulations that so restricted bank investment departments in the early '80s. Even among lawyers, few had any experience with bank regulatory law unless they were outside counsel for a bank. But the fact that I had only a glancing experience with the law of trusts and estates before I worked at the trust department only underlines the oddness of offering me the job, even though it was clear that a fruitless search had gone on for weeks before I was hired. Peter must have become pretty desperate. And I would not have taken the job if I hadn't begun to be uncertain about where I might specialize in the private practice of law.

I had been hired by the second firm to work as a tax lawyer. Although I worked for a lawyer I liked and respected, I was beginning to suspect that my mind did not operate in the right way for me to become a good tax lawyer. Of the other specialty areas in the firm—especially those of real estate and estate planning, which were, in those days, ghettos for women lawyers—only general corporate and nonprofit law interested me, and there I would be bumping up against a territorial male classmate from law school in the firm and, beyond him, my husband's preeminence in corporate and securities law.

I liked working in that firm, in my tiny office on the forty-third floor of the IDS building in the center of downtown Minneapolis, looking down on the city, the river, and beyond, all spread out before me. In my office, I hung three favorite Inuit prints. Two of them were primitive stone carvings of a caribou and a hunter created in 1965; they were images of the daily life of an Inuit artist who lived in the far northern Canadian village of Povungnituk. The third pictured an Inuit man holding another man off the ground. It was the Inuit version of the Greek legend of Antaeus. In the legend, Antaeus—son of Gaia and Poseidon, mother earth and the god of the sea—was a giant. He could not be defeated as long as he remained in contact with the earth. He was ultimately defeated by Heracles, who discovered the secret of his strength and lifted him off the ground, crushing him in a bear hug. The irony, that the print hung in my office forty-three stories above the ground, was lost on me at that point.

I must have dimly sensed something awry with my choice of profession, because I told people that I kept those prints in my office to remind me of the vastly different worlds inhabited by me and the artists, even though our lives overlapped in time. I initially rebuffed Peter's invitation to talk to him about the job because I liked working in that firm. But as I kept coming up against a dead end trying to imagine a future there, moving to the bank became more appealing.

Bank trust departments in the early 1980s were ossified by layers of hierarchy and the dead hand of tradition. Their primary business was, and still is, managing investment portfolios for families whose wealth is tied up in legal instruments called "trusts," either because they had put their investments in a trust while they were alive—usually for estate planning reasons—or because they were the heirs of a trust created under the will of someone, usually a family member, who had died. The trust department also invested assets for institutions with pension plans. There was a complex interrelationship among the managers of the trust department, the administrators of the accounts who dealt with clients, and the wealthy families of the city.

In those days, traditional bank trust departments were stuffy places, perfect for observing the dominant culture in action. Insulated from the competitive world of business, they were internally focused, obsessed with hierarchy and status, and slow to adapt to change in the world around them—change that, even then, was beginning to unsettle their business as securities investment firms began to poach on their territory.

The upper levels of the hierarchy were all men; the several layers of middle managers were mostly men; a few women appeared as the managerial levels continued to drop, down to the levels where the actual operation of the business was done, where the employees were mostly women. When all the middle managers of the trust department gathered for a meeting, there were about thirty-five people in the room, and for some time I was one of only two women, the other a longtime bond analyst in the investment department.

I remember stories that illustrated how invisible the stratification of women in the department was to the men who ran it, the men who made up the senior trust meeting. When the manager of the probate area, who had been with the trust department for many years, announced his retirement, hiring his replacement was discussed in a senior trust meeting. One of my colleagues asked, almost petulantly, if they would "have to" consider hiring a woman. No, another said, he didn't think so, because there were already so many women in the probate department. I remember suggesting, again, very gently, that if they looked at the number of the women who were at Warren's level of management in the trust department as a whole, they might come to a different conclusion.

One of the perks of being at a certain level of the hierarchy was having your own *Wall Street Journal* subscription. The lucky manager would read it first, and then it would wend its way, according to rank, through the department, eventually landing on the desk of the lowest person on the org chart. There was a period in the early '80s when an unusual number of "tender offers" occurred. In order to achieve control over a company, outside buyers of a company's stock would solicit stockholders with a tempting offer to buy their shares. Tender offers were announced in the *Wall Street Journal*, and there was a limited period, usually a week or ten days, for shareholders to take up the offer. As the trust department was in the business of buying, selling, and holding securities for its clients, they needed to be on top of tender offer information so that, if required, they could contact their clients for instructions. However, the department was missing tender offers, finding out about them too late to contact their customers, and there was consternation about how to fix the problem.

The problem of missing tender offers was discussed at a senior trust meeting. I asked, as I often did, feeling my way in a very complicated organization, how the system worked. I was told that one of the lower-level employees in the securities operations area (where the actual buying and selling of securities happened) had the job of reading the *Wall Street Journal* and notifying account administrators, in a different department, that a security held in certain accounts was the subject of a tender offer. If required, the account administrator would call the client for instructions and then let the securities operations area know whether or not to sell the stock.

It seemed that the employee who was supposed to spot tender offers was one of those lower-level employees who didn't see any particular edition of the *Wall Street Journal* for the week or more required for the paper to get to her desk. I remember asking, somewhat incredulously, since I couldn't imagine that the fix for the problem could be so simple, if it would be possible to buy that particular employee her own subscription. She was given one and the problem was solved.

COLLAPSE: THE BANK BURNS DOWN

On Thanksgiving night of 1982, a couple of trespassing children played with an acetylene torch they found in the rubble of the almost-demolished Donaldson building, which was next door to the building that housed the trust department and the rest of the bank. It caught fire and was badly damaged, and a number of floors were completely burned before the fire could be put out. The trust department executive offices on the fifth floor, the conference room where the senior trust meetings were held, the handsome wooden file cabinets behind Dorothy's desk where minutes from the senior trust meeting had been kept, all burned. Gone.

I found out about the fire the next day on the local five o'clock TV news program in Palm Springs, California. My family and I were visiting my husband's parents in their modest retirement condo. My father-in-law was in his usual spot in the lounger in the small room we called the den, watching the news, when he suddenly called out that we had to come see what was on TV. One minute I was secure in an orderly, predictable world in which I would return to Minneapolis on Sunday evening and go back to work on Monday. The next, I was watching news footage of flames shooting out of the windows of the bank building, *my* bank building, and imagining the entire trust department, my office included, going up in smoke.

It was a devastating, lonely moment. Everyone else was enjoying a rare family visit in a warm place, into which this news came as a surprising but passing piece of information. I spent the rest of the long weekend trying to pretend that everything was fine, while inside I was a badly traumatized child. What was I going to do? What if all my files and my office were completely burned? How could I be the lawyer for the trust department if everything was gone? Our outside counsel was in that building; what about their files? My favorite Inuit prints from my former law office were in that office. The thought that they had burned was as painful as imagining the loss of my files. The bottom fell out of my world and I fell with it, falling . . . falling . . . into an abyss. I couldn't control the panicky thoughts and images racing through my mind, far less coherent than I have put down on this page.

Not that I had any idea what was going on inside. It took me a long time in therapy to recognize the existence of that child, and even longer to realize which particular early trauma was being replicated that day: I must have been about two. I was standing in the living room of our duplex in Georgetown when the furnace right below me exploded, loudly blowing a hole through the floor near where I was standing. I have no memory of that moment or of being grabbed by a family friend who was staying with us and rushed outside. Everything I know about that part was told to me by others many years later. I have only a vague memory of standing in the backyard, my infant brother held and comforted by some-body nearby, a woman, hearing the sound of fire engines. How could I have known what that meant? Whatever the truth of that moment, in my memory, I am completely alone.

To this day, if something shocking, frightening, or even just com-pletely unexpected happens, my first response is to go into that traumatized place and panic. I carry that trauma in my body, in its rigidities and resistances. Years after the bank burned, I un-derstood that the destruction of the bank building in downtown Minneapolis and my familiar life in it touched that world-shatter-ing childhood moment and sent me into shock.

I called Peter as soon as I could. The sound of his voice was re-assuring. He was in endless meetings of all the senior managers of the bank. By Monday he hoped to know where the trust depart-ment would be housed. He relayed the good news that my office, including my beloved Inuit prints, was smoky and wet but un-burned. I didn't need to cut my visit short and come home before Sunday night. There would be plenty to do on Monday after the holiday weekend.

I was disappointed. I wanted to take the next plane out of Palm Springs. Pretending I was still having a nice vacation was wearing on me. I wanted to be someplace where the outside bore some re-lationship to my inside.

On Monday, I discovered that the entire trust department was going to be housed temporarily in a sub-basement of the bank's operations center, four levels below ground level. The opera-tions center was a low four-story building covered in green glass, about four blocks north of what remained of our old building. The sub-basement was an enormous, windowless room with a bare cement floor, hastily procured metal desks in rows. The desks im-mediately next to Peter were for the senior trust members, by then including me. Electrical and phone wires hung down from the high ceiling to the desks and snaked around the floor. I remember endless banks of harsh fluorescent lights and metal shelves of law books near my desk, although I have no idea where they had come from. They were not from my office.

The fourth sub-basement had been designed for computer equipment, not people. Much later, I found out that it was a month before anybody realized that in the event of a fire anywhere in the building, all the entrances would have been sealed shut and the air would have been sucked out of it.

It was days before I could write legibly on the lines of a yellow legal pad instead of scrawling huge letters and words, a few to a page. I couldn't think coherently about any problem more com-plicated than getting to work and home again. It helped that we were all together, that we were visible to each other in a way so radically different from before, when we were housed in sepa-rate offices on separate floors of the bank building. Without the structure of the building to surround and separate us, informality crept into our dealings with each other. We didn't need to leave phone messages. If the person we wanted was in and not on the phone or meeting with somebody, we walked over to talk to them. There wasn't any privacy, but there was a lot less hierarchy. We were all in this together. Peter's secretary, the legendary dragon who fiercely guarded his availability, was helpless. If he was there, everybody knew it.

The story about how the bank had implemented a comprehensive disaster plan only a short time before the fire became national legend. There might not have been a bank building, but our paychecks magically appeared in our bank accounts every two weeks. Monday after the fire, members of the human resources department were everywhere in the downtown skyways, wearing red T-shirts saying "I Survived the Thanksgiving Day Fire." For a long time, a sense of connection lingered. We bonded in our shared trauma, our sense of having been touched by something world-shattering, something so much larger than vulnerable and fragile human life, something not interested in merely human life. Just as the community bonded when the I-35w bridge collapsed.

Eventually that feeling dissipated. We found a temporary home in a building close to the center of downtown while we waited for the old building to be demolished and a new building to rise from its ashes. Offices, carpeting, and dark wooden desks returned in our quickly rented quarters, with them a sense of formality and hierarchy. For the first time in my working life, I was in an inside office with no windows, a glass wall separating me from the people who walked by, interior walls blocking light from the nearest window. A few years later, in the beautiful new building where space was at a premium, almost everybody was moved into cubicles, then a brand-new idea, now a given in office life.

By then I was gone.

After the shock of the bank burning down, my single-minded commitment to being somebody in the world of men never quite came back together. Eventually my life just stopped working. Trying to be the perfect wife, mother, community volunteer, and attorney businesswoman was enormously stressful. I was so disconnected from myself and my physical needs that I just kept piling it on. The stress built a wall that blocked me from understanding the meaning of information coming from inside and outside. I was one of those honorary men. I wasn't grounded in a relationship to my body or to a sense of myself as a woman, a wife, and a mother. I felt no connection to my real values or desires, what I really wanted out of life. I only knew that rising in status in the world of men seemed somehow important.

If I could have articulated the dream that had taken me to law school, it would have been to have an interesting job in the world of men—my mother's dream—and some measure of community visibility. I had achieved that, surely, but it wasn't enough; it didn't satisfy me. I was having health problems, one of which eventually led to surgery. I ignored the evidence that my rigid, driven, perfectionistic approach to life wasn't just injuring me but was also affecting others, who found me difficult to work with. My family found me difficult to live with, although my daughter wasn't blunt about it until she was a grown woman.

Years later, I learned about an image from the Tarot, an ancient divination system. The Tower card showed up in a reading by a friend in a women's group, but upside down. The standard interpretation of a Tarot card dealt upside down, she said, was that whatever that card might have meant in my life was in the past. I had, at that point, moved on. How could a Tarot card have such an uncanny resemblance to an actual event in my life? How could it so wordlessly and accurately sum up my experience and the meaning of that event?

There I am. A bolt of lightning strikes the King's tower and sets it on fire. I am falling . . . falling . . . falling . . . out of my forty-third-floor office, out of my fourteenth-floor office, into the abyss.

Interpretations of the Tower tell of something sudden, shocking, and profoundly life-changing that has happened or is about to happen to the person asking the question, the "querent." The Tower, in other words, is an image of the kind of shocking, apocalyptic, paradigm-changing event I'm exploring: the kind of event, like the I-35w bridge collapse or Hurricane Katrina, that affected me so powerfully as I helplessly witnessed the terrible suffering on television. The Tower is also a painfully literal image of what happened to all of us on September 11, 2001—our shared, national apocalyptic event—touching again the parallels I draw between my own story and the story I am telling about all of us.

I imagine the falling figures in the Tower are up "too high" and that, like the giant in the Inuit print in my office, they have become disconnected from the earth and dangerously ungrounded. The tower has a crown on it, a symbol of the King. Jung described the symbolic role of the King in a fairy story as the ruling principle of consciousness, the worldview that governs individual and collective psychic life, the psychic Kingdom. My ruling principle of consciousness had become the values and ideas expressed in the world of men. I was ambitious, competitive, and focused. My daily life was almost completely bound up with life in the office, its challenges and dramas. The bank trust department was, in some ways, the King's tower, a perfect expression in its hierarchy and values of the worldview I learned much later to call patriarchy.

A sudden irruption of the sacred broke through the veil between worlds, destroying the untenable structure I had created for myself and, eventually, throwing me to the ground, the ground of my real self and not the self I had unconsciously created in response to forces I had not understood. A mystery shook up my life and changed it forever. My obsession with living in a way that was out of touch with my real values and desires left me vulnerable to just such a catastrophic event. It could have been divorce, serious illness, or even the death of someone I loved. Instead it was, almost too literally, the destruction of the building where I worked, the destruction of everything I had built as a lawyer businesswoman. Whatever the burning of the bank building meant to all the other people who experienced it personally, that's what it meant to me. The moment felt ruinous and catastrophic, personally apocalyptic, but, like Betty Friedan's book a little more than a decade before, it set me on a course which probably saved my life.

It is too easy to label my creation of that self as wrongheaded and unconscious, even if I was far out of touch with my real desires. In creating that self, I had retrieved personally and culturally repressed parts of myself—my intellect; my ambition; my capacity to understand complex issues in the worlds of law, finance, and business; my belief that I could be part of that world—parts that I would need if I was to become more myself. My understandable mistake was in identifying with them, seeing no distinction between what Jung imagined as the Animus, the unconscious "masculine" part of my psyche, and myself, creating a life that served that identification rather than my real self.

If we are going to continue to think in terms of a woman's Animus, if we continue to imagine "male" and "female" culturally determined characteristics and put them into boxes, the Animus must serve the woman and not the other way around. As long as there are separate worlds in which men's and women's values operate, the domains loosely called masculine and feminine, the Anima and the Animus, will remain useful concepts. Even if the world of men now includes many women, it will be a separate world as long as the dominant values of that world remain those of patriarchy.

I am glad to have learned what I learned during that time in my life, to have had those experiences, to have been the person I was then, even with all my regrets. None of it was wasted. I can't say that I go through life without ever identifying with the driven, ambitious part of me, but when I do, I eventually realize that I'm out of touch with myself, that it's a sign that I have pushed painful feelings out of awareness, feelings that I need to unearth, hold, and explore.

After the bank burned, I put together an outer semblance of my former self, enough to fool the people in my life and, on some days, myself. But there were tectonic plates moving beyond my awareness. My world-shattering experience of the Thanksgiving Day fire parallels what I write about now, the meaning of apocalyptic collective events for a wounded collective consciousness. Just as bridges aren't supposed to fall in down in Minnesota, sturdy fifteen-story buildings in the heart of downtown Minneapolis, a short distance from the doomed bridge, aren't supposed to catch fire and burn. My experience of both events and their aftermath gives me a personal perspective on what I believe is now happening in our shared world.

Unconsciously, I had gone into the heart of our collective shadow, as one way of understanding it from inside at a very deep level. The burning of the Northwestern National Bank building on Thanksgiving Day in 1982 was, for me, the kind of dramatic, violent, paradigm-shifting experience I imagine we are having collectively, as we helplessly experience unimaginably destructive apocalyptic events. What I learned about myself from that experience has parallels to the healing process I imagine we need to go through as a society, my story giving me insights into the story I tell about our collective dream.

SPIRITUAL LIFE

The woman I was on the weekend the bank burned down had probably never heard of the Tarot and certainly would have had no interest in it if she had. I didn't have anything I would have thought of as a spiritual or a religious life. In November of 1982, I was comfortably agnostic.

I'd had an eclectic, mostly accidental, religious upbringing. My father came from an immigrant Jewish family; his grandparents arrived from Eastern Europe at the turn of the twentieth century. I have no idea how religious his childhood might have been, but moving into a WASP suburb of New York City, with its restricted neighborhoods and country clubs, made it easy for him to flee his Jewishness. My mother was not Jewish, which caused consternation among some of her Southern relatives when she and my father married. She liked to say that she was Episcopalian, but I don't have the sense that she felt connected to any church, and, long after my mother's death, my grandmother laughed at the idea that my mother was Episcopalian. She told me that my mother had been baptized by an itinerant preacher on the porch of the house in rural Dade Country where my grandparents lived when she was born. For my grandmother, my mother's baptism seemed to take care of the question.

We, the children, weren't told that my father was Jewish until I was in junior high. I still don't know why my parents sat us all down in the kitchen one day to formally announce that he was. We grew up with almost no connection to my father's side of the family or to his childhood experiences. Being Jewish was not an option for me growing up, although two of my best friends in high school were Jewish. The Jewish community of Chappaqua was invisible to me.

Shortly after my sister was born, an Irish nanny came to live with us. We quickly shortened Mrs. Darby to Darby; children of the 1940s, we would never have called an adult by her first name. Darby lived in a pinky beige-painted bedroom and bathroom on the third floor of our Pleasantville house, down the hall from the attic crawl space. She had a fascinating bathtub with clawed feet and mysterious things on her dresser having to do with her faith. We didn't think of her as a nanny. She was, for almost a decade, a member of our family, as my mother coped (her word) with having four children and a lawyer husband who was often in the city until late in the evening and worked tirelessly in his garden on weekends. I understand why my mother wanted another adult in the house.

At a similar time in my life, with a busy lawyer husband and two young children, I sometimes felt like a single parent. We hired live-in babysitters to give me freedom of movement as well as company. They were indispensable once I started law school. Darby's effect on my family—her devoted Catholicism, her stories of the Easter Rising (post office rebellion) in Dublin, her dislike of the English, her Irish accent, and her passion for opera—was formative for each of us in our own way.

Many Sunday nights, we four children sat on the floor, listening to a fifteen-minute radio program, *The Greatest Story Ever Told*, my first exposure to the stories of the Old Testament. We celebrated Christmas with Christian intensity. Sometimes we had a crèche. There was always an elaborately decorated Christmas tree, every tiny branch and space on it overfilled with ornaments, lights, and deadly, silvery lead icicles, reflected in the dark mirrors of mid-winter evening windows. For some years we listened to a record of Dylan Thomas's "A Child's Christmas in Wales" on a Victrola, waiting for each of the well-remembered lines. "And the wise cats never appeared."

My mother often played the piano while all of us, except my father, stood around her, singing from the *Fireside Book of Folksongs*, a lovingly beaten-up large book with dark green covers and a fading red graphic on the front—her reddened hands fiercely tackling the keys, hitting an occasional wrong note. Christmas carols were only for that time, and they evoked in me a sense of beauty and wonder which suffused my life at Christmas, not just at home but also in the schools we went to and the little villages—Pleasantville, Chappaqua, and Mount Kisco—where we lived. Even though it may have been an illusion, I remember it as time when the whole of our small community came together and shared something that to me, as a child, felt magical.

Only now I wonder how the Jews felt about it.

In those days, schoolchildren learned Christmas carols and sang them at school assemblies and in groups that serenaded commuters getting off the train at the little railway stations. I understand why we have collectively denatured Christmas as a shared community celebration in order not to marginalize those who don't celebrate it. I also feel my children missed something by not learning Christmas carols at school.

I went into adulthood deeply conflicted about Christmas, the magic and wonder of it, the yearning and nostalgia of it, and the memories of painful childhood moments connected to it. I became even more conflicted about it after my mother died. My mother's birthday was Christmas Eve, and we always celebrated it, making up for her having been shortchanged as a child with "Happy Birthday and Merry Christmas." I was only in my early twenties, without children of my own, when she died. It was shortly after New Year's, and my painful memories of her last Christmas were too sharp for years.

They included memories of my grandmother, who came to spend over a month in our house in Chappaqua, despite rarely having been able to take the long trip north from the small house where she lived alone in the rural outskirts of Miami. I could feel that the trip was hard on my deeply introverted grandmother, too much family for her. We all, even my normally straight-talking and acerbic grandmother, walked through that Christmas in a fog of denial that my mother, thin and bedridden, was dying.

I wish I'd been able to talk honestly with my mother, to tell her that I loved her, to grieve the utterly unimaginable together. But that conversation could never have happened, given family rules about not dealing honestly and straightforwardly with difficult or painful feelings or truths. She was taken to the hospital suddenly, just after Christmas. The last time I saw her, she was in a hospital oxygen tent, lips bright with red lipstick, feebly and unsuccessfully attempting to push the tent away and kiss me good-bye. She said she'd see me "in the spring," and my husband and I left to catch a plane home, he to go back to his law firm and me to go back to teaching English to high school seniors. An early morning a few days later, my father called to tell me that she had died during the night.

When I first became a grown-up with my own children, I annually wore myself out in a manic attempt to make magic for the people I loved, just as my mother had. I understood much later that perhaps I did that in order to keep my mother near me at the time of year when I missed her most, perhaps also because I was trying to redeem my ambivalent feelings about Christmas. I slowly, bit by bit, stopped the crazy overdoing of it, one unnecessary job—Christmas cards, Christmas baking—at a time, but that took the hope for magic out of it. Next, I flattened Christmas completely, telling myself that it had become too commercial; certainly it had in comparison to my memories of the Christmas of my childhood, with their deep yearning and nostalgia. Eventually, I released all expectations of Christmas, that I could make magic, that I had to feel magic, that it could be something so large, so much more than ordinary in my imagination—it was not humanly possible to make it all that my yearning wanted it to be.

The magic slowly returned to that flat, empty place in my heart as I began to feel something powerfully ancient and mythic about that time of year. At Solstice, there is something about the brave colored lights standing against the long, frigid darkness of my northern city, something about the hush I sense underneath the celebrating and frenzied buying, as daylight dims and shortens and the world pauses and waits for the moment when the light slowly, minute by minute, begins to return. Those lights and that hush speak to me about the millennia in which my ancestors observed and celebrated that moment of the return of the light, probably ever since we became humans.

I first touched that ancient place in me, even with the commercialism of Christmas all around, some years ago, during a Christmas season when I had no home. It was long after my husband and I had divorced. I was living in a rented apartment in downtown Minneapolis, having sold and moved out of the house I moved to after my divorce even though my new house wasn't finished. I had a few critical possessions with me, mostly clothes. The rest was in storage, waiting to be moved into the new house.

For exercise, I walked the downtown skyways in the dark late afternoons, surrounded by crowds of package-laden office workers heading to their cars or buses. As I walked, I took in the lights and decorations in the department stores and shops along the skyways, the lights visible through skyway windows as I crossed over streets.

Without my house, without my furniture, without the protective routine of my familiar life, I felt naked and alone, unusually permeable to everything around me; that unexpected vulnerability allowed a gentle, loving spirit, a sense of awe and wonder, to penetrate me, at last redeeming my childhood Christmas. Since that Christmas, it is enough that the ancient place, a religious place in the most expansive sense of the word, is reliably touched every dark, cold winter season, that I do something just a little out of the ordinary—wrap a few carefully selected presents in bright color and glitter, savor the unpredictable and poignant moments of magic whenever they appear (which they always do, especially around children) and gather to eat, drink, laugh, and hug with the most beloved people in my life.

My father participated, with enthusiasm, in our Christmas rituals. He and my mother tried to create magic for their children, even though the financial ups and downs of life in a small law firm in New York City must have made putting gifts under the tree for four children challenging at times. I don't know enough about my father's childhood to know whether or how his family celebrated Christmas, but I imagine he liked being able to enter wholeheartedly into a celebration that otherwise would have left him feeling like a second-class citizen.

When my younger brother and I were small, we were shown "reindeer tracks" one Christmas morning, in the snow on the roof over the front door that was visible from my brother's bedroom in the Pleasantville house. My father must have created them out of holiday whimsy, imagining our wide-eyed look as we saw tangible proof that Santa Claus had visited. At the same time, I wonder if he was emotionally vulnerable around the holiday. I have memories of him lashing out angrily at some childish behavior, memories that were among the reasons I faced Christmas with deep ambivalence for many years after I left my parents' house for good.

The Greatest Story Ever Told was one source of Bible stories in my childhood. The other was Sunday school. My religious education, such as it was, started when I was in elementary school. There was a brief period when I went to Sunday school in the basement of the Congregational Church, then just up the steep King Street hill from the very small town that Chappaqua was in the 1940s, for reasons which mystify me now. I can't imagine my parents going to church services. Did they, at least briefly, believe that they needed to instill a proper religious upbringing in me, not imagining that my religious upbringing could be Jewish? Whatever impelled them, my Sunday morning life in that basement didn't last long. The Congregational Church building much later became a synagogue.

Serious Sunday school started when I was in fifth or sixth grade.

A classmate had come to spend the weekend, and she sang in the Episcopal Church choir in another stone church, on Bedford Road in Pleasantville, just down the road from my elementary school. I joined the choir at that church. Shortly after that weekend, my friend left the choir, but I stayed because I loved to sing and had a decent ear for music. Sunday school was mandatory for children who sang in the choir. My memory of it is vague. It wasn't in a basement this time but in the rooms of a one-story annex to the main church. I was the only one in my family who went, and I must have heard many Bible stories, because one year I was given a Bible for perfect attendance, the only Bible I've ever owned.

However my knowledge of Christian stories and symbolism happened, I was grateful during my analytic training when I realized that I had a dimly remembered fund of Old Testament stories that suddenly became important. Something in those stories, in mythology books, and in the fairy tales from Andrew Lang's fairy story books of many colors touched a mysterious place in me that had nothing to do with anything I had obediently learned in church and Sunday school.

Otherwise, my spiritual upbringing was, at its core, agnostic. A close friend and I had a brief flirtation with the Unitarian Church when we were in high school. Although her family was Jewish, her upbringing seemed as nonreligious as mine. Our WASP suburb must have discouraged Jewishness, even among Jews brave enough to live there. We called our flirtation with the Unitarian Church "altar shopping." Our flirtation didn't last long. My father disdainfully declared at the Sunday dinner table that the Unitarian Church was just a haven for "apostate Jews," and his disapproval ended my altar shopping. I had no idea he was describing himself.

A few years ago, just as WASP culture was falling into terminal decline, a memoir by *New Yorker* writer Tad Friend about his WASP childhood woke me to a brand-new truth about my growing-up experience with my family. According to the online reviews, some readers, who apparently didn't grow up in or near a bastion of Eastern WASP privilege, found his book boring, self-obsessed, and whiny. I found his book riveting and sent it to my sister for Christmas because I wanted her take on what I learned about our family from it. Friend describes a "numbness of the soul," an emotional distancing that is both cultural and familial. I realized, and my sister confirmed, that our family had been on the far periphery of that world, perhaps yearning for inclusion in it, perhaps simply adopting its behaviors because that was what other people did. Maybe it was just about being immersed in the culture of our WASP suburb. We, too, had lamb for Sunday dinner in the middle of the day. We had no second house, but the family drove to Nantucket for several years to live in rented houses during the summer while my father stayed behind to work in the steamy city, coming up for a few weekends during our stay. My brothers were sent to day and boarding schools. For many WASPs, the Episcopal Church is the denomination of choice, so my mother's idea that she was Episcopalian would have fit nicely into an unconscious WASP fantasy. Perhaps we were WASP wannabes.

And we had the emotional distancing down pat. In my house, we had rules about proper, permissible, and acceptable behavior. People who didn't live by those rules—well, they weren't our kind of people. I don't know that anybody ever said that around me, but I understand that judgment well. It took years of therapy and analysis to undo a lethal combination of WASP repression, Catholic shame, and Jewish guilt. And I couldn't have imagined going into therapy until after the bank building burned down.

COLLAPSE: MY LIFE AS A LAWYER

In the spring of the year after the bank building burned, I had lunch with a friend who worked at the bank holding company. She was bubbling over with an experience she'd just had the weekend before, something called a Compulsivity Clinic. She urged me to go.

Something made me sign up. My experience at the clinic immediately sent me into therapy with a therapist I met that weekend, later into Jungian analysis, and from there to becoming a Jungian analyst myself. I might never have decided to go into therapy on my own, even though at that point in my perfectionistic, workaholic life it would have been a very good idea. It was one of those moments that Jung described as a "synchronicity," a meaningful coincidence, something that doesn't feel like chance. A synchronicity dissolves the apparent distinction between "inner" and "outer." I had an inner need, although I didn't know it, and the outer world responded with my friend's suggestion. It feels like something other than pure chance that we scheduled lunch for that particular Monday.

In the world I lived in at the time I signed up to go to a Compulsivity Clinic, the idea of synchronicity would have made about as much sense to me as the idea that I might learn something from a Tarot card. None. The power of a synchronicity or a Tarot reading can only be felt by someone who has temporarily suspended belief in the scientific worldview, someone who feels intuitively that an event or a card on the table in the outer world is related to something in the inner world, and I was not that person. The subjective experience of the perceiver is central to Jung's concept of synchronicity. The pattern of meaning intuited whenever a synchronicity is felt is accepted as true in a way entirely different from the way that scientific facts or principles are accepted as true.

Now, synchronicities feel slightly eerie to me. They open a crack in my everyday consciousness. I am momentarily reminded that life is mysterious. I feel something at work other than my merely human will. I remember what Jung said:

> To this day God is the name by which I designate all things which cross my willful path violently and recklessly, all things which upset my subjective views, plans and intentions and change the course of my life for better or worse.

I have experienced synchronicities that at the time did not strike me as meaningful. But looking back, I realized that I'd been given a clue about something that only later became conscious; I can still be in touch with the eeriness.

My experience at the bridge collapse site was not a scientific fact, but it was a fact. Others in the community felt something out of the ordinary at the collapse site too, even if they might not have used the word "sacred" to describe it. The uncanny experience of my friend and his wife on a boat sailing the Adriatic Sea was a synchronicity. That it suddenly occurred to my friend to tell me about it, at the end of a long lunch, also felt like a synchronicity because even then I thought that I might someday write about the bridge collapse. My friend's story said something to me about the power of the bridge collapse for everyone in the community, even for those who were on the other side of the world.

My experience at the collapse site was a mystery, a terrible, tragic mystery, a mystery that shattered our community and the lives of many of its members for some larger purpose.

Wakan Tanka in Lakota is sometimes translated as Great Spirit. More true to the actual meaning may be Great Mystery or Great Mysterious-ing, an ongoing, ever-present creative energy that embodies in the visible world. It is humbling to be touched by mystery, to realize that the control we imagine we have over our lives is an illusion. Any of us could have been on that bridge.

Going into therapy began a long, slow process of learning to trust something other than scientific certainties or other people's ideas, something other than conventional wisdom about how to live my life, things that didn't make logical sense. I had trusted something other than conventional wisdom when I reacted to Betty Friedan's book by radically changing my understanding of how married women with children could live their lives. But I didn't see then that it mattered what I was passionate about; I didn't trust myself enough to know what my passions were. I was simply determined to break out of the cultural mold that had shaped my life up until then, perhaps unconsciously connecting that mold to my mother's early death. At the time I had lunch with my friend, I often didn't know how I felt about anything. I was living on automatic pilot.

It can be jarring and disruptive to trust the small voices in our heads, to pay attention to synchronicities and dreams and change something in our lives, little or large, in response. It was jarring and disruptive to the life I had so carefully constructed in rejecting the feminine mystique when I trusted my instinct and went to the clinic weekend. The clinic shattered my sense of who I was and where I had come from, letting me focus on family and childhood experiences, that part of my life I thought I had left behind, along with its dictates about the right way to spend my days as a woman with small children.

I began experimenting with trusting my instincts in small ways. I went into bookstores and picked up books that ignited a spark of interest, what I later called my "unguided guided reading pro-gram." I devoured books on psychology. A couple of years later, an-other weekend retreat experience again left me with certainty, this time that I could no longer stay in my job at the bank.

I don't remember much about that second weekend—only that it was in a religious retreat center that had the drabness of insti-tutional buildings of a certain age, painted in leftover army green and ocher paint the hardware store couldn't sell. We were given an exercise: *What part of your past life feels the way your life feels now?* I was surprised by my answer: third grade. I hated third grade, perhaps more than any other year in school. Our teacher was a stern woman who devoutly believed in punishment. For the boys, it was sometimes a rap on the knuckles with a ruler, but usually it was being deprived of something we enjoyed or being made to sit in the corner.

I spent much of my time in school daydreaming, and I must have experienced my share of life in the corner. I only remember being sad for my friend Susan when it once happened to her, and that memory probably stands in for my feelings of shame and humiliation in Miss K's classroom.

Third grade was when my belief that something was terribly wrong with me began to solidify. Because I rode to school on the public bus and didn't live in the immediate neighborhood of the school, as most of my classmates did, I wasn't part of their everyday lives. We rarely played together or went to each other's houses after school. That may have been the reason one of my classmates invited most of the class, but not me, to a birthday party over lunch one day. I remember standing where I'd gotten off the public bus across the street from school, coming back from going home for lunch, feeling as I so often did that I didn't belong and it had something to do with me.

Now I realize that I was socially immature for my grade because I had skipped first grade. In the 1940s, the consequences of my skipping a grade would not have entered anyone's mind. I don't remember exactly what about life in the bank felt like third grade, but at the time it made perfect sense. I wonder if what I say about third grade solidifying my sense of something terribly wrong with me was the real point: that it was time to begin to heal an awful feeling no child should have.

After I had left the legal counsel office, I took a middle-management position in the trust department, overseeing the lawyers and staff who worked in the new-business (sales) department for individual trusts. I had a nice corner office, but I was in over my head and miserable. I had no idea what I was supposed to do. As trust counsel, I had learned enough about the business and legal issues involved in trust department operations to feel comfortable in my job. In a pinch, if I needed help or support, there were always the lawyers in our outside law firm to talk to. Trust counsel had been an interesting job, working with the variety of difficulties that arise in a large, operationally complicated organization. In hindsight, it may have been the legal job I enjoyed most.

I made the mistake of thinking that I needed to move out of the lawyer job and into a management track in the bank. I imagine that underneath that mistake, in addition to lawyer hubris, was an unconscious sense that I had to keep moving, keep rising in the bank, to satisfy the restless ambition that was holding my demons at bay. Peter urged me to take the job, and I did. I imagine if the job had been right for me, I would have jumped into it enthusiastically and learned what I needed to learn, just as I had when I became trust counsel. But, at that point in my life, my enthusiasm was just for a change to satisfy my restless spirit. It wasn't the right job or the right time in terms of the person I was becoming.

In third grade, I felt helpless and trapped; there was no way out other than moving on at the end of a terrible year. I felt trapped at the bank, sensing that I had come to the dead end of something; I didn't know what. I desultorily interviewed for a job at another financial institution. When the man interviewing me made it clear they were looking for an ambitious workaholic, I dimly knew I didn't want to be that person anymore, even though I was hurt that I wasn't called for a second interview.

At the barely remembered weekend in the dreary retreat center, I had the now-familiar experience of a shocking realization, this time that I couldn't go on living that way. This time I had the power to do something. When I left that workshop, joining my husband at his Carleton College reunion, a friend greeted me by asking if I'd like to join her on the board of the local psychoanalytic society; I said "yes." It was synchronistic that the experience that finally moved me to leave my life at the bank should be followed so immediately by an invitation from the direction of what became my new life, even if it was years before I made the connection.

Eventually, I dropped out of my lawyer-businesswoman world and went home. I imagine I was hoping to find out who I was and what I wanted. The creative energy was moving on from that part of my life, although I didn't understand at the time what was happening. I was exhausted and burnt out from having a job, a husband, children, and an active volunteer life, desperately unhappy and feeling deeply inadequate in my job. I took a leap of faith and launched myself into the void.

I quickly discovered that trusting that sense put me at odds with conventional wisdom. Again. This time there was no reinforcement for what I had done. When I dropped out of the feminine mystique and became a lawyer, the feminist movement affirmed my choice. Now, my fellow women attorneys and businesswomen were angry at me for betraying them. As they saw it, my personal choice implicated all women who were determined to succeed in a man's world. My decision would only give men a reason not to hire a woman.

My son had left for college, but I hoped I might be able to spend more time with my daughter, then a high school sophomore. I wonder now if she was angry at me for shattering the image of the accomplished, professional mother she was proud of and had known all her life. That image had begun to form her ideas of what she wanted from her life, just as my image of my mother had formed mine, and it must have seemed wrong to her that I would reject that life, the life I'd lived all during her childhood. And she was moving psychologically and emotionally away from home. In my memory, she spent most of her time at home on the phone, sitting on the floor next to her bed, glaring at me when I opened her closed door. My ever-present guilt for choosing to go to law school and work while she was small made me wonder if she was thinking: *NOW she wants to spend time with me!*

After I dropped out, I almost immediately became depressed. I went for help from the therapist I'd been working with on and off since the clinic weekend. I was shocked and hurt by her reaction. As she saw it, dropping out was the sole cause of my depression. Of course I would get depressed if I suddenly stopped working! I should go back to work!

How could the person who was helping me learn to trust my instincts not support my decision? I had a vague sense that I had been trying to escape a lifelong depression by living a manic, workaholic life, that it was *my* depression, and that I needed to hear what it had to say and deal with it on its own terms. And, with all my heart and soul, I did not want to go back to work. Reluctantly, sadly, I realized that I would not go on working with my therapist. In a strange, blank world, I was on my own.

I decided to go into Jungian analysis about a year after I left the bank. This time, the catalytic weekend retreat was led by a well-known Jungian analyst. I must have wanted to invite another jolting experience to help me out of a very lost place. I don't think I knew much about this particular Jungian analyst, known for her work encouraging women to follow what Jung called the path of "individuation."

As I understand what Jung meant by individuation, it is about living a life that is uniquely ours, reclaiming the parts of ourselves we have rejected and forgotten, even parts of ourselves we have never known—those parts driven underground by the dictates of our families and our culture, those parts we're ashamed of or don't want to know about. It isn't always easy to discern which voice I am listening to, which path I am following. Is it the familiar voice of family and culture? Is it a voice rooted in psychological dysfunction? Or is it a different voice, the voice speaking from my transformative edge, sometimes speaking in enigmatic hints?

Eventually, I learned to tell those voices apart more quickly and to trust, often reluctantly, the voice that speaks to me in dreams, thoughts, feelings, fantasies, and synchronicities—even if what it says goes against the part of me that believes it knows what it wants, even if it says something I don't want to hear, even if it disrupts my life. Gradually, I didn't require powerfully disruptive experiences to find my way home, to allow in what was rejected and unseen by my ordinary awareness, to break through the barriers and defenses I had erected against myself and the world.

The retreat was called "Symbolic Aspects of the Masculine and Feminine." I had no idea what "symbolic aspects" might be, but the title piqued my interest. I had left the world of men. Although it had been deeply satisfying in many ways, my way of being in it had disconnected me from essential parts of myself. Maybe this weekend could help me begin to understand what those were. The retreat might help me deepen my understanding of the different realities men and women inhabit.

Over that weekend, our small group was led slowly through the fairy tale of Cinderella as the story of a psychological journey. I had never imagined that my beloved fairy tales could be read that way! Even more startling, I saw myself and my depression in the part of the story where Cinderella has lost her mother and father and is sitting in the ashes. I was not just living *my* story; I was living a shared, collective story, a story particular to women! I had an immediate, inexplicable sense that I had come home. I decided, on the spot, that I had to work with a Jungian analyst.

I found a Jungian analyst through a stumbling process of asking around and trusting my instincts. I made a new friend at the fairy tale retreat and vaguely knew she was connected to that world. After learning that she was in analyst training and not yet an analyst, I asked her if she could recommend somebody. She suggested I talk to her analyst, but when I did, I could tell that the essential chemistry between therapist and patient wasn't there. I asked someone else, who I also dimly thought was a Jungian analyst, about working with her. She recommended somebody she knew and liked in the small Jungian community. When I went to see him, the chemistry was there.

And, sure enough, there was a synchronicity. Two women law school classmates and I had been interviewed by the *Minneapolis Star Tribune* for an article about women who had left their lives as lawyers. The article had come out only a few days before I went to talk to him. He had read it and remembered me.

Once again, I had to radically revise my stories about myself. My inner landscape melted and shifted before my eyes. I wasn't prepared to have so much of who I thought I was stripped away quite so radically. Therapy up until that point hadn't been like that. It was one thing to strip that identity away. It was quite another to start to trust what was underneath my well-put-together persona, the "me" I presented to the world, and the barriers I had erected against everything I didn't want to know about myself, against life. That person felt empty, naked, and vulnerable. A nobody. What on earth could she know?

Now my obsessive reading focused on Jung and writers about Jungian psychology. The idea of training to become a Jungian analyst came up within months and I immediately rejected it. With absolute certainty. I knew enough about transference (the way we unconsciously write our therapists into roles in our personal stories) from the reading I was doing to suspect the idea was nothing more than a side effect of being in analysis. I admired my analyst and so, of course, I would do what I had done the first time I radically changed my life. I would adopt the profession of a man in my life. Different man, same process, I thought.

I eventually trusted a halting, deeply ambivalent process enough to start to explore what I would need to do to become a therapist, although that idea still made no logical sense to me, given how much in need of therapy I was myself. I located a graduate program in psychology that would allow me to create my own course of study. That program would be the polar opposite of law school, which had poured me into a mold designed to make me a lawyer. I could be in charge of what I wanted to learn, even as I took courses to help me prepare for the psychology licensing exam. I was, by then, well beyond what would have made sense to anybody in my former life, even, I imagined, my former therapist.

While I was wrestling with the decision about whether or not to go to graduate school, she appeared in a dream. As I remember it, I am sitting on the floor in a bare room that feels like a classroom. My former therapist comes down the hall and puts her head in the door. She asks me a question about the graduate program I am thinking about. What would I do for the literature portion of the degree? She moves off down to the end of the hall and disappears through a door marked Staff Only.

Staff Only. In order to go through that door, I would have to become a therapist. The room I was sitting in was bare. I had no idea what going to graduate school would be like or what it would mean to me, but it was a first step. Now I see that having my former therapist show up in a dream after our work had ended so abruptly shifted something in me, helped me realize that I was grateful for my work with her. It started me down a path completely at odds with anything I'd ever imagined for myself. The degree was going to have a "literature portion." What was a literature portion? Might that be Jungian psychology, which was taking me back to everything I'd once loved—myths, fairy tales, stories of all kinds?

Actually putting a foot firmly on that path, applying for graduate school, took agonizing months. Was I doing the right thing? What if I was wrong? I must have been "wrong" years before when I decided that I wanted to be a lawyer. There was no feminist movement, nothing in the outside world, affirming my choice.

Finally, I had another dream. In the dream, I'm thinking about buying a bicycle from a friend, an artist. Shortly after leaving the bank, I had run into this friend on the street. She told me that she was planning to take a drawing class at an art school near her house in the suburbs and urged me to come with her. Although I didn't know her well, I liked her and I decided I would; I'd always loved art classes. I thought of her as someone who had happily made the choice not to pursue a professional career in the world of men, someone focused on her family and her creative work. In the dream, I'm trying to test the bicycle I want to buy from her while it is standing still. As I do, the derailleur chain falls off.

Eventually, the familiar "aha" jolted me. You can't ride a bicycle if it isn't moving! How could I know whether something was right for me unless I actually did it? I applied to graduate school and followed a process that, like riding a bicycle, developed a momentum of its own, a process that led me to apply for analytic training. A bicycle rider chooses her own path. The dream said I was to choose the direction of my life, not ride along as a passenger, dreaming society's dream, passively following other people's ideas about my life.

Now, I contrast that process with the one that led to the decision to build the house in which I now live, just about twenty years after I left my job at the bank and started Jungian analysis. Beginning early in the life of my older grandson, starting when he must have been about three, we had an afternoon each week that belonged just to him. I picked him up from preschool, we had a snack at a coffee shop close to his school, and then we would head back to my house to play before I took him home.

We often took walks. In the spring of 2003, a day or so before my birthday, we took our usual walk through the woods across the street from my house to the bike and walking paths that parallel the nearby railroad tracks. As we walked back, just across the street from my house, there was a fork in the path, two ways we could go. We could head back to my house, or we could turn the other way and follow a narrow path into the wooded first-ring suburban neighborhood that began right across the street from my house, a path neither of us had ever been on. When I asked my grandson which way he wanted to go, for the first time he insisted we go the other way.

Since moving into that area, I had rarely been in that little neighborhood across the street. As far as I could tell, the streets were
all dead ends. I remembered there was a walking bridge across
the railroad tracks at the end of one of those dead ends, and I
thought it would be fun for my grandson. We might see a train! We
walked up the wrong street, coming to the end of a different cul-
de-sac, but were encouraged by a friendly resident to walk down
their stairs to the next street over. There was the walking bridge.
We walked across and back, high over the railroad tracks and the
walking and biking paths, parallel stripes of tracks, grass, and as-
phalt. No train. We headed back toward my house. As we walked
by the house closest to the walking bridge on one side of the quiet
street, two boys in a driveway asked if we wanted to see a yo-yo
show. Of course we did! We watched their show, thanked them,
and walked back to my house.

That was on the outside. On the inside, something wild and
wholly unexpected was going on. I was falling in love: with the
winding streets, the gardens, the little patches of woods, the un-
pretentious small suburban ramblers, the unexpected quiet of a
neighborhood only a couple of blocks away from the busy street in
front of my house. I was having a very clear fantasy: maybe, someday, I'd find a small house on a wooded hillside in that neighborhood (not the house I'd bought after I'd moved out of my married
house, with its knee-grinding six stories of stairs between the garage and my bedroom), close to everything familiar and, yet, far
away . . . it was a compelling and unusually detailed fantasy. That
was Friday.

Monday, I had a telephone call from my architect friend, Sally.
Shortly after graduating as a Jungian analyst in 1997, I'd bought a
small, fifty-year-old summer cottage on the North Shore of Lake
Superior, right on the lake. I had renovated it as a sustainable design project, and Sally was the architect. On the phone, Sally said
that she'd just had a call from a woman who lived in the little suburban neighborhood across the street from my house, the exact

neighborhood my grandson and I had walked through a few days before. The woman said she had a vacant lot next to her house she wanted to sell to somebody who would build a "small, sustainable house" on it. Somebody had given her my architect friend's name.

At that moment, before hanging up the phone, having no idea where the lot was, I knew that I was going to build a house. What else could falling in love with that nearby neighborhood and the call from my architect friend have been about? When Sally and I went to see the lot a day or so later, I was startled to see that it was right next to the driveway where my grandson and I had watched the yo-yo show. Back from the street, under the trees and buck-thorn that covered a small lot that sloped down to a little stream, there was an almost invisible, rusted sign saying "Lot for Sale." My grandson and I had walked right by it on the way back to my house!

Much later, I found out that my neighbor had tried for a year to sell the lot and had almost given up. She had said, in exasperation, "Universe, please send me someone!" shortly before she called the person who gave her my architect friend's name.

It was all synchronicity, and by then I trusted synchronicity and the fantasies and feelings that had come up in me, the falling in love. I had become very aware of my inner life in the years I spent in analysis and training. I paid attention to it, as much attention as I paid to my outer life, once I stopped drawing hard-and-fast distinctions between them. What I had learned about myself through analysis and immersion in Jung's psychology had begun to heal the split between inner and outer and the splits that are among the most profound and destructive in Euro-American culture: the split between matter and spirit and the split between each of us and the human and natural communities in which we are always immersed.

Houses in dreams are often symbolic. They can be a visual image of the psychic structure the dreamer inhabits at the moment of the dream. Houses in life are symbolic, too. They express something essential about who we are. I'd left my married house where my children grew up, the house where I was living when my husband and I separated. It was on a well-traveled parkway around one of the better-known lakes that define city life in Minneapolis.

The house I moved to when I left that house was close to but outside of that neighborhood, off that particular beaten path but still on a very busy street: a house designed and built by an architect for his young family. It was a tree house for grown-ups and I loved it, but the six stories of stairs from the street to my bedroom became too challenging for my aging knees. The spirit that fell in love with it and bought it was out of touch with limits imposed by the matter of my body.

The house I eventually built on a wooded hillside in the neighborhood I fell in love with, the house where I now live, is my house. I was involved in every stage of the design and building of it. There is something in the symbolism of that decision about finally moving into my own psychological house, a house designed and built to suit me and the person I had become, twenty years after leaving the bank.

A critically important part of me had remained buried until the bank burned down, the part that loved singing in the Episcopal Church choir and that deeply responded, in a way I still don't have language for, to Old Testament Bible stories, mythology, fairy stories, and the brave lights shining in the darkness of Solstice. I began to rediscover that part of myself when I first went into therapy. I have no good name for that part, although there are many ways to try to describe it: religious, spiritual, ancient, mythic, or mystical, perhaps.

The moment I was introduced to Jungian psychology, I felt I had come home. I had come home to the part of me that dreams.

Whatever that part of me is, it is often dismissed by people in our society, just as I dismissed it until the bank burned down. It is particularly rejected as subjective and irrelevant by those identified with the myth of science. That part in me has nothing to do with formal religion. While a majority of people in Euro-American culture identify themselves as religious, many pay little or no attention to the part of them that loves, the part of them that dreams. Almost half a lifetime of disconnection from the dreamer and lover in me led to an unsustainable way of being, a way of being that invited intervention from something other than my conscious self, a way of being that might have taken me down the same path toward early death that my mother traveled had I not allowed that way of life, the life I had put so much effort and sincere belief into, to collapse.

MYTHOLOGY

I need to be clear about how I use the word "myth." In its most basic meaning, a myth is a sacred story. It is sacred to a particular cultural group. For that group, a myth has profound explanatory power. In my culture, the ancient myths most familiar to me are those of Greece. Gods, goddesses, and heroes enact fundamental human dramas on a stage outside time and space. Commentators on Western mythology suggest that actual historical events are embedded in many of these stories, which at some point transcended history and space-time. Jung imagined that images of ancient mythology are embedded in the psychology of all of us, that mythology describes life experiences and energies common to all humanity, developed over the thousands of years since our ancestors became human. He named those experiences and energies "archetypes."

One archetypal human experience crucial to the stories I tell is "Mother." We inevitably form images of mothering from our experiences with the particular human beings who mothered us in childhood. Every human being has experienced mothering, whether positive or negative; mother is a collective experience as well as a personal one, reaching back to earliest humanity.

To put the idea in computer terminology, Jungian psychology suggests that humans are hardwired or programmed in their inherited psychic structure to experience mothering. An innate predisposition, in some way I am not totally clear about, organizes an infant's experience, allowing her to experience life-giving psychological sustenance as she forms her most basic understanding of whether the world is a good place or a bad place, a nurturing and sustaining place or a hard, abandoning, or intrusive place. Good Mother and Bad (or Terrible) Mother are available archetypal patterns around which everyone coheres an experience of mothering, whether or not our biological mother or even a woman was the person who carried that experience for us.

That archetypal experience is cultural as well as universal, and mothering is expressed in each culture's myths and stories. Because mothers in a particular culture share ideas and images of mothering, encouraging some behaviors and not others, mothering practices reflect both our family and our culture. In some societies, for example, infants experience bodily contact with their mother or another caregiver at all times. While cultural attitudes around mothering have shifted in my lifetime, the practices I see reflected in the world around me still do not often involve continuous bodily contact between parents and infants. Shared cultural norms around mothering have a profound effect on our psychology.

Ceremonies and rituals evolve out of a culture's mythology, even for those whose mythology is out of awareness. Even if many in a culture, like mine, don't believe they have a mythology. Since the Renaissance, Western consciousness has increasingly withdrawn its psychic energies from the realm of the gods and the sacred. Contemporary meanings for the word "myth" have shifted from myth as sacred story to myth as something not to be trusted:

—a person or thing existing only in imagination
—a belief uncritically accepted by members of a group
—a visionary ideal
—a story utterly without factual basis

Some in Euro-American society imagine that humans have moved beyond irrational, primitive superstitions when it comes to stories about how the world came to be and how it operates. However, mythmaking is an innate human impulse and not so easily dismissed; it is an archetypal human predisposition. It's not hard to see how the myths of science, progress, and capitalism have become sacred stories, in both the ancient and contemporary ways of looking at myth.

To say science and capitalism are myths is not to denigrate either, both of which are ways of seeing and organizing the world. If I seem to be disparaging these ideas by calling them myths, it is because our culture now devalues mythology. Western culture tends to split the embodied world, imagining that everything has a bright side and a dark side. In the world of polarities, science and religion have been opposed, despite the way that some scientists say their scientific understanding has made them more deeply religious as they encounter irresolvable mysteries about the way the universe works. Many scientists are humble about the limits of human knowledge.

Not so the most fanatical adherents to the scientific myth. When I am in the presence of an argument that the scientific worldview or the capitalist worldview are the *only* valid ways to perceive the world, that there are no dark consequences to the way those stories organize behaviors in the actual world in which humans live, then I recognize that I am in the presence of a myth that needs no validation outside itself, a myth in both the positive sense, a sacred story, and negative sense, a belief uncritically accepted. When such a story unconsciously becomes essential to my understanding of the world, I am identified with that myth. Then there is no separation between me and the myth, and I cannot step back from it and see it for what it is.

In these times, I see identification with certain mythic stories as underlying too much of our public conversation about how best to organize society in the twenty-first century, how best to tackle the dark consequences of an unsustainable way of life. Perhaps the push to teach creationism in the public schools is a too-literal and too-fanatical attempt to right the imbalance of a too-literal and too-fanatical identification with science in our society, consciously or unconsciously a recognition that the withdrawal of psychic energy from the world of the embodied sacred has resulted in enormous loss and enormous danger for us all.

Identification with the myths of science, progress, and capitalism—and the resulting disconnection from the part of us that loves, the part that dreams, the part that is humble before the limits of our understanding—has brought the human family to a perilous place. For the first time in the experience of the human species, for the first time in the life of our mother, the earth, the activities of one her species could bring about the collapse of a beautifully balanced system of interrelationship among humans, more-than-human creatures, and plants, earth, water, wind, and stone, that complex web of relationship which has sustained life on this earth for the 65.5 million years since the last major extinction. Although I imagine the devastation that Western consciousness has visited on the earth has been deeply wounding to her, I also imagine she would survive a human-caused extinction as she has all the others. In five, ten, or fifteen million years, a beautiful, intricately woven family of life would again inhabit her lands, waters, and skies. It's humanity that's in peril.

Not everyone on the planet shares the consciousness of the Western mind, but unconscious mythologies of the Western mind have come to dominate our species' relationship to the earth and to our human and more-than-human brothers and sisters. We are on a suicidal trajectory. Many biologists believe we are already well into the next extinction event, as ever-increasing numbers of our more-than-human relatives leave the planet. No wonder we are being personally and collectively awakened by apocalyptic movements and events, shattered into a different consciousness, called to a completely different dream, a different myth, of who we are and where we belong.

I am telling two stories at the same time: my own story and the story of Western consciousness. I tell my own story because I believe that I have learned something about the transformation of consciousness since the Northwestern National Bank Building burned on Thanksgiving night in 1982, something that might help us understand what the transformation of our shared consciousness could look like, how we might open to it in our communities and as a society. I have learned to accept change, sometimes radical change, often with great resistance, living it and then reflecting on it, time after time. When whatever identity I have put together becomes too tight and constricting, fails to allow enough of what I think of as the abandoned parts of me to be lived, fails to serve my life and life itself, the process of transformation begins again.

Sometimes the process starts with a world-shattering realization. But more often, now, I have a sense that my energy, my physical energy, my psychological energy, my creative energy, doesn't want to go where I am asking it to go. I gradually lose my desire. Something that was alive in me is not quite as alive anymore. Or, as I age, something embraced by my younger physical self becomes less possible as I understand limitation more deeply in my bones, make friends with it, understand that all things are no longer physically possible. If they ever were.

THE NORTH SHORE

I dearly loved the magical little remodeled summer cabin on the North Shore of Lake Superior that my architect friend and her team designed in the late '90s, that I stayed in happily, a week at a time, for a number of years. The cabin was the result of a waking dream. The summer before I graduated as an analyst, I had gone on something described as a "vision quest" on an island in a beautiful forested lake in what became, after the settlers arrived, northern Ontario. Had I known then what I know now about how disrespected many indigenous people feel when Euro-Americans appropriate their spiritual traditions, I would not have gone on a vision quest led by nonindigenous organizers. However, that understanding was well into the future.

Groups of participants were flown by a small amphibious plane to an island, Landskib Island, on Lake Temagami. When two dozen or so of us gathered for the first time on the island, we were asked to go sit in a place that appealed to us and quietly settle into being there. From the perch that drew me, high above the rocky lakeshore, I looked across blue water to a nearby island. As I sat quietly there, I realized I was seeing a landscape that looked very much like the North Shore of Lake Superior. A little voice in my head clearly said something completely ambiguous: *You need to go find a place on the North Shore of Lake Superior and do this.*

Do what? For some time, I understood that voice to be telling me that I was to find a place on the North Shore and do something that would help connect people to the earth—perhaps start some kind of ecological education program, like the one conducted on Landskib Island. In the spring of 1997, right after graduation from my analyst training program, a little less than a year after I went on the vision quest, a good friend and I drove north to look at every piece of property that was for sale on the stretch of shore well north of Duluth. None of the houses or cabins spoke to me until we reached a cabin just outside the little town of Tofte, down a winding driveway from Highway 61.

It was tiny, well under a thousand square feet, a summer cabin that had been built in the mid-1940s by the sellers' grandparents. Now all the family members lived well south of the Twin Cities and rarely made the six-hour drive to spend time there. It was primitive and needed a lot of work. But, from a window of the small living room, it had an extraordinary view up the shore to Grand Marais, a half-hour drive to the north. A door opened to a deck which had an unimpeded view of the lake to the horizon, framed by two tall spruce trees. It felt like being on the ocean, missing only the smell of salt.

The little cabin was unusually close to the lake because it had been built before restrictions required a greater set-back from the shore. Any remodeling would be grandfathered in as long as we stayed within the footprint of the existing cabin, the restrictions ending forty feet from where the rock along the shore ended and the sparse natural vegetation began.

As my friend and I drove back up the winding driveway from the cabin to the highway, she turned to me and said, "I'm in love." So was I. I made an offer that day because the real estate agent hinted that another buyer was considering an offer. The sellers sold it to me because they knew I wanted to remodel the cabin to have a place for me and my family to visit, and the other buyer was a developer who planned to tear the cabin down and build two houses for sale on the almost five-acre lot. I met the woman who represented the family when I went up for the closing, and I remember how wistful she was, seeing the cabin for the first time in a long time and being reminded how extraordinary the views were.

I had no idea how buying the cabin fit into what the voice had said to me on Landskib Island, but running an ecological education center didn't appeal to me. I forgot about the little voice and its enigmatic message. As I write now, so many years later, I realize that I may have both understood and misunderstood the suggestion of the little voice. Shortly after beginning work with the architect who became my friend, I read a story in the *Minneapolis Star Tribune* about a couple who had built a sustainable house. I told Sally I wanted to build what gradually became in my mind a sustainable design demonstration project, an earth-friendly house.

It was the latter years of the '90s, and the idea of sustainability had not yet permeated general awareness. I understood enough about sustainability to question the idea that I should have a cabin almost a five-hour drive from my house, guiltily thinking about the size of the carbon footprint all that driving would entail. Even though many people in Minnesota either have "a cabin" or frequently go "up north" for the weekend, especially during the summer, I felt I would be hypocritical if that was all I achieved. Making a public statement about sustainable building would redeem the drive. At least the cabin wouldn't have a big carbon footprint once it was built. After it was done, we could put up a website about the process of designing and building it, an unusual idea then, greatly expanding the reach of my statement.

What we eventually achieved was one possible response to the cryptic direction "do this": let the process of building a sustainable house teach me, my architect friend, and her team about holding the earth and our fellow creatures in our minds and hearts when we build and, at the same time, give that message to a larger community, beyond the immediate community of the North Shore.

Little voices in our heads, like dreams, don't always reveal their meaning in straightforward ways. Dreams, especially, come out of our blind spots. There's a tension between believing the sense of rightness that can accompany a little voice, a dream, or a synchronicity and something I've learned the hard way: that sometimes a firm sense of rightness is the best indication that I am wrong. Distinguishing between those certainties isn't easy, but I have learned to pay attention to the quality of the energy I feel. If it comes from my ego, it has a quality of righteousness that I remember not to trust only after it has seized me, sometimes for quite a while. If the rightness has a slight quality of eeriness, the sense of something pouring through a crack in my everyday certainties, it's more trustworthy.

My sustainable design project turned out to be more of a public statement to the North Shore than I imagined it would be, and I was surprised at the hostility of some of the responses to the wind generator. I believe that connection and care for community are important, but I was a stranger to the North Shore. It wasn't my community.

I came to know the team that built the cabin and the nearby garage. Most of the small crew who worked on the cabin lived in the community or nearby, and we formed our own little community, held together by my appreciation for their craftsmanship and an ethic of care for the land and its inhabitants during construction. One of the many subcontractors who delivered material to the job site said it was the cleanest job site he'd ever seen. But I naively thought that the North Shore community at large, people who I imagined loved the earth because they lived in such a beautiful place, would appreciate my particular way of expressing that love.

Some of the people in the surrounding community, even some of my neighbors, did, but quite a few did not. One of my immediate neighbors, like me, a part-time resident, was angry that my wind generator ruined his pristine view of the high rock cliff on which it stood. I could understand his anger, but I was surprised when other members of the larger North Shore community agreed.

My neighbor invited me to his house so that he could berate me personally for putting up a wind generator, and I sat mute, feeling guilty about what I had done. He also called the local newspaper, whose reporter woke me up unexpectedly early one morning to interview me, finding me in pajamas, too early in the day to have a coherent thought. I remember one line from the story. When I was asked directly about putting up a hundred-foot wind tower in somebody else's view (we had to lengthen it from the original sixty feet after checking on the actual wind velocity near the shore), I mentioned that all the electrical energy then used on the North Shore was generated by burning coal. In my early morning fog, I said: "Coal is dirty to mine and dirty to burn, but the mess is some-place else."

I was right but, in retrospect, it was a pretty arrogant statement. After all, who was I to educate a community that wasn't mine? I was just one of many people who went to that beautiful place, bought property most of the local residents couldn't afford, did whatever we liked with it, and lived somewhere else for most of the year.

The local community derived much of its income from tour-ists. For some of the residents who lived there all year because they loved it and wouldn't live anywhere else, the wind generator was damaging the value of the community's greatest asset—even though I could have removed many of the trees on the lot and built a big house, visible from Highway 61, the two-lane highway that runs along the shore of the lake. Even though, ironically, the wind generator was invisible to most of the community and its visitors unless you knew exactly where to look or canoed near it along the shore. Later, even after all the publicity and putting up a website, my North Shore friends were very good at keeping the secret of exactly where my demonstration project actually was.

The implications of thinking of the beauty and wildness of the North Shore as an asset are shadowy. I am so accustomed to think-ing of nature in economic terms that I find that statement unre-markable. But what does it say about the way I think?

The first destructive act of imagination is to invent the word "na-ture" itself. If I think of our mother, the earth, as something other than "me," I have begun the destructive process of disassociating myself from the ground of my being. The more dissociated my

vocabulary becomes—landscape, environment, countryside—
the more I imagine myself to be separate, the more I enable the
damage, to humans and the earth, that my dissociation permits.
The best I have been able to do is to refer to what I call the "natural surround" and our devastating disconnection from "it." But
the ground of my being is still not me when I write that way, and
writing about how disconnected I am from "it" does not solve the
problem with language and imagination; it embodies the problem.

Our materialistic culture follows a logical progression: we imagine the ground of our being as a separate "it," and we carve the
ancient, rocky shores of Great-Grandmother Lake into imaginary
pieces and "sell" them to people who can afford to "possess" them.
When I purchased that particular land and cabin, I didn't pur-
chase the actual land. I purchased the right to exclude everyone
else from the enjoyment of the beauty from that particular spot,
beauty that included not just the lake views and woods but also a
stream from the nearby Sawtooth Mountains and a pebbly beach
where it emptied into the lake.

That astonishing beauty, measured in feet of shoreline, was reflected in the value of my house and the surrounding land. When
I put my cabin up for sale, I checked with the county for their re-
cords of how many feet of shoreline I owned. There was a standard
per-foot monetary value assigned for real estate purposes, and
I kept that number in the back of my mind as I evaluated offers.
In that same way, natural beauty becomes an asset to the North
Shore community, whose livelihood involves selling things and
experiences to tourists who pay to have a relationship, even a short
one, to that beauty and relative wildness, to take what they may
imagine is a tiny piece of it home.

The native peoples of this land we imagine to be "ours" did not
have the concept of owning land. They inhabited a particular place
where their ancestors had lived, in many cases for thousands of
years. Their creation stories tell of the way the people came to live
on that land. It isn't territory in the sense Euro-Americans mean

it, although indigenous nations would protect their ancestral connection to those lands from other indigenous nations when necessary. Nobody owns the land. It was given to them by the Creator.
It is shared by the people and their more-than-human relatives.
The land is alive. As a Euro-American, I have no way to understand
land as anything but a separate thing and no language for the relationship of a people to a land other than the language of posses-
sion and ownership. For many years, I couldn't tell when the land
was alive and when it wasn't. I didn't experience it in those terms.

The indigenous peoples' way of being with the land has nothing to do with claiming or buying and selling. The US government
entered into treaties with indigenous nations that disposed of
territory, but the gulf between those who thought in those terms
and those who didn't is beyond imagination. Literally. I cannot
imagine, cannot feel from the inside, a relationship to a land as an
all-encompassing, conscious presence deserving of respect. From
that perspective, the US government's unilateral declaration in the
late nineteenth century that Indian reservations, what was left of
indigenous lands after treaties were forced on their peoples, were
to be divided into parcels which were then sold to non-Indian settlers was an intentional act of cultural genocide.

The land on which my cabin was built had been Ojibwe territory
just before the land was divided up by the European settlers of that
area in the late nineteenth century. But the indigenous occupation of that land had been profoundly affected by the coming of
the colonists to the east coast of Turtle Island. Turtle Island was
originally a term used by northeastern woodland tribes—particularly the Iroquois, Lenape, and Anishinaabe—and came from stories about how the land was created and their people came to live
there. It became more broadly used in the twentieth century by
indigenous activists. As poet Gary Snyder suggests, in the quote I
included earlier, using the term "Turtle Island" for our home continent helps shift our understanding away from the Euro-American
perspective that the land of this continent is "ours."

From the very beginning of my personal and cultural ancestors' arrival on Turtle Island, as settlers drove the indigenous inhabitants off their lands, dispossessed indigenous peoples moved westward into territories of other native nations. Over many years, the Ojibwe migrated from the eastern lands of Turtle Island to northern Wisconsin and the Lake Superior area, following a collective dream that told them to travel to the land where food grows on water: *Mahnomen,* the Ojibwe word for the wild rice, which the Grand Portage Band of Ojibwe, north of Grand Marais, still harvests. But when the Ojibwe moved into the territory which became Minnesota, they bumped up against the Dakota people, whose ancestors had been there for millennia.

The result was a long war involving principally the Ojibwe and the Dakota in the territories of what are now the states of Wisconsin and Minnesota. The resulting 130 years of fighting between these nations and others were known to the settlers as the Indian Wars. Minnesota became a territory in 1849 and a state in 1858. Before, during, and after that period, native peoples were pressured to cede by treaty most of their remaining land, greatly reducing the area in which they could live. Struggles between and among the native peoples of the territory that became Minnesota became increasingly intense as the settlers claimed more and more territory as their own. I pick up the Dakota story, too, as a way to begin to understand the invisible consequences of imagining the earth in the way of Western consciousness.

The land on which my house and my home community rest was inhabited for thousands of years by the Dakota people; my country has only existed as a nation for just over two and a half centuries. The first European settlers arrived on the shores of Turtle Island five hundred years ago. Dakota lands in what is now Minnesota almost vanished in just a few decades during the settlement period. The Dakota history in what is now Minnesota ended abruptly with what the descendants of the settlers call the US-Dakota War of 1862.

That war began with the failure of the US government to honor treaty obligations to provide food for the Dakota people, leading to widespread hunger and starvation in their communities. Some Dakota men, enraged by the betrayal and fearful for their communities, attacked Minnesota settlers. The hanging of thirty-eight Dakota warriors in Mankato, Minnesota, at the order of President Lincoln, was the end of those wars, an event observed by the descendants of the settlers one hundred and fifty years later on the day after Christmas 2012. That event is still the largest such execution in American history.

After the execution, most of the remaining Dakota, feared and vilified by the settlers, were driven out of the state in a long march which proved fatal to many of the already-weakened Dakota, to settle in territories west of Minnesota. Many Dakota live outside Minnesota to this day. As I shift my focus back to the reconstruction of a cabin on a beautiful piece of land that I bought and, later, sold in the way of my people, I want to remember these stories about the almost-forgotten peoples of the land on which my cabin and my current house were built.

My architect friend, her design team, the contractor, a team of systems consultants, and I engaged in an extensive inquiry into what exactly what might constitute an earth-friendly house. In addition to designing systems to operate solar panels on the garage roof, a wind generator, and a geothermal heat pump, we used only recycled or sustainably forested wood and reused every usable part of the original cabin. The red half-log siding, typical of summer cabins from the '40s, was carefully removed, sandblasted to remove the lead-based paint, and repainted. It became the outer walls of the garage.

One of the carpenters working on the project had been hired to take down a maintenance building on nearby Sugarloaf Cove, and he told us the wood from that building was available. An organization dedicated to the preservation of the North Shore and teaching about its ecology had purchased the land on Sugarloaf Cove a few years earlier and was taking down an old logging maintenance building in order to build an interpretive center. Perhaps it was a synchronicity that the organization that made the wood available for my reuse was already doing exactly what I thought the little voice might be telling me to do.

The maintenance building had been made of lumber from the magnificent white pines which once covered all the North Shore from north of Duluth to the Canadian border. The area had been completely logged over by lumber companies in the early twentieth century, and the enormous, towering pines, similar in size to the redwoods in California, are long gone, although I have seen astonishing photos of them. We were delighted to have the wood, and it eventually formed part of the interior of the garage, the walls and ceiling open to the inside, allowing us to see the dark marks on the lumber from its former life as a maintenance building.

Of course, given my lifelong preference for doing, I would hear the voice that spoke as I sat on the shore of Landskib Island as telling me to "do" something, and I did imagine I heard it say "do this." Now I realize that the voice came to me as I was just sitting, quietly taking in the forest and waters of Lake Temagami. Perhaps the voice was also telling me just to sit quietly on the shore of Lake Superior. When I imagined I had heard a voice with an enigmatic message, I had almost finished a decade of "doing," the "doing" of graduate school and Jungian training. Going to stay in the cabin for a week out of most months for a number of years was also about just being there, letting the lake, the land, and the sky transform me. Even if I brought books and a laptop with me. Even if I used the internet, as unreliable as it was then.

It seems almost too self-centered, too human-centered, to say that living on the edge of the ever-changing ten-thousand-year-old lake, perched on billion-year-old volcanic rock, changed me. By the end of a few days there, the tensions of life in the city washed away with the sound of the waves, gentle or crashing, always there, always there, sometimes only at the very edge of awareness, the

sound coming through the open window in my bedroom, holding me as I slept. I felt close to more-than-human wildness I
experienced nowhere else when winter storms pounded the rocks
in geysers of surf, and I thought about how quickly I would die if I
fell into that frigid water. I came to know places I loved, hiking up
the Temperance River and other trails, at least until my knee gave
out. I developed friendships with people who became dear to me.
One year, I wrote poetry almost every time I was there. Another
year, I took photographs, images of my life next to the lake in all
seasons. When I was there, I was there: body, mind, and spirit.

Little by little, real life began to intrude on what had originally
been an open-hearted commitment, and my energy started to
move away from the little cabin. I hadn't known when I rebuilt the
cabin that half a dozen years later I would be inspired to build a
house in the city. When I built the house in the city, I didn't imagine that I was withdrawing energy from the little cabin in order
to build another house and live in it, but I was. I don't remember
thinking at all about the possibility of a change in the relationship
with the little cabin, but the realities of my decision started to hit
me soon after I moved into my current house.

Once again, my spirit had moved well ahead of my embodied
life, and embodied life started to catch up. I felt the burden of being
responsible for two houses by myself, one almost a five-hour drive
from the other. Life in my cabin involved unusual systems—wells
for geothermal energy, and an intricate system to feed power from
the solar panels and the wind generator to the grid when I wasn't
using it and to draw power from the grid when mine was inadequate—systems that required specialized attention. Specialized
attention was hard to come by in a remote location before experiments like mine became more common. The drive became more
and more difficult as I aged, and I was more aware of the drain on
my bank account as I took a levelheaded look at the actual yearly
cost of an experience that had once been purely an affair of the
heart.

One particularly difficult systems failure, I don't remember which one, was the end. I remember spending the night at Bluefin Bay, a nearby resort in Tofte, because I couldn't stay in my cabin. I drove home stunned, not taking in the familiar scenery of the drive, unable to think of anything other than having to let my cabin go, fighting the painful understanding that my time in it was over. I put it on the market and visited it one more time that last summer, hoping to have my usual magically restorative few days. I couldn't bear to visit it that way again. It was no longer my beloved retreat.

At the wintery end of that year, I went to pack it up and close on the sale, the small, warm sheltering space now just walls around packed boxes and the furniture I was leaving for the new owners, the view up the shore cold, gray, and forbidding. I arranged with the contractor, Greg, a lifelong resident of the surrounding community and a friendly part of my life there, to take the boxes by pickup truck to my house in the city.

Less than a year after closing, the economy melted down. If I had been able to sell my beloved cabin after that, it would have been for a much-reduced price. I had been following the economic news, and I wonder if a foreboding sense of something financially threatening in the wind played a part in the timely movement of my energy.

CITY UPON THE HILL

It has taken me a long time to learn to reliably sense when my life energy is moving on. I am more attuned to that movement these days. I feel my life energy move even when I don't consciously want to move on from a stage or a moment in my life. I was not happy to feel my energy leave something I once deeply valued, like my volunteer job as director of training for my Jungian training institute. And shifts in my energy don't always match the outer necessities of my world. But I know better than to imagine I can fight that movement or pretend it isn't happening. Moving with the creative energy of my life has brought me a joy and freedom that I could never have imagined, worth so much more than anything I have been forced to give up.

I could not have become sensitive to those movements had I not learned in analysis to pierce the veil of my illusions about myself and my story, to begin exploring my shadow, starting thirty years ago and continuing today. In the same way, the creative potential of Euro-American society at this moment in history will remain unborn until we collectively agree to pierce the veil of shared illusion that masks so much of the US story and current-day reality.

Compared to the countries in most of the rest of the Western world, especially those of our country's European cultural ancestors, we are a young and privileged nation. Our country suffered a terrible civil war, but that was long ago. Some Euro-Americans imagine that our nation has escaped the fate of so many European countries, the experience of invasion and catastrophic war. That perspective is not the point of view of those whose ancestors were here when our personal and cultural ancestors came. From their perspective, the peoples indigenous to this land have suffered five hundred years of invasion and catastrophic war. From the point of view of many of those in the other countries where we have waged war in the latter half of the twentieth century and the first part of the twenty-first, the US has devastated them and their societies, pursuing what my country imagines to be its security while destroying theirs. While I know that many in my country share my perspective, those truths are largely invisible in the country I see reflected in much of our shared public discourse. The optimism of youth, even the cult of youth, pervades Euro-American culture.

America is still a brash, young country. We declared our "exceptionalism" almost 150 years before we declared our independence. Massachusetts Bay Colony founder John Winthrop said in a sermon in 1630, before he or the other passengers of the ship *Arbella* set foot on the land they already imagined to be theirs, that the new community would be a "city upon a hill," a beacon for the world. Now that image permeates our political conversation. As President Reagan left office, he evoked it:

> I've spoken of the shining city all my political life, but I don't know if I ever quite communicated what I saw when I said it. But in my mind it was a tall, proud city built on rocks stronger than oceans, windswept, God-blessed, and teeming with people of all kinds living in harmony and peace.

President Reagan swept away the bleak presidency of Jimmy Carter, with its stagflation, energy crisis, reinstatement of the draft, toxic superfund clean-ups, and Iranian hostage crisis, removing the solar panels Carter had installed on the White House roof. Carter's presidency forced us to look too directly at the dark consequences of our way of life. Reagan floated into a two-term presidency on a buoyant wave of denial, the polished Hollywood veteran feeding on and mirroring the core American optimism that Americans can and should have whatever they want.

President Carter's fate was not lost on the Democratic presidents who followed Reagan. President Clinton and President Obama did not risk confronting America with the truth: our way of living is completely unsustainable. The current generation is robbing the working poor; what used to be the middle class of our country; the other countries in the world; and our children, grandchildren, and great-grandchildren of the good life it claims for itself, the good life that only the bravest politician dares to criticize. Fear of loss of the good life, of illusions, of status as the "world's only superpower," of an unrealistic sense of who this nation is: those fears power the momentum that keeps the country moving along a suicidal groove.

As then–Vice President Cheney declared: "The American way of life is not negotiable." I imagine Cheney was referring especially to the way of life connected to the automobile and fossil fuel, the way of life that allows him and other oil barons to be rich beyond the wildest dreams of the rest of us. He meant his way of life. He didn't mean the way of life of those who have come to be known as "the 99 percent."

Too many people in this country are reasonably afraid that they will lose their jobs, their homes, and their dreams for their children. Those who are reasonably afraid, who struggle every day to survive, are not visible in the everyday world of images and illusions. The everyday world reflects the images and illusions manufactured by those whose greatest fear is that they will lose their wealth and power if the ordinary people of the country see the ugly truths underneath the surface of our society. I know all too well that what is walled off from awareness eventually insists on being recognized, breaking through barriers erected against it. The longer it is walled off, the more explosive it becomes when it finally breaks into awareness.

Apocalyptic events are shots across our nation's bow. The longer the powerful who manage this country for their benefit fail to see that their fate and fortune are inextricably interconnected with everyone else's, the more explosive and dark that truth becomes in the shadows of collective awareness. Those of us in Minnesota who paid taxes to support state government, who elected those who were responsible for keeping us all safe, collectively failed to insist that the health and safety of our bridges and highways be one of our highest priorities. In the over thirty years in which government has been systematically attacked and denigrated, the public infrastructure that supports daily life has been underfunded and neglected. On one terrible, hot summer day in August of 2007, the community was forcibly reminded that care for all of us is care for ourselves. Any one of us, any one of the people we love, could have been on that bridge.

Vigorous repression of the fundamental truth of interconnection with each other and all our fellow beings, in service of the powerful, endangers everyone. Only transformation of our ways of seeing the world will allow our country to make the changes on which survival depends. Those changes require an economic system that doesn't oppress those within it and rape the earth. I hope that change can be brought about in ways that don't catastrophically disrupt the world I know in the process, for that world must surely come to an end. The longer we postpone change, just as I postponed necessary changes in my own life until personally apocalyptic events forced me to confront them, the greater the likelihood of catastrophe.

Our national childishness and inertia are fed daily by those who want us to be afraid. Fear and inertia keep things the way they are. Mainstream media serves those interests, and it takes a critical habit of mind to discern the subtle tracks of that subservience in that media. As I write, a story comes into my inbox that perfectly illustrates the way our media, even our public broadcast media, functions to tell us stories—dangerous stories, as Joseph Bruchac might say—to keep us asleep and to keep things the way they are. I will let the writer, Keane Bhatt, tell this story:

> Celebrating 2012's best examples of broadcast journalism, the George Foster Peabody Awards, attracted the likes of D.L. Hughley, Amy Poehler and Bryant Gumbel to the Waldorf-Astoria's four-story grand ballroom in New York this past May. In a gaudy ceremony . . .

National Public Radio's This American Life received the industry's oldest and perhaps most prestigious accolade. The 16-member Peabody Board, consisting of "television critics, industry practitioners and experts in culture and the arts," had selected a particular *This American Life* episode—"What Happened at Dos Erres"— as one of the winners of its 72nd annual awards on the basis of "only one criterion: excellence."

. . . As is typical for the program, [Ira] Glass weaved personal narratives and anecdotes together with broader context in "What Happened at Dos Erres," which focused on a 1982 massacre of 250 Guatemalan civilians at the hands of their government's elite military commandos—the Kaibiles.

But in his hour-long treatment of a savage period of Guatemalan history, Glass and his producers edited out essential lines of inquiry and concealed a key aspect of the bloodshed and its import for U.S. listeners: Washington's continuous support of Guatemalan security forces—including the Kaibiles at Dos Erres—as they killed tens of thousands of largely indigenous civilians in 1982 alone. Moreover, by distorting the historical record, Glass performed an impressive feat of propaganda—he sensitively related Guatemalan victims' harrowing personal stories while implying that the only fault of the United States was that it had simply not done enough to help them.

Bhatt's opinion piece, first published on the website of the North American Congress on Latin America and picked up by progressive internet news outlets, goes on in horrific detail about all the ways in which our government knowingly participated in the genocide which killed up to two hundred thousand Mayans in Guatemala. The genocide conducted against peaceful Mayan villagers was carried out by right-wing death squads, similar to those in other Central American countries, death squads that were supported, trained, and financed by our government in our name, with our tax dollars, as a key part of a Central American policy designed to keep things the way they are. It was President Reagan's "city upon the hill" that began that policy in the 1980s.

I heard a few of those "harrowing personal stories" directly from survivors. Over a decade ago, I went to Guatemala with a colleague and friend as part of supporting indigenous community-healing work by Mayan activists whose lives, families, and communities had been shattered by decades of assassination, imprisonment, torture, and the slaughter of innocents in an all-out genocidal war. One of those activists, who had lived in exile in fear for his life for more than a decade, was to speak in one of the hundreds of small rural villages that had suffered that genocide. He invited us to come with him.

There was a community gathering with speeches; then a procession to the church and a ceremony to consecrate and bury the bones of victims from that village, bones that had been gathered from all over the countryside, bones of countless bodies left to rot where they fell. I heard stories of men being flung into the ocean from helicopters; of women, children, and babies raped and slaughtered in front of their mothers, grandmothers, aunts, sisters, and cousins; of villages razed to the ground and burned. These stories were told in Spanish and haltingly translated for me and my colleague, including a story told to us by one particular mother. She had witnessed the killing of her husband and her sons and the burning of her house in just a few terrible hours. Perhaps on an ordinary, peaceful, sunny day, just like the day we were there.

As I looked around at those gathered that day in the small Mayan village, I could see that there were no men of a certain age, only the young and the very old.

All the rest, murdered. Gone.

Bhatt goes on:

During his brief 17-month rule from 1982-83, Guatemalan military dictator Efraín Rios Montt escalated to its grim apogee the state terror regularly employed during a decades-long attack on leftist insurgents, suspected sympathizers, and Mayan communities. *This American Life* correctly described the directives of the Army High Command's scorched-earth campaign, in which soldiers burned farmland and homes, slaughtered animals, raped and mutilated women and children, and exterminated entire communities like the hamlet of Dos Erres. Glass concluded that state-led massacres "happened in over 600 villages" and added that an overall accounting of the larger conflict by "a truth commission found that the number of Guatemalans killed or disappeared by their own government was over 180,000."

Bhatt's story is only one of many stories detailing the horrors of the Mayan genocide in Guatemala that have long been a matter of public record and were revealed again in the monthlong trial of Rios Montt in Guatemala in the spring of 2013. Even the *New York Times* remarked on the absence of testimony in that trial about the way the US supported that slaughter, an act for which President Clinton apologized in 1999. Why was there no testimony about US involvement at the trial? At the close of his trial, a three-judge panel found Rios Montt, then an elderly man, guilty and sentenced him to eighty years in prison. On May 20, Guatemala's highest court threw out the conviction, citing irregularities in the trial. Rios Montt died in his own bed in the winter of 2018, and the victims of his terrible ruthlessness have little reason to believe that things have truly changed in their country, that their government will ever acknowledge them and what they endured. Their suffering, like the suffering of the African and North American indigenous peoples who experienced five hundred years of genocidal policy on the land we call ours, remains largely invisible.

The truth remains unspeakable. Not to be spoken.

All the information in Bhatt's story is available in the public record, but I run into people who aren't aware of it. I ask you to think with me about the absence in our shared discourse of the Mayan genocide we supported and to wonder what kind of a society bestows an important award on a documentary producer who leaves out the ugliest truth of what he reports. Perhaps a society that wants to stay in denial about the indigenous holocausts in its own history.

The damning detail in Bhatt's story and Glass's explanation to him that US involvement was "not the focus of what we were doing" say something about the ways our shared stories serve the forces that want things to stay the same. US involvement in right-wing repression in the Americas is ongoing. President Reagan is a hero. No radio producer who wants to win a Peabody Award will tell that story. Ira Glass's documentary exploits the appalling suffering of Guatemalan villagers for his professional benefit.

Still in the middle of my shock and horror on a peaceful sunny morning in a remote Mayan village, I asked our translator: Why? What could these people possibly have done that deserved this?

They were believed to be communists, he said.

That simple statement echoes the ancient story that I imagine underlies our five-thousand-year-old civilization: a story that I believe carries the heroic mythic image that threatens human life on our planet today. If we do not become conscious of that myth, if we do not understand the ways in which it continues to warp our lives into dangerous and unsustainable patterns, I believe we will fail to dream a different dream. I do not want to imagine that we will fail.

CREATION STORIES

In the beginning, Eurynome, the Goddess of All Things, rose naked from Chaos, but found nothing substantial for her feet to rest upon, and therefore divided the sea from the sky, dancing lonely upon its waves.

—Robert Graves, *The Greek Myths*

Like all dualities under heaven and on earth, beginnings and endings are not easy-to-separate moments of space-time. Endings contain the seeds of new beginnings. Each new beginning on this embodied earth carries the seeds of its ending, no matter how far away and remote that ending may be.

My high school Latin teacher once translated *Lacrimae rerum* as "the tears in things." The older I get, the more I understand that there are always tears in things, just as T. S. Eliot wrote seventy years ago:

In my beginning is my end. In succession
Houses rise and fall, crumble, are extended,
Are removed, destroyed, restored, or in their place
Is an open field, or a factory, or a by-pass.
Old stone to new building, old timber to new fires,
Old fires to ashes, and ashes to the earth
Which is already flesh, fur and faeces,
Bone of man and beast, cornstalk and leaf.

What end am I witnessing now? What seeds of a new beginning can I barely imagine as I live through the fear and anxiety that endings bring? I learned much of what I understand about beginnings from creation myths, like the creation image at the beginning of this chapter. The story of Eurynome creating the earth by separating sea and sky and dancing the world into being takes me back to pre-Hellenic times, her image arising out of the earliest stories of my most remote cultural ancestors, brought into Western imagination by Homer and Hesiod.

Like apocalyptic events, creation myths are also collective dreams.

I wonder if the blank-page anxiety I encountered as I started this chapter was, in some small way, akin to the widespread fear and anxiety arising in many of us at this moment of pregnant death in our shared life. Reading fragments of creation stories puts me in touch with the dreamer who is writing this book and quiets my anxiety. Still, there is the waiting.

I said to my soul, be still, and wait without hope
For hope would be hope for the wrong thing; wait without love,
For love would be love of the wrong thing; there is yet faith
But the faith and the love and the hope are all in the waiting.

Creation stories don't take place in space-time. They are not about a long-ago event. They take place in timelessness, sacred time, the eternal Now. They invisibly inform our imagination every time we set out to make something that didn't exist before, today or thousands of years ago, the words on this page as I write.

In the world of embodied form, death and destruction often precede creation; endings precede beginnings. I felt timelessness at the site of the I-35w bridge collapse shortly after it happened. I wondered if the sacred had irrupted through a rift in the wall between worlds in the service of something so much larger than merely human meaning, something we, the community, couldn't possibly imagine or understand in our shared grief. At a very particular moment, midafternoon of September 10, 2007, at a very particular place, the 10th Avenue bridge in the city of Minneapolis, I sensed timelessness arising out of and hovering over our shared experience of trauma and loss, hovering over the rubble of lives and certainties, of concrete and metal. *Takuskanskan.* Everything that moves is sacred.

Creation stories contain mythic images that, subtly, out of aware-ness, inform beliefs about how creation happens in the here and now. Reading creation myths puts me in touch with the dreamer in me. I hope you, too, can feel the power of these images and stories, for they reverberate down through human history, in some cases for thousands of years, some reaching back to what I imagine to be the very beginning of the Western mind. I hope you will feel the power of one particular ancient story known as the *Enûma Eliš*. It is a violent, matricidal story, a Babylonian creation story in which the Hero, Marduk, kills the Mother-of-all and makes the world out of her pieces. I see that story being lived out everywhere around me at the particular moment of space-time I inhabit as I write.

Before the splits I am describing as the split between matter and spirit and the split between human and community, human and nature, at the very beginning, ages ago, as human consciousness be-gan to emerge, my most distant human ancestors must have won-dered about the miraculous world that held and sustained them and the unseen forces alive in that world. I don't know exactly how they imagined that world came to be, but I have read creation myths from various cultures and societies, ancient stories about what might exist before form or behind form. My language does not easily grapple with this most essential mystery. Every indigenous nation has its own story about how the ancestors came to be on a very par-ticular land, sometimes beginning before the creation of the earth. If I can suspend my scientific certainties about how the world came to be, I can learn from creation stories about living in a nonlinear world, the world our science is now describing to us.

Stories about the world of space-time begin with creation be-cause creation is the beginning of form, the beginning of space-time. Western consciousness is still imagining new creation sto-ries. Some contemporary science takes me to the big bang at the very beginning of the universe. Science can't take me any further back. To go further back, I need other myths and stories, myths and stories that humans have told each other throughout space, time, and, now, history. The further science penetrates to the beginning of the universe—if the universe has a beginning—the more limitations to human understanding I bump up against. Those limitations are sometimes expressed in ideas about dark matter and dark energy, which are said to make up much of the universe I see and try to understand—dark because they aren't illuminated and visible, dark because I cannot penetrate their mystery.

Many possible images of creation inform humans when we, in a multitude of places, times, and cultures, begin something new, in touch, consciously or not, with particular ideas and images of the way creative energy manifests through action into the material world of space-time. At the beginning of this chapter, lonely Eurynome, goddess of all things, emerges naked from chaos and divides all that is into sea and sky, looking for a place to rest her dancing feet. Pre-Olympian, pre-Indo-European languages, Eurynome is older than old. Where did Eurynome come from? What did she divide into sea and sky?

If everything starts in the beginning, what was there before? How do I imagine it?

1. In the beginning God created the heaven and the earth.

2. And the earth was waste and void and darkness was upon the face of the deep: and the spirit of God moved upon the face of the waters.

—Genesis

There was something formless and perfect
before the universe was born.
It is serene. Empty.
Solitary. Unchanging.
Infinite. Eternally present.
It is the mother of the universe.
For lack of a better name,
I call it the Tao.

—Tao te Ching

The Lakota (Sioux) people say that in the beginning everything was in the mind of Wakan-Tanka. . . . All things which were to be existed only as spirits. Those spirits moved about in space seeking a place to manifest themselves. They traveled until they reached the sun, but it was not a good place for creation to begin because it was too hot. Finally, they came to the Earth, which was without life and covered with great waters. There was no dry land at all for life to begin upon. But then, out of the waters, a great burning rock rose up. It made the dry land appear, and the clouds formed from the steam it created. Then the life on Earth could begin.

—J. Bruchac, 1991

How can I imagine *something* before time and space when that which precedes form can't be said to exist? How can I imagine what exists *before* time and space when there can be no *before*, an idea born of space-time? Dark matter and dark energy are only the latest ways of grappling with that mysterious conundrum.

In my imagination, bound as I am by the world of form, I insist that *something* must precede form. Is it nothingness? Emptiness? The infinite? The mind of Wakan-Tanka? Or is it chaos? And how do I imagine chaos? Does a creation story portray heaven and earth as emerging naturally and peacefully out of chaos, chaos being only the name for a mythic, form-preceding state, or does the disorder of chaos require the intervention of a creator god? How is that creator god imagined? Does that creator god have a gender? Do I imagine inherently emergent form? Or do I imagine that the creator god imposes form onto something else, something I imagine as threatening to form itself, something that must be conquered and subdued that will always lurk nearby, requiring heroic intervention, over and over again?

I look up synonyms for chaos as I write: disorder, confusion, bedlam, anarchy, disarray . . . If those words inform my imagination about the state before the manifestation of form, then I must also imagine a heroic creator god to battle and subdue the forces of anarchy and disorder. And so, the Hero enters imagination at the very beginning of the consciousness which now rules the world. Along with the Hero come linear time and history. I lose my sense of being part of great cosmic circles and the endless cycle of birth and death. I imagine history and progress instead.

Over time, I have moved from imagining that I impose form in order to write to waiting until a vague sense emerges, waiting until I notice a thought, idea, image, feeling, or memory arising in the blank space in which I anxiously sit. Am I, the heroic writer, imposing form on the unfocused chaos of my thoughts and feelings? Or am I waiting for thoughts, images, memories, and feelings to spark my waiting fingers on the keys, taking a leap of faith and beginning to write, no matter how much I doubt that what has emerged in the empty space is worth putting onto the intimidating blank screen?

If I imagine that my fragmentary thoughts, feelings, memories, and images are just chaotic mind stuff getting in the way of my ability to impose form, writing is a lot harder and a whole lot less satisfying, at least to me. If I let form emerge, stories ask to be written in loops, circles, and spirals, not in straight lines of logical, linear progress from one idea to the next, just as the form of this book has emerged in loops, circles, and spirals in the months and years in which I have been writing it.

When I imagine I impose form on chaos, I attempt to draw a boundary between the two. Ideas about boundaries and linearity are inherent in the way my Westernized mind works, and they are alive and well in conventions about writing and reading. This particular writing demands that I flout the boundary between you and me, nullify it to a certain extent, to make at least a little transparent the process of creating what you see on the page.

I ignore that imaginary boundary to allow us both to observe the creative process at work. I struggle to make real and embodied in a disembodied medium what is otherwise an abstract idea about how the manifest world emerges from the elusive *before*. I tell stories about my life because I want to give you some sense of how ongoing creative energy has moved in my life, inviting you to see your life from that perspective, to remember when and how you experienced that energy and what happened when you did.

The idea of boundaries will be one of the themes that emerge as I explore the Western mind and other ways of being human in the world. Imposing form on chaos; drawing boundaries; imagining that things in the manifest world are just exactly what they seem despite all the scientific work of the twentieth century that says they are not; imagining that there is a boundary between us and the world, between writer and reader . . . keep track of these ideas as they appear and disappear in what may sometimes feel like the disorganized flux of this writing. I try to leave breadcrumbs, signposts, markers to help both of us, because this story is, in a very real sense, telling itself. I will try to let it tell itself, to stay out of the way. Yet if I don't shape it and give it form, it won't make sense to anybody but me. I write this story and it writes itself and me. The tension is always there.

Two different mythic creation images, creation requiring form to be imposed on chaos and form as simply emerging out of chaos, take me from the dawn of Western consciousness in ancient Mesopotamia to the most recent developments in Western science, currently known as chaos theory and complexity theory. Thanks to the amazing technology at my fingertips, I have help explaining creation from the perspective of contemporary science.

Chaos theory is the field of study in mathematics that studies the behavior of dynamical systems that are highly sensitive to initial conditions—a response popularly referred to as the butterfly effect. Small differences in initial conditions (such as those due to rounding errors in numerical computation) yield widely diverging outcomes for such dynamical systems, rendering long-term prediction impossible in general. This happens even though these systems are deterministic, meaning that their future behavior is fully determined by their initial conditions, with no random elements involved. In other words, the deterministic nature of these systems does not make them predictable. This behavior is known as deterministic chaos, or simply chaos.

How interesting that the science of the twentieth and twenty-first centuries has validated the nonlinear ways of experiencing the world of my indigenous ancestors and of indigenous peoples today. Linear thinking says that cause A leads to effect B. Newtonian physics tells me that if measurements are precise enough, I can predict that effect B will always follow cause A. How humbling to find that human understanding is actually more limited than I imagined, that I cannot predict the behaviors of the systems, natural and human, in which I am always immersed. But how comforting to know all systems obey laws which constrain their results, even if humans will never fully understand them.

In 1972, Edward Lorenz, the founder of chaos theory, introduced the now-famous idea of the "butterfly effect":

> The butterfly effect is the concept that small causes can have large effects. Initially, it was used with weather prediction but later the term became a metaphor used in and out of science. . . . In chaos theory, the butterfly effect is the sensitive dependence on initial conditions in which a small change in one state of a deterministic nonlinear system can result in large differences in a later state. The name, coined by Edward Lorenz for the effect which had been known long before, is derived from the metaphorical example of the details of a hurricane (exact time of formation, exact path taken) being influenced by minor perturbations such as the flapping of the wings of a distant butterfly several weeks earlier.

From the linear perspective of the myth of progress, I have little to learn from my ancient ancestors. It's true that I belong to the most technologically advanced society the world has ever known. At the same time, there is another story moving into global awareness. This story is one of limits to human power and understanding, limits to the ability to expand indefinitely. Part of this story is a growing awareness of the potential destructiveness of climate change, part of it is beginning to understand that the earth's resources and carrying capacity are finite, and part of it involves waking up to the reality that humans cannot endlessly throw waste into the biosphere without dire consequences. I have been reluctant to accept that we humans cannot technologically fix our way out of these challenges. I don't want to believe we have to radically change the way things are. I want to keep my illusion that clever humans can figure out a way to fix this.

Where did the illusion of human power and control come from? Western society has learned a great deal from being able to isolate pieces from the whole and study them. But how did I come to forget that there is a larger whole of which everything I know and touch is only a part? Contemporary climate science tells me that scientists can't predict what will happen as the globe warms and that human ingenuity is inadequate to the task of finding a successful technological intervention to stop it—that the only way forward is to change what we are doing to bring it about. Global climate is a complex, chaotic system with rules humans don't understand. We know that everything we do has an effect. We just don't know what those effects will be.

It is not an accident that science is being frontally attacked in our shared conversations, that fewer people believe global climate change is a problem than did a decade ago. Some of us don't want to hear what it has to say.

For me, images from an ancient Mesopotamian creation myth illuminate this question. I imagine that we began to forget that we are part of a larger whole a very long time ago, with the consciousness that emerged in the lands around the Mediterranean Sea. I see the origins of that consciousness, what I call Western consciousness, in an ancient creation story from the city known as Babylon.

In that story the hero, Marduk, kills the Mother, Tiamat, and makes the world of her pieces. The *Enûma Eliš*, named from its first words, "when, on high," was found in the mid-nineteenth century, written on clay tablets, in the ruins of an ancient royal library in a place once known as Nineveh. The ancient city of Nineveh is now Mosul, Iraq. Some of the best evidence there is of the emergence of Western consciousness was found over a hundred and

fifty years ago in a place now witness to the horrors of what I imagine to be the death throes of the willful Western mind taken to its
logical, terrible extreme.

The ancient images that may unconsciously inform the devastation of twenty-first century Iraq arose in one of the places where
my country is perhaps most guilty of treating other peoples and
their lands as disconnected, unrelated things, home to the most
precious commodity our suicidal society knows: oil. Hundreds of
thousands of Iraqi civilians have died and millions have become
refugees. Institutions and buildings that preserved the earliest
evidence of the beginnings of Western culture have been destroyed
in acts of violence, ignorance, and selfishness. The invasion of Iraq
in 2003 triggered an ongoing sectarian war that threatens to spiral
out of control, in Iraq and the wider Middle East.

The myth of Manifest Destiny justified my Euro-American ancestors' desire to sweep from coast to coast on Turtle Island, pushing
the original inhabitants aside and claiming the land and all that
lay on, above, and beneath it for a brand-new country. The myth of
Manifest Destiny now seems to describe the relationship of the US
with the world. A Euro-American rancher attending a resistance
training workshop organized by indigenous activists and communities in the path of the proposed Keystone XL pipeline spoke to
that reality: "We are all Indians now."

The discovery and translation of the *Enûma Eliš* and other myths
written on those clay tablets introduced the myths of Mesopotamia
to modern Western consciousness. The myths have similarities to
the myths we in Western consciousness know so well, the myths
of the ancient Hebrews which were eventually incorporated into
one of the world's most important religious texts. French poet and
essayist Yves Bonnefoy's encyclopedia of mythology, *Mythologies*,
says about the myths of Mesopotamia (taking into account his
Western bias that no civilization existed before Western civilization):

Starting with such poor materials as reeds and clay, in a difficult and oppressive climate, the Mesopotamians created one of the oldest, if not the oldest, civilizations, whose impact on civilizations that arose subsequently even quite far to the east and to the west is every day revealed to be more profound.

Stumbling across the *Enûma Eliš* as I was writing my thesis for Jungian training in the early '90s was a seminal moment for me, a moment when the seed of all the thinking and writing I have done since, including the writing which you now read, was planted. This seed, this mythic image, comes from the very beginning of the consciousness that now rules the world, the consciousness that runs amok and threatens our survival. I want to examine the mythic image of the Hero killing the Mother and making the world of her pieces and suggest that it underlies many of our shared assumptions about how to live on and with our mother, the earth.

Western consciousness dreamed this world into being almost five thousand years ago. The apocalyptic nightmares of our twenty-first century world tell me this dream of the world is coming to an end.

KILLING THE MOTHER

The myth begins:

> At the very beginning, before time and space,
> When on high the heavens had not been named,
> Firm ground below had not been called by name,
> Naught but primordial Apsû, their begetter,
> (And) Tiamat . . . she who bore them all,
> Their waters commingling as a single body;
> No reed hut had been matted, no marsh land had appeared,
> When no gods whatever had been brought into being,
> Uncalled by name, their destinies undetermined—
> Then it was that the gods were formed within them.

Just as Eurynome dances lonely above the waves, the myth of the *Enûma Eliš* begins beyond time. "When on high" there was no firm ground; there was only Apsû, the sweet water of the rivers, and Tiamat, the salty water of the sea. Tiamat and Apsû are Mother and Father. Nothing has yet been brought into being and named, for naming happens when One becomes Two and the world begins.

As often happens in creation stories, including the creation story told by Western science about life on earth, life begins in the sea. In this particular image, the gods simply arise out of the commingling of the sweet waters of a river and the salty waters of the sea. Father water and Mother water are pregnant with possibility, pregnant yet unchanging, empty and full. Two forms of water, river and sea, central to the lives of the Assyrians, Akkadians, and Sumerians, are commingled and inseparable, yet they are a two between whom there can be a third thing, a creative interaction. Paradox baffles my logical, linear mind, so it is a good place to start. Light is both a wave and a particle. It is just so.

The seeds of Western civilization sprouted in Babylon and its neighbors along the shores of the Mediterranean. If this myth were a dream, it would be a dream of the Western mind. We trace much of Western culture back to the Greeks, yet the images of this myth have an uncanny persistence alongside, or maybe underneath, the philosophical and theological systems of Plato, Aristotle, and the Greeks, extending into my own time.

In this myth, like so many others, the One becomes Two, pairs of polarities, for twoness is in the very nature of space-time: light/dark, male/female, good/bad . . . The gods are created in pairs, beginning with the upper and lower worlds, earliest forms of earth and sky. While Apsû and Tiamat represent the unchanging stillness of that which precedes form, the offspring, who represent the polarities of space and time, are all about change; they create agitation and instability. Their commotion disrupts Apsû's stillness. Angry, he insists to the mother, Tiamat, that these noisy gods be destroyed. Tiamat protests. Their son, Ea, sees the scheme and, immobilizing Apsû with sleep, kills him.

Then Ea and his wife, Damkina, have a son, Marduk, described as "created in the heart of Apsû," a reincarnation of the original masculine/Father principle which Apsû represented in its earliest form before time and history began with the gods of polarities. Marduk is the Hero, the "loftiest of the gods" who enters Western mythology and imagination at this moment. I am so accustomed to thinking of myself, my life, and my world in terms of the hero myth it is difficult to imagine how humans might live without it. The hero myth underpins the idea of individualism, rejecting the reality of our profound interconnection and interdependence on each other and everything else. In the Western imagination, the community doesn't channel creative energy into form through its individual members; only the individual can create.

The hero myth is reflected today in the veneration of the individual and capitalism, an economic system based on individual choices. The idea of capitalism assumes a marketplace in which an aggregate of individual decisions creates the best of all possible worlds, itself a creation myth that many accept as simply how the world works. Capitalism is only one of many possible economic arrangements, all of which have flaws, but the degree to which capitalism is revered and other economic arrangements are denigrated in public conversation is, to me, a sign of mythological thinking.

When I am told, as I often am, that our current system is the only good way to organize an economy—when the imagined rationality of the aggregate decision-making of buyers and sellers, the "market," is placed on the highest pedestal in our political discussions—I know I am in the presence of something non-rational. It is non-rational in the same sense in which some of those identified with the unconscious myth of science denigrate everything that lies outside its explanatory powers.

When a story becomes a myth, it gains a timeless power. That the idea of capitalism can connect with the mythmaking part of those who hold it dear says something to me about how dangerous it has been to forget that humans are inherently mythmaking creatures. The myths of science, progress, and capitalism leave no room for the power of the sacred and so deny the power of myth. An unconscious myth can do damage because it is not subject to examination. The myth of capitalism is perpetuated, perhaps knowingly and cynically, by those who benefit most from the system as it is. What I find most truly irrational is not the idea of myth; it is our suicidal trajectory, our collective willingness to take the risk that, in the not-too-distant future, humans will no longer be able to sustain life as we know it, all in the name of a fiercely held idea.

When I realized that many, many thousands of Mayan villagers in Guatemala had been slaughtered in service to political and economic interests, I saw exactly how powerful and dangerous unconscious mythmaking could be. My government decided in the 1980s that American corporate interests in Central America dictated a policy of supporting right-wing governments engaged in the vicious repression, torture, imprisonment, and murder of their people. That policy was justified by claiming that these rural villagers, like the villagers in Vietnam, were communists. That mythic idea underlies unspeakable atrocities in the small Mayan village I visited only a couple of decades later.

There is mythic truth to that story, thus its power. It is no accident that innocent lives in the indigenous community my colleagues and I visited were destroyed under that name. Communism. Community. The similarity of those words is not accidental. The glue that holds us together as human communities, the understanding that we are all connected to and responsible for each other and the beings with which we share our lives on the earth, that most essential glue, has been rendered invisible by the myth of the heroic, self-sufficient individual who holds transcendent importance in Western cultural imagination.

Economic theory has been perverted to that end. The social safety net, Medicare, Social Security, health insurance, unemployment insurance, food stamps, student loans—these expressions of our collective responsibility to support and care for each other are politically fragile, always on the verge of destruction by those whose ideology is identified with the myth of the hero. Those who want the destruction of these programs say openly that they don't want their tax dollars to go to support anyone they imagine to be unwilling to pull themselves up by their bootstraps, Mitt Romney's imaginary "47 percent" who sit around passively waiting for the government dole. The myth of the hero lies invisibly under Romney's heartless story.

As I worked on this chapter, a minority of Republicans voted against funding Obama's signature health care act, shut down the government, and took four billion dollars out of the food stamp program during a time when the economy did not support the working poor. Representative Paul Ryan argued that reducing the social safety net is a Christian act because, in his words, "We don't want to turn the safety net into a hammock that lulls able-bodied people to lives of dependency and complacency."

Almost a year before Ryan made that statement, researchers published a study that conclusively showed that, over a fifty-year period, access to food stamps for women led to "increases in economic self-sufficiency (increases in educational attainment, earnings, and income, and decreases in welfare participation)," the exact opposite of what Ryan and others insist. Moreover, the study's author, Hilary Hoynes, an economist at UC Berkeley, said that her work indicates that there are important benefits of the safety net that have been ignored. She posits that a more generous safety net could reduce health disparities, that the emerging evidence points to an important role for investments in early life—and that those investments generate important returns in terms of better health and economic outcomes in adulthood.

The policy Ryan so vocally and publicly supported is not only cruel; it exists in a fact-free zone where ideology trumps common sense. Ryan was carefully tailoring his image as he nursed presidential ambitions. If he were to become president, whose interests would he represent?

Obscenely wealthy people are a small minority of our political universe, but their voices have increasingly dominated the national conversation and the behavior of our government since the time that President Reagan was swept into office by a collective unwillingness to face the dark side of the dominant Euro-American way of thinking about and organizing the world. The world of the powerless and the voiceless has, during that time, become increasingly dire.

I have no quarrel with our support of European resistance to the imperial ambitions of Joseph Stalin in the years following World War II. But that wasn't how the story was told. I don't support the ruthlessness that went under the banner of communism in the Soviet Union and China in order to exercise dictatorial control over helpless and intimidated people. But the ruthlessness

of capitalist societies in protecting the interests of their financial
elite, *our* imperial ambition, has been rendered invisible. Soviet
society, Chinese society, and my own are all inevitably flawed attempts by humans to organize collectively.

You might be thinking, *But, but, but what about the gulags?
Tiananmen Square?* I am not suggesting that dictatorial violence
and terror by nominally communist societies have ever been justified. However, neither was nor is the slaughter of innocents when
we are the ones supporting or carrying out the slaughter, a truth
we are only able to see when we surrender our illusions about who
we are and how we act in the world. Soviet society was a deeply
flawed totalitarian regime in the name of the collective, but perhaps we could also see in its insistence on government by "the collective" a reaction against the cult of the individual. Tearing the
world into opposites, we and they danced a terrible dance on the
brink of global destruction for too many years, each creating the
other as the monster threatening the world, each becoming the
monster threatening the world.

As Jung pointed out, the other often provides a "hook" for our
shadow projections. When I project my shadow, I imagine the
darkest parts of myself to belong to somebody else. Not me. Them.
I criticize or hate those behaviors and the person carrying them
so that I don't have to criticize or hate myself. Just as I said earlier
about distinguishing between different kinds of certainties by their
energy, I have learned to recognize my shadow projections by the
fierceness and anger I direct toward somebody else. Another person. Another society. If I mentally turn people into abstractions
such as Republicans, black people, or welfare recipients, there is
almost no limit to the amount of my own darkness I can see in
them.

When I finally see my own dark side, when I finally admit those
attitudes and behaviors I hate the most are mine, when I can finally love and accept those behaviors as part of my own flawed
humanity, I can accept, even love, those who have been carrying

my dark side for me and turn them into real people. And I can do my best to stop behaving in ways that offend my most moral aspirations. It's hard to see and accept my darkest acts and thoughts. It requires a lot of humility about the particular imperfect human being that I am.

While the psychological dynamics of individuals, communities, and nations are essentially the same, the collective energy invested in shadow projections by groups is much stronger, often to a terrifying degree. The list of genocides and holocausts in the twentieth century bears witness to whole societies caught in murderous fury and carrying out atrocities almost beyond imagination. The slaughter of indigenous villagers in Guatemala is just one of those stories.

In the years following World War II, we were told a story that served the interests of our corporate military establishment. We were to base much of our economy on the expansion of the military-industrial complex. We were to imagine that we were in a state of permanent war, a war against "godless communism" which threatened each of us individually and the entire "free" world. How better to do that then to anchor our nation's fears to a myth underpinning five thousand years of Western consciousness? Communism. Community.

The collapse of the Soviet empire required that fear and hatred be directed at a different target, and the idea of "terrorism" allowed us to maintain our collective psychological primitivism. We made our fear, our own terror, into the target. My country once again constructed foreign policy out of deepest irrationality and hatred, creating another unending feedback loop in which we kill them, they kill us, and countless innocents are caught in the crossfire. My fear, my terror, as I watch my government bomb one country after another in the Middle East, after invading two of them, is that this insane feedback loop cannot be stopped.

I continue with the story of Marduk and the Mother-of-all, Tiamat, as I suggest that the myth of the Hero, whatever its demonstrable and manifold benefits, has brought the world to the brink of disaster and beyond. Tiamat, the mother, rises to avenge Apsû's death and, surrounded by monsters, goes into battle. She challenges Marduk, who destroys her.

> The lord spread out his net to enfold her,
> The Evil Wind, which followed behind, he let loose in her face,
> When Tiamat opened her mouth to consume him,
> He drove in the Evil Wind that she close not her lips.
> As the fierce winds charged her belly,
> Her body was distended and her mouth was wide open.
> He released the arrow, it tore her belly,
> It cut through her insides, splitting the heart.

After dispatching her warriors and her consort, Marduk makes the world out of Tiamat's torn and bloody pieces:

> The lord trod on the legs of Tiamat,
> With his unsparing mace he crushed her skull.
> When the arteries of her blood he had severed . . .
> Then the Lord paused to view her dead body,
> That he might divide the monster and do artful works.
> He split her like a shellfish into two parts:
> Half of her he set up and ceiled it as sky,
> Pulled down the bar and posted guards.
> He bade [the fathers] to allow not her waters to escape.

Marduk puts the heavens in order, establishing the zodiac and the calendar and telling the moon how to shine. With the pieces of dead Tiamat's body, he performs other acts necessary for the creation of the world. Splitting the Mother-of-all like a shellfish, he firmly divides the world into opposites. He is honored as the creator.

According to the encyclopedia of mythology edited by Yves Bonnefoy, the purpose of the Babylonian creation myth, the *Enûma Eliš,* was to legitimize the reshuffling of the existing gods in response to political revolution. Marduk was the special god of the city of Babylon, which had risen through the use of force to become the capital city of the surrounding area of Mesopotamia, the land which is now the theater for endless war.

Marduk's promotion to chief among the gods was designed to establish Babylon in the minds of its people as the center of the world. The daily life of the city was organized by annual festivals involving Marduk, ritually celebrating the wresting of civilization from the forces of nature that threatened to pull the structures of the merely human back into the primitive chaos of storms, winds, and sea, an ever-present reality in the ancient world. In the myth, the gods unanimously place Marduk above them because he saved them from annihilation by the monstrous and primordial Mother, Tiamat, or perhaps Marduk asks them to make him supreme in order to have the power to vanquish Tiamat. (The Bonnefoy encyclopedia contains both versions.)

In the same way, my culture's mythic veneration of the individual and the capitalist system is connected to a need to cement the existing power structure. Marduk's story was told as propaganda, transposing a particular power structure into mythic time. I don't need to go back to Mesopotamian civilization to see that that temporal power is frequently justified by connection to divine power. Communist regimes in Russia and China repressed religions, fearing them as alternate allegiances for their people, wary of the power of their stories to inspire and create meaning when the state was to be the source of all meaning.

The idea of "godless communism" has its own kind of connection between temporal power and the divine. Reagan's city upon the hill was just the beginning of the most recent attempts to blur the boundaries between church and state, a condition rightly warned against by the framers of the US Constitution. Politicians today invoke a Christian nation, saying that our country is blessed by God and everything done in our name is sanctified.

Connecting temporal power with the divine may have begun two thousand years before Christ in the ancient cities around the Mediterranean. Before we imagine the priests of the long-ago city of Babylon were exploiting ignorance and superstition, we might take a good look at ourselves.

The images of the *Enûma Eliš* dramatize the battle between the unruly power of wild nature and the order of civilization and its laws. Bonnefoy's encyclopedia states: "The defeat and death of Tiamat signify the end of one world and the birth of a new world." There were and there are other ways to imagine the creation of the world. But this bloody image, this violent dream, this matricidal act, this is the beginning of monotheism and Western patriarchal culture. It is a synchronicity that the lands of Mesopotamia, which originated these violent images at the beginnings of Western civilization, are now the place where we witness the overwhelming violence that tells us it is about to end. We too are at the end of one world and the birth of another.

The hero, Marduk, becomes the creator in his story. Violent matricide is the foundational necessity for creation, the beginning of all things. It is the story that the Western mind has told itself for thousands of years. The earth-and-creature-annihilating trajectory of Western culture is only the latest, most terrible, consequence of Tiamat's murder and dismemberment at Marduk's hands: *killing the Mother and making the world of her pieces.* Our world has become Marduk's world, a world in which healthy, intact ecosystems and the aliveness and beauty of intricately interwoven and interdependent dances of plant, animal, and human, are slashed, scraped, bulldozed, polluted, and destroyed in the name of progress and profit. It is a dog-eat-dog world in which the most vulnerable members of the human community are sacrificed to the greed and self-interest of a few.

In Marduk's story, in the imagination of the hero, the Mother-of-All becomes monstrously threatening. She is cut to pieces, and from her flesh and blood the world is created. She is our mother, the earth, *mater*, etymologically linked to "mother" and "matter." She is the substance of all we see, touch, and experience, all that supports and nourishes us. But in Marduk's story, she is dead, disappearing from the story the Western mind tells. Marduk believes that he, the Hero, is the creator, and so does the Western mind. Along with her, all human maternal experiences—connection, community, interdependence, and nurturing—are rendered invisible. I no longer understand my connection to and dependence on all life. That sense of interconnection ceases to exist when I imagine that only ongoing heroism protects me from violent and dangerous nature, "red in tooth and claw," as Tennyson imagined.

In the consciousness that rules the world, the Hero of our imagination is dependent on nothing and no one other than himself. He is born alone and he dies alone. That heroic consciousness blasts the tops off mountains, dumps toxic chemicals into our waters, and pollutes the air we breathe. When I imagine myself as separate from the earth and not dependent on her, I don't understand that everything that poisons the earth poisons me and the people I love. Toxic chemicals are found in the breast milk of mothers nursing their children at the farthest reaches of the globe. Our bodies give mute testimony to the truth that we are the earth and she is us.

Mater, matrix, our mother, is now visible only as all-pervasive *mater*ialism which obsesses our culture as a poor but compulsively embraced replacement for what we really want and need: to belong to each other and the earth. The source of our world is barely visible as the ancient root of the word "materialism" itself. Our world, our unsustainable world, is now literally made of her pieces. Only the deeds of the Hero remain. Yet, just as Marduk's triumph ended one world and began another, the apocalyptic events of our time are telling us that the world born from the death of Tiamat is coming to its end. How else have humans imagined creation?

CREATION BY EROS

Western creation stories without heroes are found at the very beginnings of the world that is ending, even in the *Enûma Eliš* itself. From the erotic commingling of Tiamat and Apsû, the gods who represent the twoness of the embodied world simply arose. Other erotic images emerged at the dawn of Western culture, like that of Eurynome dancing the world into being so that she would no longer be alone. Stories from the earliest days of the Western mind imagine creation as originating in relationship: connection, care, desire, passion, Eros—the "molten core of the heart's desire," as theologian Catherine Keller says. From Greek mythology:

> The Orphics say that black-winged Night, a goddess of whom even Zeus stands in awe, was courted by the Wind and laid a silver egg in the womb of Darkness; and that Eros . . . was hatched from this egg and set the Universe in motion.

The Orphic creation myth imagines the erotic joining of Night and Wind, the maternal womb of Darkness, and the silvery egg moon, producing the god Eros, who sets the universe in motion. This story of erotic creation, found at the beginnings of Western consciousness, imagines a universe founded in love, the movement of the god Eros in his many aspects: connection, passion, desire, love, care, nurture, relationship, affection . . . The foundation of community is Eros, love and care for one another.

When we associate those who live in community, like the Mayans in rural Guatemala or the villagers in Vietnam, with the myth of communism, we are back at the beginning of historic time, killing the mother. We are only now coming to know that there were many incidents like the infamous My Lai massacre during the war in Vietnam. Our soldiers were complicit in horrific war crimes, fighting shadows—our shadows, the shadows of the Western mind, the enemies imagined to be hiding among rural villagers who lived in community.

President Reagan let the right-wing death squads of repressive dictators commit the war crimes for us in Central America, rather than risk the public rising up in revulsion at "another Vietnam." Better to raze the countryside and murder the people in it than to allow the possibility that some of those resisting state terror might live in those simple villages. It's not hard to see the monstrous Terrible Mother lying just under the surface of those appalling acts, not hard to see how our young men could be caught up in those stories and commit the atrocities our nation asked them to commit when we sent them far from home to a strange land, where the shadowy enemy blended into peaceful villagers, to kill and die for abstract ideas like "freedom" and "the domino theory."

Fighting terrorism is a continuation of the same dangerous story. Our media- and government-produced fear leaves too many passive and unable to fight the forces that mold the world in response to dreams of endless power and wealth, the dreaming that dominates our world. Certainly there are those in the world who wish us harm, who may decide to act violently and terrifyingly on that wish. But, until we understand the world holistically and systemically, we and they will only create more death and destruction as we fight the shadows created by simplistic fundamentalist stories.

In a holistic world in which everything is connected to everything else, we would, in all humility, acknowledge the ways in which we act collectively to create our darkest nightmares: the systemic causes of neglect, poverty, oppression, violence, destruction, and death, and the dangers of ever-expanding empire. Images of Eros and our connection to the earth might begin to calm our fears and direct our imaginations to a different story. We might imagine that the Eros we experience in our lives, our personal lives, our lives in community, tells us something fundamental about all that is created in our world.

Eros appears throughout my personal story, weaving in and out: the wandering unpredictability of my life; my unguided-guided reading program; my desire to become a Jungian analyst; my falling in love with a little cabin on the North Shore and, later, with the neighborhood in which I now live. The mythological images of creation by Eros sound in a core truth that has a particular kind of feeling, a truth of both heart and mind. There are a thousand ways to say and, yet, no way to adequately say: when I feel the fire, the desire, the passion at the center of my heart, I know I am connected to ongoing emergent energy, the creative energy that is the universe. That energy and I cocreate my life and my work, arising in the spaces within me, between me and another, and in the spaces among all of us when we are in community, cocreating our shared world.

Still at the very beginnings of Western consciousness is Hesiod's *Theogony*, another mythological dream of Eros catalyzing the world into being, this time with Chaos and Gaia each playing a role. Hesiod was a Greek contemporary of Homer, living in the first century BCE. Gaia is our mother, the earth. Gaia sustains human life and offers matter for the realization of human creation in space-time. Eros is the catalyst for the emergence of Gaia's space-time reality out of the formless potential of Chaos. Eros moving through us is the passionate energy that uses Gaia's generously given matter to create in the service of life.

If this creation story is a dream, then it is the dream of a different dreamer. Here is Hesiod's creation story from Bonnefoy's encyclopedia of mythology:

> Thus before all else, there came into being the Gaping Chasm (Chaos) . . . but there followed the broad-chested Earth (Gaia), the forever-secure seat of the immortals who occupy the summits of snowy Olympus . . . —and also Love (Eros), the most beautiful of the immortal gods . . .

Chaos, Earth and Love thus constitute the triad of Powers whose genesis precedes and introduces the entire process of cosmogonic organization.

Western consciousness seeks to solve what it sees as a problem, creating Chaos and Gaia as opposites, attempting to resolve the fertile paradox I described earlier with the world parents, Apsû and Tiamat. In Hesiod's imagination, as in the beginning of the *Enûma Eliš*, Chaos and Gaia simply arise in a single act of genesis, two powers forever joined in relationship by the tension that sets them against each other and keeps them always attached, differentiated but not divided, just as Tiamat and Apsû are both separate and commingled at the beginning of the *Enûma Eliš*. In Hesiod's universe, Chaos, the mythic form-preceding state, is both the reality against which Gaia defines herself and the support without which she could not have come into being. Chaos and Gaia are connected, but do not unite, "two strata that envelop one another and prop one another up, without ever mixing together."

Eros in Hesiod's story does not represent the attraction between opposites in the way those in Western consciousness have come to understand erotic attraction, embodied in the Greek myth of Aphrodite. The Western story of erotic attraction relies on first splitting the world into opposites. Then a longing for completeness gives rise to a powerful attraction to the split-off other. For Hesiod, the god Eros is a more ancient power, preceding the creation of opposites. Chaos and Gaia bring forth the world from themselves. Eros, in Hesiod's cosmogony, is

> older than Aphrodite. . . . Eros represents a generative power which precedes the division of the sexes and the opposition of contraries. This is a primordial Eros like that of the Orphics—in the sense that he expresses the power of renewal that is at work in the process of genesis itself.

Leroy Little Bear, Blackfoot, says about renewal:

> Renewal is an important aspect of the Native American paradigm. From the constant flux, Native Americans have detected certain regular patterns, be they seasons, migrations of animals, or cosmic

movements. This gives rise to the view that creation is a continuous process but certain regularities that are foundational to our continuing existence must be maintained and renewed.

Scientists wrestling with chaos theory and complexity theory, just two of the latest paradigm shifts in the way physicists and mathematicians are beginning to look at creation, say that creation is an ongoing, inherent emergent process. There are rules underlying what appears chaotic to our limited human understanding; we just don't know what they are. Creation-destruction-creation: these are cyclic realities, occurring over and over again.

From the Western linear perspective, destruction and renewal aren't forever inherent in the creation of form. Renewal in historical linear time requires apocalyptic destruction, catastrophic endings instead of never-ending cycles. An apocalyptic ending to the world that began with the death and resurrection of the son of the Christian god has been in Western imagination for two thousand years. The kingdom of heaven is imagined as lying beyond death and endings; the embodied world is no longer pregnant with divine emergence. In the last two thousand years, monarchs, empires, and institutions have come and gone, changed form, decayed and renewed, but the archetype of catastrophic endings has seized our imagination, and some of us cannot let it go. If I identify too strongly, too fiercely, with the way things are, I cannot let in the awareness that it is time for something to pass, that the energy in the embodied world is moving on.

Again, Little Bear:

From the very limited and restrictive perspective of the human, the big picture looks chaotic. It may have an underlying order, but it is too vast for us to see . . . This view of the universe as chaos is manifested in the notion of the trickster figure in Blackfoot mythology. In a nutshell, the trickster is chaos. From a Western point of view, trickster stories seem outlandish and farfetched. From a Blackfoot view, the trickster is the manifestation of the flux . . .

. . . Looked at in the view of the concept of constant flux/motion, one can readily see the perspective of Aboriginal people: all of creation is forever moving and changing. Nothing remains forever. There is no finality. A human being may be a human being today or look like a human being today, but may become something else tomorrow. A rock may change into an animal, an animal into a tree. In other words, the Aboriginal way of thinking is that there is animate potential in everything . . . the only constancy is non-constancy . . . that is the trickster. He or she is a culture-hero, an ignoble, stupid character, a transformer, a gift-giver, and an enemy of boundaries. He is a creator, and a teacher. He is constant flux.

Trickster stories abound in North American indigenous cultural imaginations. He or she is the antihero to the hero of Western consciousness. Vulgar, deceitful, thieving, clever, shape-shifting, cunning, foolish, funny . . . the trickster defies limits and rules, boundaries and categories. The trickster image reminds me again of what Jung once said about God:

To this day God is the name by which I designate all things which cross my willful path violently and recklessly, all things which upset my subjective views, plans and intentions and change the course of my life for better or worse.

If I accept what new paradigm science and Trickster stories are trying to tell me, that the world of my senses is nothing but constant flux, then I must face a profoundly disturbing idea. Everything I think is stable and permanent is an illusion, *maya,* as I understand that concept from Hinduism and Buddhism. We and all that is are in a constant state of creation and destruction. Again, Little Bear, on flux:

The constant flux notion results in a "spider web" network of relationships. In other words, everything is related. If human beings are animate and have spirit, then "all my relations" must also be animate and must also have spirit. What Blackfoot refers to as "spirit" and energy waves are the same. All creation is a spirit. Everything in creation consists of a unique combination of energy waves. In other words, what appears as material objects in space is simply the manifestation of a unique combination of energy waves.

Conversely, all energy wave combinations do not necessarily manifest themselves in terms of material objects. . . .

   If one were to imagine this flux at a cosmic scale or at a mental
level consisting of energy waves, one can imagine him- or herself as
a surfer: a surfer of the flux. While surfing, one goes with the flow
of the waves, becoming one with the waves . . . in the process of
surfing the flux, one takes in and experiences all different combinations of energy waves.

If everything is energy flux, then we and everything else are
completely interconnected. We and our familiar world are simply
a momentary manifestation of a process going back to the beginning of time. What happens to the separate self, to our sense of our
unique identity, when we imagine the world, the universe, in this
way?

When I imagine I am a separate self, I limit my focus and awareness to what I imagine is just me. That feeling is inside and about
me. That tree is outside and is not me. Yet how do I know anything
I imagine to be outside me except by my perceptions, which are
mine? I imagine my perceptions to be inside me. Yet, depth psychologists, those who followed Freud and Jung, tell me that when
I pay attention to my perceptions and experiences, I receive information about the other, sometimes another person, sometimes
the world. The idea that there is a separate world inside me that is
not also the world outside me or that "me" and "you" are not always "we"—that fantasy is Marduk's fantasy, not the reality of the
interconnected, embodied world in which I live.

I remember one of my very first patients when I started my private analytic practice. I met with him in an office I rented from another therapist a few hours a week. It was a synchronistic meeting
because he was newly graduated from a master's program and I
was at the very beginning of working privately as a Jungian analyst.
I later learned from experienced therapists that when a therapist is
working on a particular psychological problem for themselves, often the people who come into their offices at that time are working

on the very same problem. It might have helped if I'd known that then, but I didn't.

My patient told me that he wanted me to give him some techniques to help him reduce his stress. I was overwhelmed by my inadequacy. I was in a training program which did not teach "techniques" to manage feelings or stress. What could I tell him? As I remember, we stumbled through the hour, perhaps one or two more, and then he didn't return.

Only later, with supervised help, did I realize that I was being taught the profound psychological truth on which analytic work rests. My patient was overwhelmed by feelings of inadequacy that were causing him what he thought of as intense stress. He was trying not to feel those feelings because they didn't make sense; after all, in his mind, he had just completed a master's program; he shouldn't have such feelings. I was picking up his rejected feelings of inadequacy through my own vulnerability around adequacy at that moment.

If I had been more rooted in my analytic seat, I might have recognized my feelings of inadequacy as both mine and his. I might have understood them as a doorway to understanding my patient from the inside in service of helping him discover that he was, in fact, feeling stressed and why. And I might have given some attention to the stresses my own feelings of inadequacy were creating in me. Instead we both sat helplessly in a miserable field of inadequacy that filled the room. We were living out the truth that "me" and "not me," "inside" and "outside," are only mind constructions made necessary by the fantasy of separate selves.

As I began writing the last paragraph before this story about my patient, I was anxious. I had come to something that felt like a jumping-off place, the end of my thoughts about the myth of Tiamat and Marduk. For the several days, the half-filled page looked like a cliff, a place where I could fall over the edge, while I went back and edited sections I had written before. I tend to write that way, going back and moving forward, editing as I go, hoping to get to that inevitable cliff with enough momentum to sail into the empty unknown and find firm ground on the other side rising up, like the burning rock in the Lakota creation myth or the sea that Eurynome creates for her dancing feet.

An image of my experience in that hour of felt inadequacy came up. Only as I finished writing about my early days as an analyst did I realize how my memory of that incident so mirrored my sense of inadequacy as I approached the half-filled page. The experience with my patient felt like the perfect illustration of an idea that had come to me fully formed more than a week before I first wrote this section, something I had written down with no clear sense of what I would do with it—an orphan thought sitting in my notes, waiting to be woven into this story. It was a way out of the stumbling around about "me" and "not me," which there is no easy way to talk about: a way to leap off the cliff into space and have something rise up to meet my feet.

The story about my patient and my experience with him illustrates something almost impossible to talk about abstractly. Imagining I am an isolated, separate self flies in the face of what I experience in my waking life at every moment. What part of what happened in that room was me? Was my patient? In my everyday world, I often have experiences that belie my rigid identification with an isolated, separate self; I just can't see them for what they are. When I lose myself in the beauty of a sunset or a misty morning in the forest, I don't imagine I have ceased to exist as a separate self. When I find myself swept up in a sense of intimate connection and creative purpose with others in a group, I don't lose my sense of who I am. When completely engrossed in a task, I lose awareness of everything else as I become one with the task. But when I am caught in Marduk's fantasy of separateness from all that surrounds me, I don't let those experiences tell me something I urgently need to know.

I wonder about deliberately imagining another kind of focus or awareness. One Buddhist teacher suggests that "I" am only an

ongoing point of awareness. Everything else about the way I imagine myself is a story created by my ego, that identity-creating place
that wants to retain its all-important role in my life. What if I imagine expanding that point of awareness? Outer? Inner? Experience?
Memory? What if, in truth, all those experiences and more that
have been rejected by my culture, just as I rejected parts of myself
in response to my family, are always mixed together, and I unconsciously choose which part of that experience gets my attention at
any given moment?

Writer and Jungian analyst Jerome Bernstein invites me to expand my awareness, to take in a way of being human he believes
Western consciousness has lost, what he calls "the borderland."
He has experienced an entirely different kind of consciousness
spontaneously arising in his patients, a discovery that required
him to throw out at least some of what he understood about psychology. People who experience what he describes as "borderland
consciousness" have almost unbearable feelings of empathy with
the fellow creatures in our natural surround, almost unbearable
feelings of grief with the earth in our times. How do I consciously
expand my limited awareness and allow in psychic energies and
perspectives that peoples in other places and times would have
known so familiarly that they would not have named them, just as
I don't name my awareness because it is just so?

INDIGENOUS AWARENESS

With the wisdom of hindsight, I realize that for over twenty years I have been trying to understand in my limited way what I first thought of as indigenous awareness. My experiences as a woman in the man's world of law and business taught me that there could be profoundly different perspectives among members of the same culture and social class based just on gender. In the early '90s, I was moving toward the Jungian theory exams that mark the midpoint of analyst training in my training institute. I knew I would write a thesis as one of the requirements for graduation. I was in another unguided-guided reading program, like the one I entered when I dropped out of the worlds of law and business, when I stumbled on the mythic images of the *Enûma Eliš* in a book by feminist theologian and philosopher Catherine Keller, *From a Broken Web*.

At the same time, I stumbled onto work by indigenous and non-indigenous writers that helped me understand that there are profoundly different perspectives between nonindigenous peoples and traditional indigenous peoples, still living on the land where their ancestors' bones are buried. I wondered what I could learn about that difference in awareness that would help me understand what was missing in mine. I thought the missing something might be connected to the idea of community, and I chose "community" as my thesis topic.

Community was not something I could define. Most often I thought of it, with longing, as a sense of absence, something that I imagined must exist in another time, another place. The word "community" touches something in me, perhaps the dreamer and the lover, and must have over twenty years ago when I began thinking about it.

As I first wrote this section, I asked my word processing program to come up with synonyms for the word "community." I was struck by how untouched that place in me was by the definitions and synonyms I found. Public, civic, municipal . . . these words do not resonate in the way the word "community" does; they feel flat. I think about what my friend Rosalie Little Thunder said about "strange, flat words":

> It's not just how the language functions, but takes the lead. We learn through the senses, the smells, the sounds, the feelings, the relationships. The senses embrace the energy and the experiences. When understanding is demanded of strange, flat words, it's like trying to compose music without emotion.

As I worked on my thesis, I ran across an autobiography by Malidoma Patrice Somé, *Of Water and the Spirit.* When I first read about his heartbreaking early life experience, I imagined his life was unusual. Certainly, I thought, it must be a situation particular to the indigenous inhabitants of Africa:

> Somé, who was born about 1956 in Upper Volta, was close to his shaman grandfather. But this relationship and his tribal way of life was destroyed when, at age four, he was kidnapped by a French Jesuit missionary and raised in a seminary, from which he escaped at age 20. Returning home to his Dagara village, he was viewed by some as too tainted by white knowledge and ways to be able to join fully in tribal life; nevertheless, he underwent an intensive and dangerous six-week shamanic initiation that thoroughly established him as a member of the tribe.

Somé's ability to walk in two worlds, indigenous and nonindigenous, drew me to his work and what he had to say about "community."

> The drinking had opened up people's throats and they began to sing. It was the sound of homecoming, the kind that tells you that you are linked to people who care. I liked what I heard, a melody

never experienced before, so peaceful it produced within me a joy beyond definition. I understood that what makes a village a village is the underlying presence of the unfathomable joy of being connected to everyone and everything.

Homecoming. Coming home. People who care. The longing for community beneath my everyday awareness is a longing for home, the place I most deeply belong, where I am "connected to everyone and everything." I don't know I am missing anything until I feel that sense of coming home and realize I have been longing for it, just as my fellow "white person" outsider Peter and I realized at breakfast during the Seventh Generation Fund gathering on the Northern California coast. That sense of coming home weaves in and out of the personal story I tell about what I believe is missing in my cultural awareness.

Somé's autobiography tells of his experience of being torn from his family and community and the dangerous initiation he endured in order to reclaim the home he had lost when he was educated out of his indigenous language and identity. I later learned from indigenous friends and colleagues that Somé's experience as a child in Africa was also the experience of generations of indigenous children on Turtle Island during the long period that the official policy of the US government was "Kill the Indian . . . and save the man." Little Thunder, who spoke only Lakota until she was forced to attend boarding school as a child, said that being required to speak English made her world much smaller.

In the US and Canada, schools—particularly boarding schools, called "residential schools" in Canada—were created for the express purpose of "civilizing" and Christianizing young Indian children. For generations, children were seized and removed from their families, their people, and their lands. Their hair was cut, their clothes were taken away, and they were punished for speaking their language. They were physically, psychologically, and sometimes sexually abused, made to work as servants for the school and nearby townspeople, and given barely adequate food and clothing. Many of them died. The traumatized survivors, with a deeply internalized sense of their Indian "badness," were returned to their people, unable to communicate or participate in traditional lifeways, their sense of identity as a member of a particular community on a particular land stretching back hundreds, if not thousands, of years utterly destroyed. Their families and communities must have been devastated by their loss.

That story is such a painful story; it's hard for me to let it touch me too deeply. I can barely imagine what it might have felt like to be taken away from home and family in early childhood and sent to a strange place where I was stripped of everything familiar, to be treated strictly and unempathically, if not worse. And I can never truly know what a small child growing up in a world where she felt connected to everyone and everything else must have suffered. What, in some forgotten ancestral place I have lost connection to, I suffer. When I experience an unexpected sense of coming home, I have a dim idea of what I am missing.

Once I graduated from analyst training, I was able to engage more seriously with the question of what was missing in my cultural awareness. If the individual is ill because the community is ill, how could I apply what I learned during my training in service of healing my own community, the Euro-Americans who come to Jungian analysts for healing? Pursuing that question took me to indigenous communities on the lands that are now Canada, the US, Mexico, and Central America: the lands of Turtle Island. It introduced me to indigenous artists and activists. I became aware of the ways indigenous activists struggle against the ongoing forcible imposition of Marduk's mother-killing worldview onto their lands and communities.

Indigenous activists work to heal their broken communities, reweaving the torn pieces of language, ceremony, and lifeway destroyed by deliberately cruel policies of forced assimilation. Because their struggles against colonization and their ways of seeing the world are almost invisible in the dominant culture, it gradually became clear to me that indigenous peoples are among those who live in the shadow of Euro-American consciousness, that in our collective imagination they carry the knowledge of interconnection and interdependence that has been largely lost to Euro-American consciousness.

Living in that shadow forces Indians and others grouped under the fantasy of "race" to carry all we have lost by identifying with Marduk's murder of the Mother for the sake of creating our world. In overvaluing the individual, many in my culture denigrate and persecute those who value community. When Jung said that shadow is a moral problem, I believe he meant that only when I stop making others carry my personal and cultural shadow do I stop persecuting them and become complete. I come home to myself.

Our Euro-American society marginalizes indigenous peoples, their history, their lives, and their concerns. It renders real Indians invisible behind stereotypes and misconceptions. Some of us imagine Indians still to be a twenty-first-century version of the "primitive savages" we have been told our European ancestors met. Some of us imagine Indians in the traditional dress of 150 years ago. Others of us are stuck in the fantasy of the mystical, eco-sensitive Indian and try to appropriate indigenous traditions and lifeways to fill the empty places our culture so often leaves in us.

Since I first began exploring Indian Country over twenty years ago, indigenous concerns and expressions of contemporary Indian life, particularly in writing and visual arts, have become more visible to those willing to explore outside the boxes created by Euro-American cultural stereotypes. I went into Indian Country with all my preconceptions intact and had to learn, slowly and often painfully, this lesson: if I were to learn what I wanted to learn from a world so far outside my own, it would be necessary to approach that world with eyes, ears, and heart open and mouth closed. Even today, years later, I forget that lesson and catch myself, with embarrassment, imposing my stereotypical ideas onto someone else. I needed to withdraw my projections and fantasies about Indians, to learn what I could about contemporary Indians and about what is missing in my awareness. I had to learn the ugly truth underneath our whitewashed history of who we are as a nation.

I have learned from speakers of indigenous languages that English is not a good language with which to think, write, or speak about all that lies in our cultural shadow. English was forced on inhabitants of indigenous communities, and it fragments indigenous reality. The more time I spend in Indian Country, the more I understand how thinking and speaking in English has fragmented my reality. I see how orienting my relationship to the world by imagining separate things keeps me from experiencing the ongoing, ever-moving flux of the moment. I remember how I taught high school students in my classroom to diagram sentences: separated things, nouns, acting on other nouns, verbs describing that action. I see how thinking in abstractions distances me from my sensuous experiences in the moment, how easily and often I wander around the alive and sensate world lost in my head.

Indigenous activists see English as a tool of colonization. Before I began to get a sense of how indigenous language speakers might have experienced being forced to learn English, I saw their world through the lens of my own language and culture. Just as I learned that I need to get outside my sense of entitlement as a white, middle-class woman, my belief that I could understand indigenous otherness from outside it, my so-called objectivity, created an unconscious Euro-American mental privilege, a belief that I knew something I did not in fact know, that I did not need to try to understand someone else's perspective and experience in their own words and not impose my abstract ideas on them.

Languages don't just describe what the speaker thinks of as reality; they create it. Indigenous language speakers have taught me that English describes and creates a reality of separated things. It chops the alive-and-always-moving world into disconnected pieces, objects to be manipulated, with language and in the world. Leroy Little Bear has said that his Blackfoot language has no nouns and consists of a relatively small number of sound syllables. Nouns, he says, are created for small children and others just learning the language.

Here is Jeannette Armstrong, native speaker of Okanagan, a language whose speakers are indigenous to that part of Turtle Island we call British Columbia, describing her experience of the difference between English and her natal language:

> I believe it may be wise to question the idea that language is a system of sound symbols, that is, that the word, as a sound, represents something definable. My thinking is that symbols, seen as compact surrogates of things, seem to take on a concreteness in and of themselves that supplants reality. *Words in that sense define the reality rather than letting the reality define itself.* Language sounds would be better regarded as patterns that call forth realities, as a sort of a directional signal to a time and place. . . . The Okanagan language creates links by connecting active pieces of reality rather than isolating them. . . . If we put aside designations like nouns and verbs and think simply of sounds that revive components of reality from that in which we are all continuously immersed, then we can think of a language that remakes little parts of a larger ongoing activity. *[Emphasis added.]*

I first read that passage years ago, and I still find it difficult to understand. I am not sure what Armstrong means when she says: "Language sounds would be better regarded as patterns that call forth realities, as a sort of a directional signal to a time and place." I imagine it has something to do with her idea that words in English define the reality rather than letting that reality define itself. I wonder if she is saying that indigenous languages are little recreations of the energetic properties of the particular time and place to which they refer, a particular moment in the ongoing energetic flux of constant change that Little Bear and contemporary science describe. The energetic properties of the moment are incorporated in the language itself. The listener doesn't just think about that moment, they experience and feel connected to it.

If you also find that passage of Armstrong's writing difficult to understand, then you have some idea of the distance between Armstrong's experience and ours. I find it similar to others in which Native speakers struggle, in my language, to say something about the utterly different reality their language creates. Leroy Little Bear gave me a glimpse of the reality that his Blackfoot language creates:

> Blackfoot philosophy includes ideas of constant motion/constant flux, of all creation consisting of energy waves and imbued with spirit, of everything being animate, of all of creation being interrelated, of reality requiring renewal.

Indigenous languages are different one from another because they come directly out of the relationship between a particular people with a particular land. I know that I can't make abstract generalizations about them, despite the urge to do so coming directly out of my Western psychological structure. But I can learn about English language and reality when I try to understand as much as I can about the realities indigenous languages create in their speakers.

In *Braiding Sweetgrass: Indigenous Wisdom, Scientific Knowledge, and the Teachings of Plants*, Robin Wall Kimmerer describes her struggle to learn the language of her Potawatomi ancestors. Kimmerer is a highly educated professor, enrolled member of the Citizen Potawatomi Nation, and accomplished speaker of English and what she calls the "lexicon of science." She recounts being baffled by the complexities and subtleties of her ancestral language until she realized that she was trying to learn something she had never before known, something she calls the "grammar of animacy."

One day, in frustration and sheer fatigue, she was paging through an Ojibwe dictionary her sister had given to her for Christmas when she ran across a verb, "to be a Saturday."

Pfft! I threw down the book. Since when is *Saturday* a verb? Every-one knows it's a noun. I grabbed the dictionary and flipped more pages and all kinds of things seemed to be verbs: "to be a hill," "to be red." "To be a long sandy stretch of beach," and then my finger rested on *wiikwegamaa:* "to be a bay." "Ridiculous!" I ranted in my head. "There is no reason to make it so complicated. No wonder no one speaks it. A cumbersome language, impossible to learn, and more than that it's all wrong. A bay is most definitely a person, place, or thing—a noun and not a verb."

And then I swear I heard the zap of synapses firing. An electric current sizzled down my arm and through my finger, and practically scorched the page where that one word lay. In that moment I could smell the water of the bay, watch it rock against the shore and hear it sift onto the sand. A bay is a noun only if the water is dead. Then bay is a noun, it is defined by humans, trapped between its shores and contained by the word. But the verb *wiikwegamaa*—to *be* a bay—releases the water from bondage and lets it live. "To be a bay" holds the wonder that, for this moment, the living water has decided to shelter itself between these shores, conversing with cedar roots and a flock of baby mergansers. Because it could do otherwise—become a stream or an ocean or a waterfall, and there are verbs for that, too. To be a hill, to be a sandy beach, to be a Saturday, all are possible verbs in a world where everything is alive. Water, land, and even a day, the language a mirror for seeing the animacy of the world, the life that pulses through all things, through pines and nuthatches and mushrooms.

The Potawatomi language doesn't describe the world; the world in all its aliveness pulses through the language, describing itself.

As Kimmerer goes on to say, speakers of Potawatomi and other indigenous languages use the same words to address the living world as they use for their family. "Because they are our family," she writes. The Potawatomi language extends the language of animacy far beyond what someone like me who thinks and writes in English can imagine.

Of apple, we must say, "*Who* is that being?" And reply *Mshimin yawe. Apple that being is.*

Yawe—the animate to be. I am, you are, s/he is. To speak of those possessed with life and spirit we must say *yawe*. By what linguistic confluence do Yahweh of the Old Testament and *yawe* of the New World both fall from the mouths of the reverent? Isn't this just what it means, to be, to have the breath of life within, to be the offspring of Creation? The language reminds us, in every sentence, of our kinship with all of the animate world.

Kimmerer describes the profound gulf between her ancestors' language and English.

In English, you are either a human or a thing. Our grammar boxes us in by the choice of reducing a nonhuman being to an *it*, or it must be gendered, inappropriately, as a *he* or a *she*. Where are our words for the simple existence of another living being? Where is our *yawe*?

One afternoon, sitting with her field ecology students near where water was momentarily a *wiikwegamaa,* she shared her ideas about animate language. One of her students asked what Kimmerer calls the "big question,"

"Wait a second," he said as he wrapped his mind around this linguistic distinction, "doesn't this mean that speaking English, thinking in English, somehow gives us permission to disrespect nature? By denying everything else the right to be persons? Wouldn't things be different if nothing was an *it*?"

Kimmerer understands her student's awakening to be also a re-membering. We educate our small children out of their instinctive understanding of their kinship with all things. We explain that the pronouns we use for other beings are not "he" and "she" but "it."

When my older grandson was small enough to be carried around by adults, we noticed that when other people approached, he would tilt his head forward, touching their forehead with his, in what appeared to me to be an instinctive gesture of affection and respect. In the family, we referred to that gesture as "head bonking." As we pushed him around the neighborhood in his stroller, he would incline his head in the general direction not just of people, but also of dogs, squirrels, and trees. When he began to master language, that gesture disappeared.

Linguist Mathew Bronson also points to the use of the English word "it" as one way in which Marduk's perspective on my world is enabled:

> Animacy as a category of human thought is deeply entwined with the pronouns we use every day as speakers of English. It . . . has implications for the current environmental crisis and for attempts to cultivate a more intimate relationship with the more-than-human world. . . . If you are talking about a bug, a whale, a tree, a mountain lion, a spirit or any single non-human entity whose sexual gender you do not know or perhaps even care about, you are forced by the patterning of the English language to use the pronoun "it". In order to say that something is animate, a speaker must know and care about the sexual gender, otherwise the referent is automatically demoted to the pronoun we reserve for inanimate things. English grammar does not easily allow a plant or insect or animal or spirit or planet into our conversations without automatically demeaning it. . . . This is evidence to support the suspicion that the English language is currently complicit in it-ing Mother Earth to death. . . . Poignantly, 90% of the world's languages are dying and will be gone within decades, displaced by the cold, placeless tongues of global commerce and colonization. Millions of voices . . . are going silent and with them the local wisdom borne of millennia of intimate and sustainable communion with place. . . . The very fabric of life on the planet is . . . under siege.

LOSING INDIGENOUS AWARENESS

"*Wouldn't things be different if nothing was an* it?"

How did our personal and cultural ancestors lose touch with that instinctive human understanding? I am deeply indebted to philosopher and magician David Abram for his work on perception and language. I was introduced to it in his book, *The Spell of the Sensuous.* Abram works both theoretically and experientially to deconstruct my most basic assumptions about how I perceive the world. He asks:

> How did Western civilization become so estranged from nonhuman nature, so oblivious to the presence of other animals and the earth, that our current lifestyles and activities contribute daily to the destruction of whole ecosystems—whole forests, river valleys, oceans—and to the extinction of countless species? Or, more specifically, how did civilized humankind lose all sense of reciprocity and relationship with the animate natural world, that rapport that so influences (and limits) the activities of most indigenous, tribal peoples?

Abram's question is the one that fascinated me in the early 1990s, the question that impelled me to read work by indigenous writers as I tried to imagine realities other than those undergirded by Marduk's story. Abram answers his own question by looking at the development of written language, asserting that the decisive shift was the shift of our energy, once in a reciprocal relationship to the land and our fellow beings, to a relationship with the written word. He suggests that in oral cultures, the contour and scale of the landscape and the calls and cries that pervade the local terrain are attuned in the rhythms, tones, and inflections that play through the speech of the culture, because members of a subsistence culture must be exquisitely attentive to subtle shifts in the patterns of weather, landscape, and animal movements.

Perhaps, in Armstrong's way of saying it, "language sounds would be better regarded as patterns that call forth realities." The energetic realities of particular times and places are communicated in language that brings them to life in the relationship between speaker and listener. About the land, Abram says:

> A particular place in the land is never, for an oral culture, just a passive or inert setting for the human events that occur there. It is an active participant in those occurrences. Indeed, by virtue of its underlying and enveloping presence, the place may even be felt to be the source, the primary power that expresses itself through the various events that unfold there.

I don't want to pass too quickly over that statement, for Abram is describing an experience profoundly difficult for me to understand. Because I believe events in human history to have been created by the people involved in them, I understand history as a series of human-centered events, removed from any sense of a land on which those events occurred. Even if I connect events to a place, it's a geographic place name, an abstract idea, not an embodied sense of a particular land. In an oral culture, Abram says, the land creates and stores the events.

I have difficulty imagining that the land creates the events. Yet I have no trouble imagining what someone sensitive to the energies of the earth once told me: that before our personal and cultural ancestors arrived on the lands on which my community sits, there were an unusual number of sacred places. Our treatment of the indigenous peoples who were here and our mistreatment of the land as we have lived on it have been and still are toxic, first to the land and then to the activities taking place on that land. The toxic energies held in the land affect those of us now living on it, whether we are aware of it or not. I remember a speaker at an indigenous gathering describing a place by saying: the land is still alive. I had never thought of land in that way, but I instantly knew that I had

experienced both the aliveness and the deadness of land. I just
hadn't ever thought about it.

Indigenous speakers transmit their knowledge of the power of
particular places through story. The function of story is vastly different from the function of story in a culture oriented around written language, as Bruchac says:

> Just like the people of European descent who came later to North
> America, the aboriginal people sometimes forgot the role they were
> supposed to play in the natural world and forgot to respect their
> elders or to share with others. However, the native people had the
> benefit of thousands of years of living *with*, not just *on*, this place
> they called Turtle Island, this land balanced on the back of a great
> Turtle. As a result, they developed ways of living and ways of teach-
> ing that enabled them to blend into the land, to sustain not just
> themselves, but generations to come. The knowledge that native
> people obtained from thousands of years of living and seeking bal-
> ance, was, in a very real sense, quite scientific. But it was not
> taught to people in classrooms or in books; instead it was taught
> in two very powerful ways. The first way was through experience,
> the second through oral tradition, especially through the telling of
> stories.

It may be impossible for me to imagine the experience of language and story in an oral indigenous culture. In words that echo
the earlier passage from the writing of Little Bear about experiencing the world as ongoing flux, Nalungiaq, an Inuit woman interviewed by ethnologist Knud Rasmussen early in the twentieth
century, describes it:

> In the very earliest time
> When both people and animals lived on earth,
> A person could become an animal if he wanted to
> And an animal could become a human being.
> Sometimes they were people
> And sometimes animals
> And there was no difference.
> All spoke the same language.
> That was the time when words were like magic.

The human mind had mysterious powers.
A word spoken by chance might have strange consequences.
It would suddenly come alive
And what people wanted to happen could happen—
All you had to do was say it.
Nobody could explain this:
That's the way it was.

What happened when written language intervened in the relationship between the land and its peoples? Abram traces the development of written language, beginning with pictorial systems
that directly related to objects in the material world. Then, around
1500 BCE, about the time that Babylon became the center of the
Mesopotamian world and Marduk killed Tiamat in the Babylonian
imagination, Semitic scribes invented the first alphabet. The first
written language had consonants only, the omitted vowels requiring the presence of the reader who would bring words to life
with breath. The phonetic alphabet moved the focus away from
the phenomenal world to the sounds of the human voice, creating
words as symbols of something else. Even so, Abram says, early
Greek literature retained a preoccupation with and connection to
sensuous nature.

The creation of written language, Abrams says, was the beginning of separating humans from the earth as their focus shifted
from the ever-changing animate world to the world of abstract
ideas. As humans became separated from the earth, cities and
power hierarchies arose. I understand the story of Marduk killing
the Mother and making the world from her pieces as a mythical
metaphor for that separation, directing my attention to the earliest
times in the evolution of our current way of seeing the world, re-
minding me that Marduk's story was inextricably connected to the
rise in power of the city of Babylon.

By the time of Socrates and Plato, a psychological realm of
unchanging ideas, separate from an experience of the ever-
changing material world, became well established. Or, as

Armstrong suggests in the earlier quote: language became a system of sound symbols that represented "something definable," something to be thought about rather than experienced. The focus of the Platonic Dialogues was to substitute this realm of abstract, disembodied ideas for the older oral languages which embodied lived situations, the lived situations of my indigenous ancestors in whom the language and the land were interconnected and alive.

I quote Abram at length here because in his description of the impact of the Greek alphabet on what he calls the "literate self," I hear a description of the definitive separation of matter and spirit, of our minds from our bodies, of our minds from the ongoing, ever-changing flux that is the embodied world. Only in the living, embodied world are there tears in things, *lacrimae rerum*:

> The letters of the alphabet, like the Platonic Ideas, do not exist in ordinary vision. The letters, and the written words that they present, are not subject to the flux of growth and decay, to the perturbations and cyclical changes common to other visible things; they seem to hover, as it were, in another, strangely timeless dimension. . . . The process of learning to read and to write with the alphabet engenders a new, profoundly reflexive, sense of self. The capacity to view and even to dialogue with one's own words after writing them down, or even in the process of writing them down, enables a new sense of autonomy and independence from others, and even from the sensuous surroundings that had earlier been one's constant interlocutor. The fact that one's scripted words can be returned to and pondered at any time that one chooses, regardless of when, or in what situation, they were first recorded, grants a timeless quality to this new reflective self, a sense of the relative independence of one's verbal, speaking self from the breathing body with its shifting needs. The literate self cannot help but feel its own transcendence and timelessness relative to the fleeting world of corporeal experience.

In the embodied world there is growth, ripeness, decay, and death. Nothing stays the same, everything passes. As I carefully read Abram's words, I am struck by the sense of transcendent power that written language confers. When I read, when I write, I leave the constraints of space-time and embodiment. I am immortal and invulnerable. How seductive written language must have been when humans first discovered it. How seductive it is when each of us achieves it.

In his last work, *Man and His Symbols*, Jung describes the consequences of that shift of human attention away from the sensuous world of nature to the reflective, literate self, movingly describing what "man" has lost. Losing a connection to the embodied world has made many in Western consciousness very, very lonely.

> Man feels himself isolated in the cosmos, because he is no longer involved in nature. . . . Thunder is no longer the voice of an angry god, nor is lightning his avenging missile. No river contains a spirit, no tree is the life principle of a man, no snake the embodiment of wisdom, no mountain cave the home of a great demon. No voices now speak to man from stones, plants, and animals, nor does he speak to them believing that they can hear.

As Abram sees it, the consciousness produced by developing and using written language radically separated Western consciousness from its natural surround, leading to the split between matter and spirit, as our language focused on the inner, abstract world of ideas. The splitting may have originated with written language, as Abram suggests, but I can see how that radical split has come to be reflected in our spoken language as well. When caught in the inner world of abstract ideas, I describe what I imagine to be reality rather than letting reality describe itself, just as Armstrong says about the English language above.

It's only a short distance from not letting reality describe itself to using language in a manipulative way to create realities completely untethered from the sensuous, animate world. Our language has so lost its connection with the world of experience, as its speakers manipulate language in their own self-interest, that I am now accustomed to living with lies. A "Healthy Forests Initiative" allows logging companies to clear-cut forests of ancient trees. A "Clear Skies Initiative" allows industry to poison the winds. The words "peace" and "democracy" hide war and imperialism. Many of us in Western consciousness are outraged by these lies yet are often unaware that we are all caught in a language and a worldview that enables them.

The story Nalungiaq told to Rasmussen almost a hundred years ago about the way things were "in the very earliest time" is a story about what linguist Bronson calls "the old language," which united the human and more-than-human worlds. The idea of a long-ago shared language is an extremely common one, common enough that I imagine it to be archetypal or universal. It appears in the stories of indigenous peoples and in the mythologies of Western consciousness, especially the story in Genesis about the Tower of Babel.

Bronson gives us the Cheyenne version of that story:

> Long ago, people and animals and spirits and plants all communicated in the same way. Then something happened. After that, we had to talk to each other in human speech. But we retained the "old language" for dreams and for communicating with spirits and animals and plants.

Bronson goes on to say that today words can retain their power, even if we have forgotten to respect that power or are accustomed to having it used to manipulate us:

> The word in its primordial force runs through us like a current: what we say still comes alive, as in Nalungiaq's story, or dies in the telling. Indeed, the power of language to create reality is a constant of the human experience. But this and other lessons of the old language have been largely obscured in the transition to modernity and industrial-technological civilization. When we contrast indigenous and western languages and worldviews, we can begin to reclaim aspects of the old language that undergirds both.

The word is a primordial force, an energetic reality. That life force, that energetic reality, can be engaged in the service of stories that heal or stories that destroy, stories that connect or stories that separate. Bronson says:

Words matter, literally, in that what is said becomes true if someone is willing to believe it. Madison Avenue has not forgotten the
principles of the old language and we forget them at our peril. The
rapport between words, between sentences, between people and
groups that allows all communication to take place is an energetic
phenomenon. Rapport is the vestige of the old language. In an indigenous view . . . this rapport can extend to the living world.

My Western story about the "old language" Bronson describes
is the story of the Tower of Babel in the book of Genesis. It takes
me back to the beginnings of Western consciousness and the land
we now think of as the Middle East. The story in Genesis 11:1–9 is
familiar to me from my childhood:

Now the whole world had one language and a common speech. As
people moved eastward, they found a plain in Shinar and settled
there.
    They said to each other, "Come, let's make bricks and bake them
thoroughly." They used brick instead of stone, and tar for mortar.
Then they said, "Come, let us build ourselves a city, with a tower
that reaches to the heavens, so that we may make a name for ourselves; otherwise we will be scattered over the face of the whole
earth."
    But the Lord came down to see the city and the tower the people
were building. The Lord said, "If as one people speaking the same
language they have begun to do this, then nothing they plan to do
will be impossible for them. Come, let us go down and confuse
their language so they will not understand each other."
    So the Lord scattered them from there over all the earth, and
they stopped building the city. That is why it was called Babel—
because there the Lord confused the language of the whole world.
From there the Lord scattered them over the face of the whole
earth.

Although I first heard this story as a child, I understood it differently when I put it in the context of the collective story I am telling. One thought was that even if the idea of an "old language" is
archetypal, the ancient Hebrew story does not tell the same story
that Nalungiaq told Rasmussen. Her story says that animals and

humans spoke the same language; the Tower of Babel story speaks about a language common to all the peoples in the newly created world, not a language shared by the human and more-than-human inhabitants of that world.

The biblical story is about the children of the three sons of Noah, who had survived the great flood in the Ark—the ancestors of a united humanity who all spoke the same language. When I imagine that the earliest Western culture of Mesopotamia profoundly influenced the ancient Hebrews from whom the Tower of Babel story came, I wonder if the story of Marduk's triumph over Tiamat and the disappearance of the Mother invisibly underlies the Genesis story of the ancient Hebrews.

Feminists have long noted the absence of powerful feminine energy in Christian stories; Mary is Christ's human mother, not a maternal power on equal footing with a father creator god. Marduk becomes the sole creator god in his story. His story is said to be the first evidence of the idea of monotheism, as the many gods of Babylon and its surrounding area became one. The Tower of Babel story in Genesis also imagines the world to have been created by a sole creator god. In the Tower of Babel story, we imagine a world in which the Mother-of-all has died and disappeared, the creation of the world is no longer connected to the Earth Mother and the Sky Father. In Nalungiaq's story a divine magic permeates the visible world:

> That was the time when words were like magic.
> The human mind had mysterious powers.
> A word spoken by chance might have strange consequences.
> It would suddenly come alive
> And what people wanted to happen could happen—
> All you had to do was say it.
> Nobody could explain this:
> That's the way it was.

In the Biblical story, the creator god is in the heavens, and humans are discouraged from cooperating to reach for the divine;

they are scattered over the earth, forced to speak different languages and to misunderstand one another. The divine no longer animates the embodied world but is reserved for the creator god, far away in the sky, beyond human reach.

One message of that story seems to be that for humans to work cooperatively to reach for the divine on their own is hubris. The first peoples of the newly created world are put in their place by a divine act which echoes the story of Adam and Eve being driven from the garden as punishment for wanting to know. Here the next-to-original sin is working cooperatively; for if humans speak one language, "nothing will be impossible for them." Hold that thought; it will come up again.

All conclusions about ancient Mesopotamian culture are tentative because evidence is so limited. However, there is one understanding of the actual historical event that may have been mythologized in the story of the Tower of Babel. When the descendants of Noah came to the land of Shinar, they settled there and decided to build a tower. To the best of my understanding, Shinar was the ancient region of Mesopotamia which contained Babylon. Towers built in that region are known as ziggurats. Perhaps one piece of evidence for the accuracy of this story is the name for the Tower of Babel, possibly taken from the name of the city of Babylon in which an actual event took place. The ancient Hebrew word for confusion is "babel," and the contemporary English word "babble" references that word and this story.

One likely candidate for the tower that eventually figured in the story of the Tower of Babel is Etemenanki, temple of the "foundation of heaven and earth." That tower is referred to in the *Enûma Eliš*, suggesting that it may have existed as early as the second millennium BCE. A number of references to that tower suggest that it was destroyed at least once deliberately by invaders and, given its impermanent structure of sun-dried clay, continually eroded by the elements. It was rebuilt in the sixth century BCE for the final time before its destruction by Alexander the Great in the third century BCE, along with the city of Babylon. That ancient tower was dedicated to the Babylonian god, Marduk.

I wonder if the story of the Tower of Babel in the book of Genesis was in its origins as political as the story of Marduk apparently was. Is it only coincidence that this story depicts the jealous god of the Hebrews destroying the temple built to honor the Babylonian god Marduk? It seems synchronistic that thoughts about the different realities created by indigenous and nonindigenous languages end up at Marduk's door. I have come full circle. The next circle starts with linguist Bronson's thought that the "old language" was about something he calls "rapport."

PRECONQUEST CONSCIOUSNESS

The rapport between words, between sentences, between people and groups that allows all communication to take place is an energetic phenomenon. Rapport is the vestige of the old language. In an indigenous view . . . this rapport can extend to the living world.

Bronson's thoughts about the "old language" invite me to think about erotic creation mythology in relationship to groups and communities. *Rapport* is one of many synonyms for Eros, the ever-moving energy that sparks creation in the visible world. Wikipedia defines *rapport*: "Rapport is a close and harmonious relationship in which the people or groups concerned understand each other's feelings or ideas and communicate well." I understand Bronson's use of the word *rapport* to be about something deeper and more powerful than that definition suggests. Perhaps the synonyms *bond, connection,* and *empathy* come closer to what I think Bronson means when he uses the word *rapport.*

Armstrong says about the English language: "Words . . . define the reality rather than letting the reality define itself." Perhaps Bronson's "old language" allows reality to define itself. For the world to describe itself to me, I need to approach all that I experience empathically and respectfully, with open heart and open mind. In Martin Buber's language, the world becomes a "Thou," not an "It."

When I empty my mind of thoughts and ideas and open myself to the land at a particular moment in a particular place, the land and its more-than-human inhabitants may speak to me through my experience in the moment and, sometimes, in visions and dreams. The world speaks to me in the old language. Is "the old language" of "rapport" another way of saying what erotic creation myths express, that love of and in the world sets it in motion?

I imagine my passion to be a divine spark, the place where, through me, the creative energy of the universe meets matter. When I express that divine spark, I bring something unique and brand new into the visible, embodied world. It is the moment when the world expresses through me a need only I can fill. It is the moment when the human surroundings in which I am always embraced—a group, a community, a society, or my culture—express through me a need only I can fill. If, as the story of the Tower of Babel says, nothing is impossible if humans speak the same language and work cooperatively, perhaps nothing is impossible if humans work together and speak the "old language" of rapport. I imagine that working together and speaking the old language of rapport, of Eros, is one of many ways of reaching for the divine which suffuses the world of matter, taking me back before the time when the divine became located in a remote sky god and humans were told to worship that god, not feel a spark of divinity in themselves. Bronson's writing evokes thoughts about community.

Some years ago, I ran across a paper that presents the most intriguing contemporary nonindigenous thinking I have found about what communities untouched by Marduk's story might have been like. The author, anthropologist E. Richard Sorenson, describes the many remote indigenous communities all over the world in which he had lived and worked for over thirty years at the time he wrote the paper. Those communities were very different from one another but similar in one respect; they had experienced little or no contact with what I am calling Western consciousness.

Over many years, Sorenson gradually became aware of an interconnected awareness among the members of those communities. One of the words he uses to describe that awareness is "rapport." He says his Western consciousness blocked understanding of what he was experiencing for a long time, but he eventually understood that the awareness shared by the members of those remote indigenous communities was radically different from his own. He named that awareness "preconquest" consciousness, describing Western consciousness as "postconquest" consciousness.

Although Sorenson writes in postconquest academic language, I hope I am able to penetrate it to the essence of what he is saying as he describes his experiences. It is hard to convey the impact of this paper in isolated segments. I am being true to my own post-conquest consciousness in attempting even to convey a flavor of Sorenson's work.

Sorenson describes what he believes are the necessary conditions for what he calls preconquest consciousness.

> The outstanding demographic condition required for such life is small populations surrounded by tracts of open territory into which anyone can diffuse virtually at will. This allows those discomfited by local circumstance, or attracted by conditions further on, to move as they wish with whoever might be similarly inclined.

Preconquest groups are small. Their members are able to evade prolonged contact with unwelcome circumstances by leaving. If the communities Sorenson studied managed to avoid significant contact with postconquest peoples, at least until Sorenson came to live in them, they would have been exceptionally isolated geographically, on islands or in remote mountainous regions.

Of course Sorenson would have brought postconquest consciousness with him, but he was uniquely trained and personally inclined to affect the communities he lived in and studied as little as possible. He wanted those communities to describe themselves to him, not impose his understanding on them. Even so, as he says in his paper, his Western cultural blinders kept him from understanding what he was seeing for years. Becoming emotionally connected with the members of those communities was essential to his eventual understanding.

> The outstanding psychological condition is heart-felt rapprochement based on integrated trust. . . . The outstanding economic condition is absence of private property, which allows constant co-

operative usage of the implements and materials of life for collective benefit. The human ecology engendered by the interactions of
these outstanding conditions makes the forcing of others (including children) to one's will a disruptive and unwholesome practice.
It was not seen.

In addition to being geographically isolated, preconquest communities share community resources. Children in those communities are raised in constant bodily contact with caregivers.
Members of the community live in a state of unconditional open
trust and rapport. Sorenson's use of that word suggests to me that
he is describing something that might be connected to linguist
Bronson's thoughts about the "old language."

Any form of subjugation, even those barriers to freedom imposed
by private property, are the kiss of death to this kind of life. Though
durable and self-repairing in isolation, the unconditional open trust
this way of life requires shrivels with alarming speed when faced
with harsh emotions or coercion. Deceit, hostility, and selfishness
when only episodic temporarily benumb intuitive rapport. When
such conditions come to stay and no escape is possible, intuitive
rapport disintegrates within a brutally disorienting period of existential trauma and anomie.

Sorenson did not observe the harsh emotions or coercion taken
for granted in Western culture. When people from postconquest
cultures like mine enter preconquest communities, particularly
when they are in search of "resources" they might exploit, the
Western consciousness they bring with them destroys the essential interpersonal trust and rapport. The extinction of preconquest
consciousness in the members of those communities often fore-
shadows the extinction of the communities themselves, as those
in postconquest consciousness assert control over the community
and its living context of plants, animals, and lands.

Once their preconquest consciousness is destroyed, the members of those communities quickly display the awareness so familiar to me as a member of Euro-American culture. They develop

abstract ideas about themselves and the lands on which they live. They draw boundaries and attach rights to those boundaries. As I understand it, they begin to live in a hostile competitive world of separated things.

What I understand of contemporary indigenous activism suggests that often the nonindigenous people to whom these remote communities are first exposed are those who are there to seize and exploit what their postconquest minds imagine to be *resources* that, they imagine, *belong* to the people in those communities. Deceit, hostility, and selfishness drive those encounters. A *resource* to somebody in Western postconquest consciousness might be a plant or animal relative to the members of those communities, the word *relative* coming to my mind as the way the Lakota people traditionally describe their relationships with all other beings in the human and more-than-human worlds. I am emotionally connected to *relatives*; I possess and dispose of *resources* when I become emotionally disconnected from them.

The bonds among the members of preconquest communities are both physical and emotional. A profoundly erotic sensuality communicates without words as effectively as spoken language and is often preferred. Members of the community have an empathic intelligence which enables them to pick up the slightest emotional nuance in each other. Strangers are enveloped in their embrace as readily as members of their own community. Sorenson was often aware that his needs were being met without effort on his part to communicate them. When negative emotions among community members arise, they fade in the warmth of intuitive rapport.

> In those isolated hamlets . . . emotions such as anger, if inadvertently induced by rough-and-tumble play, quickly faded in the ambiance of constant empathetic rapport and tactile stimulation. Getting angry among confreres was like one hand getting angry with the other. So they were not accustomed to full-blown expressions of negative emotions. When confronted with our photographs of full-blown anger, many were stunned, frightened, and disoriented. Even in photographs not intended to show anger, they sometimes

noticed subtle traces that are so common in the West that they are
not even considered anger there.

They had other reasons to be frightened of negative emotions.
They had no formal social structure, therefore no stable social safety net to hold them all together when affect-rapport gave way. When
it did . . . they were bereft, existentially desolated.

When the openness and trust essential to their preconquest
awareness cannot be sustained, their preconquest awareness
fades away. Sometimes the disappearance happens gradually and
sometimes something resembling a community-wide psychosis
will, in a very short time, overwhelm the entire community, leaving its members in a dazed, traumatized state, with total amnesia
as to the nature of, or even existence of, their former state of consciousness. Sorenson includes his field notes from a time when
he happened to be present in one community when their preconquest consciousness gave way. His description is personal and ag-
onized, and so was my reaction when I read it for the first time.

Only by pure chance did I happen to be there when their extraordinary intuitive mentality gave up the ghost right in front of me, in
an inconceivable overwhelming week. I'm almost wrecked myself,
in a strange anomie from having gone through that at too close a
range. . . . *I never was much good at keeping research distance,
always feeling more could be learned close in.* . . . There really was
no way to have predicted that, just after I arrived, the acute phase
of their ancient culture's death would start. To speak abstractly of
the death of a way-of-life is a simple thing to do. To experience it
was quite another. I've seen nothing in the lore of anthropology
that might prepare one for the speed by which it can occur, or for
the overwhelming psychic onslaughts it throws out. . . . Yet this is
just what happened when the traditional rapport of those islands
was undone, when the subtle sensibility of each to one another was
abruptly seared away. In a single crucial week, a spirit that all the
world would want, not just for themselves but for all others, was
lost, one that had taken millennia to create. It was just suddenly
gone. . . . When the mental death had run its course, when what
had been was gone, the people (physically still quite alive) no lon-

ger had their memory of the intuitive rapport that held them rap-
turously together just the week before, could no longer link along
those subtle mental pathways. *[Emphasis added.]*

Sorenson witnessed other instances of the death of that ancient
preconquest rapport, not always as swift and dramatic, which happened whenever a domineering or abstractly focused alien culture
(whether Western, Sinic, Indic, or Islamic, he says) fatally impacted
preconquest communities. He believes that such a profound psychological adjustment results in brain changes, causing physi-
ological as well as psychological changes. Sorenson anticipated
contemporary neuroscience which is now exploring exactly this
connection between environment, mind, and body. For Sorenson,
for me, and for others who have read his work, the destruction of
preconquest consciousness he describes raises "important questions about the promise and condition of the state of humankind."

Sorenson says that the cognitive gap separating preconquest
and postconquest life is probably responsible for "the conquerors" not recognizing what it was. After all, it had taken him a long
time to understand what he was experiencing in the communities
he studied. In light of the Euro-American history with indigenous
peoples on Turtle Island, I imagine that even if "the conquerors"
had recognized that they were in the presence of a vastly different
consciousness, they might have assumed it was inferior, primitive,
or savage, and the result would have been the same.

Postconquest approaches to truth are what Sorenson calls "dialectical." I understand what he means by dialectical as the split
approach to truth in the world of Western consciousness. In that
world, ideas oppose each other, and the thinker is forced to choose
one or the other. Either one is true or the other is. It can't be both.
Light must be either a wave or a particle. Sorenson's use of what he
calls "non-dialectic techniques" allowed him to finally understand
what he was seeing.

One technique involved viewing research films of childhood in a
very remote New Guinea community over and over, allowing what

Sorenson calls his "pattern-recognition capability" to see recurring patterns of behavior. Once he recognized those patterns, he could see them in other preconquest communities. Living in those communities allowed him to develop spontaneous, instinctive friendships despite the language barrier, to build cross-cultural bridges beyond language.

Sorenson's close friendships with members of preconquest communities became the other crucially important "non-dialectical" approach to understanding their extraordinary way of being in the world. They and Sorenson came to love and trust each other, and it was that erotic connection that allowed Sorenson finally to understand what he was seeing from inside his own experience and not as an academic idea.

I believe Sorenson is describing a shared experience of unconditional love and trust in which members of the preconquest communities he visited always move. When he talks about "affect coordination" and the "heart-felt liking" between him and the members of preconquest communities, I imagine he's saying that the connection among the inhabitants of the preconquest communities and between them and their surroundings is Eros in all of its forms: attraction, affection, friendship, trust, deep intimacy, delight, joy, and love, the "old language" of rapport. Eros sets their world in motion.

Sorenson describes what he calls a "liminal awareness" in the individuals of those preconquest communities:

> In the real life of these preconquest people, feeling and awareness are focused on at-the-moment, point-blank sensory experience – as if the nub of life lay within that complex flux of collective sentient immediacy. Into that flux individuals thrust their inner thoughts and aspirations for all to see, appreciate and relate to. This unabashed open honesty is the foundation on which their highly honed integrative empathy and rapport become possible. When that openness gives way empathy and rapport shrivel. Where deceit becomes a common practice, they disintegrate.
>
> *Where consciousness is focused within a flux of ongoing sentient*

awareness, experience cannot be clearly subdivided into separable components. With no clear elements to which logic can be applied, experience remains immune to syntax and formal logic within a kaleidoscopic sanctuary of non-discreteness. Nonetheless, preconquest life was reckoned sensibly – though seemingly intuitively. *[Emphasis added.]*

A "flux of ongoing sentient awareness" that can't be subdivided into clear elements to which logic can be applied suggests what Armstrong, Little Bear, and contemporary science describe as the energetic reality of which everything is a part. My Western post-conquest mind wields Marduk's sword, cutting energetic reality into inert pieces that I name, imposing order onto what I unconsciously imagine to be chaos.

In the preconquest communities Sorenson observed, self and community were not imagined as opposites. The community spirit in which its members moved was absolute trust. Everyone could be completely open about their thoughts and feelings. In such a community, there would be no need to hide anything from others. The idea of deceit, that somebody could conceal thoughts and feelings from others in order to manipulate them, was inconceivable.

Preconquest groups are simultaneously individualistic and collective – traits immiscible and incompatible in modern thought and languages. This fusion of individuality and solidarity is another of the profound cognitive disparities that separate the preconquest and postconquest eras.

When I am caught up in Marduk's way of seeing the world, I imagine that I can serve the needs of the community or serve my own. Not both. I don't need to look any further than Jung's comments about the way individual consciousness can be extinguished in a group to find examples of how community is viewed from Marduk's splitting and polarizing perspective.

The bigger the group, the more the individuals composing it function as a collective entity, which is so powerful that it can reduce individual consciousness to the point of extinction, and it does this the more easily if the individual lacks spiritual possessions of his own with an individual stamp.

I know from my own experience that powerful emotions can sweep a group possessed by a bad story, creating dangerous levels of groupthink, as Jung describes here. However, being in a group does not necessarily and invariably extinguish an individual's independent sense and judgment. A group can also be a community in which each individual makes a unique creative contribution to the moment or the task at hand. When the group openly and nonjudgmentally accepts each contribution, group members discover essential parts of themselves that blossom only in a group. My friend Kent Lebsock, a Lakota activist, gives voice to that other possibility: "I am most fully myself in my community." Self and community are necessarily one when both are at their most connected and most creative. *Self* and *community* become nothing more than different perspectives on the ongoing, ever-moving energetic flux of the world.

Sorenson's work and the work of indigenous language speakers like Little Bear and Armstrong suggest to me that what Sorenson calls preconquest consciousness is focused on movements of energy. In my dominant consciousness, especially when I think and speak in English, isolated objects are related to each other by cause and effect. Thinking in terms of cause and effect creates a world in which I imagine either that I make events happen or that events happen to me. One view imagines too much human power, the other not enough.

A language that, as Armstrong puts it, "remakes little parts of a larger ongoing activity" incorporates movements of energy into the language itself, removing events from the realm of human control. Accepting that humans do not control the always-moving energy of the world requires living with humility and acute awareness that every act in the world has consequences. Human agency requires human responsibility to all life as reflected in the Lakota word for that always-moving energy: *takuskanskan*. Everything that moves is sacred. It is a very different world from the one in which I think, speak, and write.

With the judgments inherent in the nature of my consciousness, it's hard for me not to take a position on whether the obliteration of preconquest consciousness by postconquest consciousness is "good" or "bad." Certainly, the encounters between postconquest cultures and indigenous cultures have created immense suffering. I need only understand what happened, and is still happening, to the indigenous inhabitants of Turtle Island to see that suffering written in blood and tears. But I am not making a judgment, at least not here, about those encounters.

All of us, not just the contemporary indigenous inhabitants of Turtle Island, have indigenous ancestors. I tell these stories because I want to suggest that encounters between the consciousness of *my* indigenous ancestors, founded on a core experience of being part of all that is, and a worldview founded on separation and disconnection drove that part of *my* psychic inheritance out of the everyday awareness of my remote ancestors, out of my everyday awareness, and out of the everyday awareness of many of us in the Euro-American society in which I live.

When he uses the words "liminal awareness" to describe preconquest awareness, I believe Sorenson is describing awareness somewhere between what he calls "supraliminal" Western consciousness and the alive-and-always-moving world, the world of flux. The word "liminal" comes from the word "limen," which is the transverse beam above a doorway or a threshold. It is a between place, neither in one space nor another. Around the turn of the twentieth century, Arnold van Gennep first used the term in writing about rites of passage he observed among the Ndembu of Zambia. Sorenson would probably have been aware of the work on liminality by his fellow anthropologist Victor Turner, who explained that those who were in a liminal state during a rite of passage were neither here nor there. In a coming-of-age ritual, for example, the initiate would no longer be an adolescent and not yet an adult.

In Sorenson's description of the shift from liminal awareness to supraliminal awareness in those communities that lost their preconquest consciousness, I see how the unexamined assumptions of my world come out of postconquest consciousness, a world in which I look outside myself for rules about how to behave, jostle with others over status and prestige, and argue with others over what is *right* or *wrong*.

> With preconquest consciousness largely unencumbered by abstract concepts, it remained unconstrained by formal categories of value and cognition (i.e., rules and stable cognitive entities). Only when awareness shifted from liminal to supra liminal did the notion of 'correctness' become a matter of concern – e.g. behaving 'properly,' having 'right' answers, wearing 'appropriate'; clothes etc. 'Improper' aspirations, inclinations, and desires were then masked as people tried to measure up to the 'proper' rule and standard. They used rhetoric and logic argumentatively with reference to norms, precedents, and agreements to gain and maintain dignity, status and position. It was an altogether different world from that of the preconquest era where people freely spread their interests, feelings and delights out for all to see and grasp as they lurched toward whatever delightful patterns of response they found attractive.

I imagine Sorenson is talking about a consciousness immersed in the immediacy of experience without a distancing filter of abstract ideas. Once their preconquest consciousness faded, community members judged themselves and others by a set of abstract rules that may have derived from their observations of those in postconquest consciousness. For example, sensing that Sorenson was made uncomfortable by public displays of their erotic tactile communication, preconquest community members hid it from him for a long time so as not to make him uneasy, not because they felt there was something wrong with their behavior. Once their preconquest consciousness collapsed, their experiences with

Sorenson and others in postconquest consciousness informed their sense of how to be in the world.

When their preconquest consciousness disappeared, their instinctive trust in their own spontaneity went with it, as they began to look outside themselves for rules and norms upon which to base their behavior. Some of my sense of what Sorenson describes as a "pervasive intrinsic spontaneity" emerges from his descriptions of the behavior he observed.

> One day, deep within the forest, Agaso, then about 13 years of age, found himself with a rare good shot at a cuscus in a nearby tree. But he only had inferior arrows. Without the slightest comment or solicitation, the straightest, sharpest arrow of the group moves so swiftly and so stealthily straight into his hand, I could not see from whence it came. . . . At the same moment, Karako, seeing that the shot would be improved by pulling on a twig to gently move an obstructing branch, was without a word already doing so, in perfect synchrony with Agaso's drawing of the bow, i.e., just fast enough to fully clear Agaso's aim by millimeters at the moment his bow was fully drawn, just slow enough not to spook the cuscus. Agaso, knowing this would be the case made no effort to lean to side [*sic*] for an unobstructed shot, or even slightly shift his stance.

Sorenson uses this example to describe what he calls an "individualistic unified at-oneness," which he says cannot be represented in English because of its self-contradictory nature, the paradox that one is simultaneously an individual and an inextricable part of their human and natural surroundings. It was very difficult, first, to understand what he was seeing and, then, to hold onto that experience once he returned to Western culture:

> When I first came face-to-face with these experientially-based modes of cognition wherein logic was irrelevant, they slid right past me. I did not even see them. Even when I did begin to catch on, I tended to doubt such perceptions once I was again within the confines of Western culture. It took years of repeated, even dramatic exposure before these initially fragmentary mental graspings were able to survive re-immersion in Western culture.

Sorenson is telling me that the gap between my Euro-American consciousness and preconquest consciousness is an abyss. He is testifying to the degree to which his return to Western consciousness after a profound immersion in a preconquest community at first destroyed his confidence in his experience of preconquest consciousness. It made him doubt his memory of being in these communities.

I imagine that experience was painful.

Describing Sorenson's work to friends and colleagues helps me imagine what might have happened when Sorenson tried sharing it with others. Sometimes, friends and colleagues react by imagining that Sorenson is idealizing the communities in which he lived for thirty years and that a shadow side of those communities must also exist. As they imagine that shadow side, preconquest community members who didn't meet community norms would be punished or banished.

It is important not to idealize indigenous communities and their lifeways. But how can my colleagues assume something about the communities Sorenson describes when they have not been to those communities? When they have not read Sorenson's work? It fascinates me that my colleagues' abstract fantasies about the shadow side of preconquest communities fit so perfectly with Western ideas about community destroying individuality, ideas expressed in the statement from Jung I quoted earlier.

Sorenson is not just presenting ideas about preconquest consciousness; a student of Margaret Mead's, he's a trained and experienced observer of non-Western cultures. In over two decades of exploring the shadow side of Western culture, I have never run across anything quite like his paper. He deepens my limited understanding of what still exists of indigenous consciousness. For those of us in Western consciousness, understanding indigenous awareness as an experience and not an abstract idea is hard. I seem to be barred from experiencing what Sorenson describes as preconquest consciousness. Remnants of that awareness have

been fading in the many indigenous communities radically trans-
formed by Western consciousness.

I mentioned earlier what I called the unconscious mental privilege of my Euro-American awareness, the way in which I can assume that my ways of knowing are the only valid or legitimate ways
of knowing. When I am in the grip of that privilege, I believe I can
understand others and make judgments from outside their experience, from the so-called objective stance of Western culture. I impose my reality on the reality of others, instead of letting them describe their reality for themselves. In their reaction to Sorenson's
work, my colleagues are privileging an abstract idea, a theoretical
assumption, over Sorenson's description of his own experience.

Some critics may reject Sorenson's work because they believe
we cannot trust the observations of someone who so openly ad-
mits that his ideas come out of subjective experience. Sorenson
insists that he could only have discovered what he did from an immersion in his own subjectivity and in the communities he studied. As he says in the field notes I quoted earlier, "I never was much
good at keeping research distance, always feeling more could be
learned close in."

Sorenson's field notes are written in direct and personal language about the trauma of witnessing the abrupt collapse of a
preconquest community he had come to love. His erotic connection to the members of that community made him vulnerable to
experiencing their profound trauma through his empathy. The
language of his field notes is very different from the abstract and
academic language in which most of his paper is written. I have
long imagined that Sorenson wrote in a particularly abstract and
academic way about his observations because he wanted his academic colleagues to pay attention to what he had to say.

I wonder if they did.

I believe that objectivity is a central fantasy of Marduk's world.
Abstract ideas, based on imagined objectivity, are believed to be
more important and credible than direct experience, which can

be dismissed as personal and subjective. When my personal and subjective observations are couched in impersonal, abstract language, they take on an illusory quality of authority and credibility. It takes a kind of humility, which I often experience when I am with indigenous people but find hard to sustain in Marduk's world, to accept that there are profound limitations to what I can know or understand and that, despite my best efforts, much of what I experience will always be mysterious.

When I'm in Marduk's world, I imagine that I know and create by cutting the sensate material world into separate pieces with my objectivity, just as my society often does with bulldozers and chainsaws: *Killing the Mother and making the world of her pieces.*

From the very beginning of my attempts to enter and explore the worlds of past and contemporary indigenous peoples, when I tried to describe what I was learning there, I often experienced defensiveness in the reactions of my non-Indian friends and colleagues. At first, I felt helpless, invisible, and angry when that resistance came up. That experience allowed me to understand, if only a little, how my indigenous friends feel when they experience all the ways in which they, their communities, and their struggles have been erased from the Euro-American story. I didn't understand that defensiveness and judgment at first, but now, they tell me I have crossed into shadow territory.

I have also come to understand that when I experience that resistance, I may be bumping up against a defense to a shared cultural trauma.

POSTCONQUEST CONSCIOUSNESS

I have run across little in Jungian and post-Jungian literature about colonialism and globalization, other ways of thinking about the consciousness that threatens the world. I was delighted to find work by Mary Watkins and Helene Shulman asking the same questions I am from a Jungian critical perspective, especially in their book *Toward Psychologies of Liberation*.

Their writing was strongly influenced by the writing of Ignacio Martín-Baró, a Jesuit priest and psychologist, who was murdered along with the other members of his household by right-wing death squads in El Salvador in November 1989. Those death squads, like the ones I described earlier in Guatemala, were operating with arms, financing, and training support from the Reagan administration. Martín-Baró asked in his own work, *Writings for a Liberation Psychology*, what good psychology was if it left repressive social and institutional structures intact. Martín-Baró lived that question, joining the Salvadoran people in their resistance to oppression and their struggles for peace and justice. That commitment cost him his life.

Watkins and Schulman help me think about why my country's dark past with the indigenous inhabitants of Turtle Island has largely disappeared from contemporary Euro-American cultural awareness and how that disappearance damages us, personally and collectively. When I attempt to tell friends and colleagues what I have learned from travelling in Indian Country, I imagine their defensiveness and judgment come, in part, out of what Watkins and Schulman call "cultural amnesia" about the genocides carried out by my personal and cultural ancestors against the indigenous

peoples and communities of Turtle Island and the African indigenous peoples who were kidnapped, taken far from their home-
lands and communities, and sold as property.

I imagine that to admit that our actions in Central America supported genocide would threaten a collective dissociation from our
country's genocidal history. As a society, we have driven a heartfelt and immediate knowledge of that genocide deep into our cultural shadow. I find it hard to maintain an everyday awareness of
who we as a nation have been and who we continue to be. For a
long time, I understood abstract ideas about our dark past but pre-
vented that awareness from reaching my heart.

That was a long time ago, some of my Euro-American friends
say. Or it wasn't *their* ancestors.

As long as our nation's historical and present-day assaults on
indigenous peoples, cultures, and communities remain invisible in my cultural conversation, I am complicit in genocide. As
long as I forget that our nation is built on and continues to benefit from land and resources obtained by violence, deceit, murder,
and theft, I am complicit in genocide. Cultural amnesia is not just
a moral problem; it is a profound psychological trauma. As Jung
made clear a century ago, when I fail to bring the contents of my
shadow, all I disown about myself and my society, into conscious
awareness, I will act out of ignorance and malice, harming myself
as well as those who carry my shadow projections. When I resist
allowing the contents of my shadow into awareness, when I resist
knowing and accepting my inevitable flaws, the first injury is to my
humanity.

Watkins and Shulman speak of disengaged witnessing as "bystanding":

> Those who have profited most from colonialism and transnational
> capitalism have had disincentives to reflect on the psychological
> correlates of being involved in oppressive structures. In large-scale
> industrialized societies, it has been hardest to recognize, describe,
> and begin to address the pathologies of bystanding. These patholo-

gies are often normalized. . . . Bystanding allows status quo distri-
butions of power and privilege to go unchecked, giving rise to what
Arno Gruen (2007) has called the "insanity of normality." To question the psychic damage exacted through bystanding often requires
unflinching examination of the psychic cost of privilege. . . . For
those in colonizing cultures, colonial ideologies have contributed
to dissociating the personal from the political, building a sense of
private interiority that is strangely disconnected from historical and
cultural context.

I believe Watkins and Schulman are saying that if I focus only on
my inner world with its stories and dramas, I am separating myself
from essential context. I talked earlier about my tendency to pull
myself out of the context of my community and the land where I
live. As Watkins and Schulman see it, I need also to be aware of
my historical and cultural context. I need not to sleepwalk through
a landscape littered with historical and present-day violence and
injustice. The point is not to walk around feeling guilty; the point
is to understand that there is a personal and collective cost to my
privilege. Becoming aware of that context has required me to take
responsibility for telling my story, to say something about what I
have learned and how it has affected me.

Watkins and Schulman examine at length the wounding effects
of what they call "bystanding." They include: disconnecting oneself from nature and community; preoccupation with personal
survival; constant comparison with others leading to profound
anxiety, loneliness, and narcissism; the mutilation of a grounded
sense of oneself in order to destroy empathic connection to others and allow them to be degraded; profound anxiety caused by
loss of the qualities of oneself which have been projected onto the
degraded others; greed and addiction to consumerism and materialism; and psychic numbing, especially numbing to violence,
in order to continue to overlook the violence, both obvious and
subtle, inherent in colonization.

Patients bring these psychic wounds into analytic consulting
rooms. I have these wounds. When I understand my wounds only

in terms of "private interiority," divorcing them from historical and cultural context, I limit the possibilities for healing. I know as a matter of theory and from personal experience that those who experience trauma in childhood often want to forget the feelings and memories associated with those experiences. I have difficulty looking at my shadow because of a cruel inner voice that makes me ashamed of any behavior which doesn't fit with a too-perfectionistic sense of who I should be.

Cutting off parts of myself in order to manage traumatic feeling leaves an inner emptiness that I attempt to fill in unhealthy and ultimately unsatisfying ways. When I travel a healing path to all I have refused to know about myself, the empty space gradually fills with a grounded and realistic sense of the particular human being that I am; my wounds and my gifts. It takes courage I can't always find to face those painful feelings and memories, the reality of how I behave with other people and myself, the knowledge that I am a broken and imperfect human being.

The healing I may experience as an individual in Western culture will be incomplete until I travel the same difficult route into my country's darkest, most shameful, and most painful places. The psychological symptoms explored by Watkins and Schulman are so pervasive in Euro-American culture that I see them as descriptions of the culture itself. My cultural wounds will not heal until I have the courage to fill in the emptiness left by cultural amnesia and begin to feel empathically, painfully, and sorrowfully what the invasion of this continent by my European ancestors must have meant to the indigenous peoples who had been here for thousands of years and what the capture and enslavement of indigenous African peoples must have meant to them and their home communities.

I need to understand and feel what the ordinary peoples of the rest of the Americas have suffered, often those in indigenous communities, as they experienced violent repression at the hands of their governments, supported invisibly in the shadows by the US government, my government. I need to understand and feel the immense suffering that waging endless war for over sixty years has visited on my country and the world. I need to listen to those whom we, as a nation, have wounded, hear them speak about their reality in their own words and not defensively try to impose my reality on theirs. I need to allow them to describe their own reality, especially when it is difficult for me to hear.

For an illustration of our collective inability to hear these stories, I look no further than the controversy over sports teams with racially offensive names. I am glad to see so many of those with Euro-American ancestors are able to understand what is wrong with those names, to empathize with those who are deeply offended by them, and to understand that if team names offend indigenous peoples, they need to be changed for that reason alone.

As Peggy Flanagan, member of the White Earth nation of Ojibwe and mother of a small child, says:

> I've never felt as powerful and proud of my community as I was while walking down the middle of Franklin Avenue in Minneapolis on a cold evening in November with hundreds of other Native activists and allies. We were marching from the heart of the Minneapolis American Indian community to the Hubert H. Humphrey Metrodome to speak out against the Washington Redsk*ns mascot.
>
> Hundreds of American Indians and allies rallied outside the Metrodome to demand that Dan Snyder, owner of the Washington professional football team, change the team's name and mascot in spite of Snyder's dissent. The owner's unwavering commitment to keeping the Redsk*ns name became evident when earlier this year he stated, "We'll never change the name. It's simple. NEVER. You can use caps."
>
> . . . For me, though I am hopeful, the change isn't coming quickly enough. As a Native American woman and mother, I am concerned about how my infant daughter will see herself represented and portrayed in popular culture and the media as she grows up. Multiple studies have shown that American Indian sports mascots and other negative stereotypes are detrimental to the self-esteem and development of Native American youth and exacerbate racial

inequities. The continued use of the Washington Redsk*ns mascot sends my daughter, and other Native and non-Native youth, the message that somehow it's okay for her to be called a racial slur. In her formative years, she will continually see herself portrayed as less than human.

. . . I am not a mascot. My daughter is not a mascot. My people are not mascots. We are human beings. We are still here.

I am sad to see non-Indian people insisting that the objections by Indians are irrelevant and that the team, their owners, and their fans are entitled to keep those names, imposing their reality on native people who are deeply hurt, treating the use of those names as property they own and are entitled to keep. One way to see this reaction clearly is to imagine how we would judge a "white" sports team that called itself the N-word that is no longer acceptable in most Euro-American conversation. The failure to open minds and hearts to someone else's experience when it implicates our dark side is a direct and ongoing consequence of shared cultural amnesia about the treatment of indigenous people on this continent by the European invaders.

In psychology, there is a well-understood concept called "reaction formation." One definition is:

Reaction formation is a type of defense mechanism in which a person acts in the exact opposite manner to his own disturbing or socially unacceptable thoughts or emotions. This behavior is often unconscious and appears exaggerated, perhaps in an effort to over-compensate for the embarrassment, guilt or repulsion the person feels regarding his private thoughts.

I compulsively embrace life while denying death. I imagine life to be all about exciting beginnings, not sad endings. I fiercely declare and cherish my independence while banishing my secret desire to be dependent.

For me, the current passionate insistence on American exceptionalism feels like a reaction formation to an unconscious understanding of just how dark the US history on the lands of Turtle

Island has been and how violent and selfish have been many of our collective twentieth- and twenty-first-century actions in the world. As journalist Bill Moyers put it, just after a speech by President Obama in which Obama heralded American exceptionalism, perhaps as a way to salvage his credibility after announcing that he was not immediately going to order the bombing of Syria:

> (Exceptionalism's) hidden core of arrogance has often turned it into a kind of nationalism-on-steroids that carries with it imperial swagger, the itch to crush dissent at home, and a defiant statement to the world that we're free to ignore what Jefferson called "a decent respect to the opinions of mankind." Re-branded as "Manifest Destiny," it was used to justify unnecessary invasions of Canada and Mexico, the eventual establishment of colonies in the Pacific and a period as the de facto suzerain over the weak governments of the Latin American nations of this hemisphere.

Each of us sees the claim to American exceptionalism through our own lens. For me, it is important not to fall into the split worldview of Western consciousness but instead to hold both points of view, to see American exceptionalism from both sides, as Moyers does in the piece I quote from above. The positive side of American exceptionalism is our highest moral aspirations for our country in its relationship to those within its borders and the rest of the world and the way those aspirations have inspired those who fight, in our country and all over the world, for equality and justice for marginalized and powerless groups.

However, when I read or hear a reference to American exceptionalism, I often feel in it a refusal to take our place as an equal among the other nations in the world, aware of all we have accomplished and all we have yet to achieve.

If I focus on the negative in this writing, I hope you understand it as my attempt to bring the forgotten dark side to your attention, to remember that direct experience is always ambiguous and there are no truths for all time, only the truth of our unique and momentary point of awareness in the ongoing flux of the world. Only if we hold all possible ideas about the reality of our history and present-day actions as a nation will we be able relate to the rest of the world with a profound humility about who we are and have been, open to hearing in others' own words what they might want or need from us, rather than acting from an imperial assumption that we know what is best for them, which often seems to end up being best for us.

I have gradually come to understand my distant ancestors' loss of their preconquest consciousness as a pervasive, unrecognized, and unhealed trauma that has travelled from one generation to another, down to my postconquest consciousness today. Because it was not his focus or area of expertise, Sorenson doesn't talk about the ongoing psychological trauma experienced by those who lost their preconquest consciousness, but, as a psychologist, I read it in between and underneath the words of the painful story he tells. I was profoundly and unexpectedly affected when I read his paper for the first time, and so were a number of the colleagues I recommended it to. I felt a despair for what we had lost and what we had become. It was only after more than a decade of working with Sorenson's ideas about preconquest and postconquest consciousness that I began to see that understanding the dark side of Western consciousness as a trauma opens up the possibility that it can be healed.

Many Euro-Americans living today are inheritors of intergenerational trauma from at least two sources, both of which are grounded in an ancient disconnection from the land and fellow beings. One is the trauma of what Watkins and Schulman describe as "bystanding," witnessing the violent treatment of others but not being able, or willing, to act to stop it. Our Euro-American ancestors on Turtle Island witnessed the indigenous and African holocausts which are fundamentally woven into who we are as a nation. That witnessing has been and is traumatic.

Some of us also inherit the trauma experienced by ancestors who came to Turtle Island from Europe. Our personal and cultural

ancestors left everything: their homes, communities, fellow creatures, familiar weather and seasons, and the lands where their
ancestors' bones were buried. Many imagined they could begin
new lives on "empty" land Europeans had "discovered"; theirs by
Divine dispensation. However they came to leave their ancestral
lands, I see no evidence in our shared cultural consciousness that
our ancestors' wrenching separation from land, community, and
ancestors has ever been mourned in an ongoing and communal
way; this has created a profound intergenerational trauma that
finds its way to their descendants and to all those who are and
have been traumatized by our unconscious violent and destructive actions as a nation.

As a Euro-American, I am an inheritor of a particular strain of
Western cultural trauma. I am a restless, unrooted person de-
scended from generations of restless, unrooted people. Without
a grounded and realistic understanding of my history and the
humility which would accompany that understanding, I don't
know who I am, and I often believe that I am something I am not.
Euro-American society becomes ever more dangerously inflated,
xenophobic, and narcissistic. Lacking a vital connection to land,
community, and ancestors, many live in an unconscious existential state that Jeannette Armstrong calls "displacement panic." She
says about her own experience:

> I have always felt that my Okanagan view is perhaps closer in ex-
> perience to that of an eyewitness and refugee surrounded by ho-
> locaust. . . . I have felt that crisis as a personal struggle against
> an utterly pervasive phenomenon. . . . Through the lens of that
> perspective, I view the disorder that is displayed in our city streets,
> felt in our communities, endured in our homes, and carried inside
> as a personal pain.

The pain Armstrong and her community feel is inextricably connected to the pain many Euro-Americans are not able to feel because its existence and the reasons for it cannot be explored. When
I am disconnected from my personal pain, I unconsciously act it

out, inflicting it on the people in my life. I imagine that my personal and cultural ancestors acted out their unconscious inherited
trauma against those who had been here for thousands of years,
living on the lands where the bones of their ancestors were buried.
I imagine that genocidal violence on the lands we call ours was,
among other things, an act unconsciously designed to exterminate
indigenous consciousness because the indigenous consciousness
of our European and Mediterranean indigenous ancestors had
been exterminated.

Trauma, unless remembered, consciously explored, and healed,
begets more trauma. Extermination of indigenous consciousness
was an explicit policy of the United States government after the
years of direct conquest were over. Ongoing racism, neglect, and
brutality continue the work that official policy no longer openly
embraces. I have learned from indigenous friends and colleagues
that their ancestral trauma at my ancestors' hands is alive in their
communities, where members of those communities act out their
"internalized oppressor" against each other and the community.
In the American political system, I see profoundly disrespectful,
hostile, self-aggrandizing behavior poisoning our shared public
discourse.

I imagine my colleagues' resistance is also a psychological defense. When I accept Sorenson's view that there is a kind of consciousness I do not understand as lived experience—a consciousness that exists in communities where open honesty, empathy,
trust, and love are community norms, where community members live in a state of profound and joyful interconnection with the
human and more-than-human worlds, a consciousness that long
ago was driven into my cultural shadow—then I mourn the loss of
that consciousness and all that I have lost with it. A heartfelt understanding of that loss shakes me to my personal foundation.

When friends and colleagues react to Sorenson's work by assuming that he has neglected the darker aspects of life in preconquest communities, I imagine that reaction also comes out of the

psychological splitting that occurs so often when I am in Western consciousness. In Marduk's world, the splitting of the world into polarities and the repression, or forgetting, of one side of the polarity creates the psychological state Jung called shadow. Could preconquest communities exist wholly outside Marduk's realm of splitting and forgetting? Sorenson's particular focus when observing preconquest communities was their child-raising practices. Looking closely at the way he describes preconquest child nurturing, I can see how such a culture would be sustained and how radically different it would be from mine.

Sorenson confesses to being "dumbfounded" by the lush sensuality of infant care he saw in one extremely remote community in the New Guinea forest. Infants were in continuous bodily contact with their mothers or their mothers' family and friends. They were never deprived of body contact, not even under challenging conditions.

> Eliciting delight from babies was a desired social norm, and attentive tactile stimulation was the daily lot of infants. It included protracted body-to-body caressing, snuggling, oral sensuality, hugging, fondling or kissing.

The entire community was involved in this erotic, sensuous play with infants. Infants quickly became as skilled as adults in this form of communication. They learned as they grew that their needs and their reality would be accepted unconditionally by those around them.

> When I first went into their hamlets I was astonished to see the words of tiny children accepted at face value – and so acted on. For months I tried to find at least one case where a child's words were considered immature and therefore disregarded. No luck. I tried to explain the idea of lying and inexperience. They didn't get my point. They didn't expect prevarication, deception, grandstanding, or evasion. And I could find no cases where they understood these concepts. Even teenagers remained transparently forthright, their hearts opened wide for all to gaze inside.

Given Sorenson's precise and nuanced observations of the way that infant consciousness emerges into erotic, completely attentive and accepting surroundings, it is possible that in such a community the darker aspects of human interaction such as deceit, hostility, selfishness, and greed are rare. Adults who grow up in a community in which the growing child is completely loved and accepted would, in turn, raise all the children in the community that way. There would be no imagined division between individual and community because both exist simultaneously and nourish each other. Such a culture would not create rigid polarities, splitting the world into dualities, as mine has, just an ongoing dance between and among possibilities.

Some in Marduk's world imagine that such a community would thwart and punish individual expression, coerce individuals into following community norms, and punish or banish those who didn't. That fantasy is simply not supported by Sorenson's precise observations. If I believe that a preconquest community would *always* have a dark side, I am imposing an abstract idea onto Sorenson's work and privileging that idea over his description of his experience. When my colleagues insist that the communities Sorenson describes *must* have a dark side which punishes individuality, I hear the sound of Marduk's sword splitting the Terrible Mother like a shellfish, reverberating down through the centuries.

Perhaps my personal experiences as a child in Euro-American culture cause my reactions to the thought of such a community. Until recently, psychological ideas about the development of human consciousness, beginning with the infant's earliest days, have unconsciously incorporated Marduk's eternal mythic drama. Some of my Jungian colleagues still insist that our everyday sense of identity and self must break free of the monstrous "Terrible Mother" unconscious, assigning gender to ideas about a sense of self and its origins. As they see it, the "unconscious"—whatever we have forgotten, never consciously knew, or aren't focusing on—is a threatening state of chaos, not the fertile source of all that emerges into awareness. If I believe that an infant's sense of a self in the world cannot be born without withdrawing nurturing and support at some point, then Marduk's mother-killing act becomes a necessity.

When I imagine myself as an ongoing point of awareness in a flux of memory and experience, I reimagine ideas about psychic structures engaged in an ongoing battle for supremacy. I understand that children who grow up in a world of adults in traumatized postconquest consciousness may become adults with a damaged sense of self, feeling an intense, largely unconscious, loneliness and longing, a profound emptiness. Such adults would be easily overwhelmed by inner and outer circumstances.

I wonder if I cannot imagine communities such as the ones Sorenson describes because the very idea of such nakedness and vulnerability, such absolute and unconditional trust in the human and more-than-human surround, arouses an instinctive response in me. I find it hard to imagine living without the psychological and physical defenses I use to protect myself against invasion or abandonment by a hostile and uncaring world, against my need for belonging in relationship and community. There may be something inherent to my culture that I have absorbed from my earliest moments in it as an infant that gives rise to the fantasy that I am an independent, separate self. Something that cuts me off from experiences that could reconnect me to an immediate and embodied knowing that I am completely interconnected in and to a world of fellow beings in which I always belong.

After years of exploring the possibilities of consciousness other than that created by the dominant culture, I have to wonder, with Sorenson, if the creation of the Western sense of an isolated, individual self doesn't often begin with the earliest moments of an infant's experience in our culture. The physical and psychological connection between mother and infant is not nearly as intense as that between mother and child in preconquest communities. Mothers in our culture are sometimes afraid to allow that bond

to become "too intense" for "too long," an insistence on independence pathologizing what they imagine to be "too much dependency."

If mothers put children in infant beds to sleep alone instead of
maintaining bodily contact during sleep, or refuse to come to them
when they cry at night, they subtly discourage infants and young
children, especially young male children, from having dependency
needs. Most infants in Western culture don't experience anything
like the kind of erotic tactile surround Sorenson describes, responsive to every need before it is vocalized. Too many of us experienced hostility to our childish behavior when it violated an adult's
sense of what should be permitted and what shouldn't.

Joseph Bruchac says that in traditional indigenous life, children
are not punished for misbehaving. Instead, they are told a story designed to teach, for punishment not only doesn't work to change
childish behavior but teaches children the wrong lesson. I know
from my own experience that memories of punishment and my
child's sadness and sense of injustice persisted long into adulthood.
I know those painful experiences were a primary cause of the defenses against others and against life which took so many years of
therapy and analysis to begin to undo. In my pain and sadness, I was
utterly alone, all sense of connection to the adults in my life and the
joys of my world shattered. My escape from sadness was reading.

Unless they also experience love, care, and nurturing, children
who have those experiences grow up to raise their children the
way they were raised, creating in them a drive for an exaggerated
independence and an inability to feel needs for relationship and
community. It is not accidental that some of those in our collective
conversations who advocate the strictest and most punitive kinds
of social policy also express support for strict and punitive behavior toward children.

Finally, we are reimagining the theory which says that infants are
psychologically and emotionally merged with their mothers and
must be deprived of experiences of nurturing and care in order

to become healthy adults. Toward the end of the last century, infant researchers—for example, Daniel Stern—noticed that, from birth, infant and mother engage in an ongoing dance in which the mother both reflects the developing infant's new capacities back to her and moves just a slight step ahead of where she is to encourage her to try something new. Engaging in that dance gives the infant, from birth, a sense that she will always be connected to her mother as she develops her capacities as a separate self. The Stone Center psychologists of Wellesley College were among the first to argue that the developing sense of oneself as an individual does not require separation from relationship but rather differentiation within relationship, noting that difference between oneself and another becomes the basis for relationship.

I have learned that healthy infants are adept from birth at sorting out elements of experiential flux and making sense of them. When I watch an infant joyfully discovering the delights of her world, I am witnessing her innate capacity to relate to an ongoing experience of flux, energized by her love for the world and its love for her. Sometimes the infant is hungry, tired, or in pain. But if she experiences a reasonably good (what British psychoanalyst D.W. Winnicott described as "good enough") experience of love, nurturing, and care, she learns, over time, to trust that it will be there and to carry it with her wherever she goes.

In the communities Sorenson observed, an infant would have few of the distressing experiences that are common in our culture, but even in our world, experiences of love and nurturing in response to an infant's distress can support her developing sense that the world will receive her with love. An infant won't develop a trusting, curious, and loving approach to her world if her parents instinctively, acting perhaps unconsciously out of their own wounded infancy, withhold that nurturing and care in response to ideas influenced by Marduk's mythic matricide.

As I understand Sorenson's work, those living in a preconquest world would experience a deep, erotic interconnection with their community and the natural world at all times. For some in Western consciousness, such a state feels like an unhealthy loss of individual identity. Instead, our experiences in natural and human surroundings could be doorways to an awareness in which the imagined boundaries of individual and community are far more permeable than the separating logic of Marduk's world would allow. We could dismantle the theory that tells us that our human and more-than-human surroundings are the engulfing Terrible Mother and soften the edges of defensive fantasies of independent separateness that may have been reinforced since early infancy.

That theory not only profoundly affects our psychological development as individuals; it also affects our understanding of what happens to us in groups and our ability to understand how we might nurture the emergence of community in those groups.

IMAGINING LIFE IN GROUPS

I found Sorenson's work and began to imagine what it might say about community a number of years after I originally became fascinated with the psychology of groups, around the time I started Jungian analyst training in the late '80s. By then, I'd had enough good and bad experiences in groups to wonder what might account for the difference.

I participated in Tavistock Groups, weekend group learning experiences based on the theories of psychoanalyst Wilfred Bion, and I was intrigued with Bion's ideas. Bion wrote about his observations of groups while doing group therapy work in England in the 1940s with soldiers who had been diagnosed with what we now call post-traumatic stress disorder (PTSD). He described those observations in his book, *Experiences in Groups*, which became the foundation of what is now known as "group relations theory."

As Bion saw it, the ideal group becomes a successful "work group" that competently and effectively performs the group's task. Unfortunately, as many of us who have done work in groups can testify, groups can be easily distracted from their task. Bion's revolutionary idea was that dysfunctional group behaviors result from shared unconscious group stories he called "basic assumptions." At any given moment, a group could be a work group, one of three "basic assumption groups," or in some transitional phase between any two of them.

The traditional Tavistock group, based on Bion's theories, meets all day for two or three days. Eight to twelve group members arrive to find a room with a circle of chairs. There are enough chairs for every group member plus one extra. In my experience, the group sits nervously waiting to find out what they are supposed to do. Precisely at the announced starting time, someone arrives and silently takes the empty chair. The group expectantly waits for instructions, which come in the form of a paradoxical assignment: "the task of this group is to observe its behavior as a group in the here and now." This person, the consultant, then becomes silent and remains, during the allotted time for the group to meet, outside the interaction of the group, sitting quietly much of the time. They occasionally make a comment about the group behavior they observe. Precisely at the end of the allotted time and with no comment, the consultant gets up and leaves the room.

The A. K. Rice Institute for the Study of Social Systems continues to support this powerful approach to learning about group dynamics. Here is their recent description of the assumptions that underpin group dynamics learning and the shift in perspective necessary to see any group as a whole and not just a collection of individuals. In their view, the individual is always expressing something on behalf of the group as a whole, and a shift in awareness can enable group members to understand what that might be:

> In a Group Relations, or Tavistock, conference, exploring the group-as-a-whole requires a perceptual shift on the part of group members and the consulting staff who work with them. *This shift requires limiting, if not discarding, an emphasis on individual separateness and a readiness to see the collective motivation expressed in the activities of individual group members.*
>
> Under the lens of the Group Relations framework, individuals are recognized as voices of the collective that emerge from time to time on behalf of the whole. *This perspective implies that members of a group . . . depend on each other to express the dilemmas actually belonging to the whole group. [Emphasis added.]*

About the role of the consultant they say:

> Consultants consult only to a group, not to individual members, and only within the time boundaries prescribed. . . . The consultant does not engage in social amenities, advice giving, or

nurturing, but performs his or her task by providing interventions for the group's consideration and reporting his or her observations back to the group. Thus, the consultant confronts the group by drawing attention to group behavior.

In my experience, the paradoxical task and the consultant's behavior immediately throw the group into a state of perplexed disorganization, especially when the members of the group don't know each other. As these groups begin, their members discover that devoting themselves to the task they have been assigned seems impossible. My experience of these groups, especially as the consultant enters the room and assigns the impossible task, even if I have been in such a group before, is that they can be almost unbearably tense.

As Bion saw it, every group unconsciously searches for a leader who will meet its needs. Each member must find a relationship to the group culture. Individuals in the group play roles in the group's shared unconscious stories, based on an unconscious attraction to a particular role. Bion's assumption is that a group member's sense of being a mature self is always under threat in a group and the difficulties of group life are almost impossible to avoid. Such a negative view of group life is consistent with Jung's comments I quoted earlier that the group can overwhelm individual consciousness.

In a paper published about twenty years ago, based on my master's thesis, I challenged the prevailing presumption among group relations theorists that the group, in its fundamental nature, is *always* threatening to an individual's sense of themselves and that group life *necessarily* involves a great deal of off-task dysfunctional behavior. I also wanted to challenge the assumption among the group relations theorists that what they called "work group," the group that is able to focus on its task effectively and efficiently, is the most creative possible result of coming together in a group.

I had stumbled across the *Enûma Eliš* in the early days of my Jungian training. I wondered if images of maternal slaughter in the Western unconsciousness might be relevant to the work of Bion and his followers. It seemed possible that theories that emphasized negative experiences in groups were influenced by the unconscious mother-killing image that I imagine has had such a profound effect on Western awareness. The early group relations theorists thought that being in a group and feeling the need to relate to all the other individuals in the group at the same time was an overwhelmingly difficult psychological task. As they saw it, the group *always* threatens an individual's sense of identity, a very different perspective from the one my Lakota friend expresses as a sense that he is most truly himself in his community.

Bion and his followers imagine that the challenge of relating to a number of others at the same time throws each group member back to her earliest awareness, the consciousness of an infant relating to those who mothered her, that archetypal experience all humanity shares. In that fantasy, the individual would unconsciously experience the group as one psychic entity and that entity would feel maternal. As the early group relations theorists saw it, any experiences touching that unconscious memory of early mothering must necessarily be threatening to a sense of oneself as an individual, causing group members to suffer painful experiences of anger, sadness, abandonment, envy, competitiveness, and fear of retaliation. As a consequence of those difficult feelings, they argued, the individual experiences a profound and unresolvable ambivalence and anxiety about the choice of joining the group or leaving it physically, psychologically, or emotionally.

Later group relations theorists described the urgent problem of the individual in the group to be one of "belonging" and, again, those theories come out of the assumption that group experiences must be negative and that all sense of individuality is lost.

One of these theorists, Kenneth Eishold, imagines that wisdom lies only in the creativity of the individual and that belonging to a group extinguishes that wisdom:

Society is an association of diverse groups and our need to belong to at least some of these groups is as profound as our need to sleep and dream. And yet, what we give up to belong! Some of us have more to give up than others, to be sure—certainly from the perspective of society that stands to lose precious contributions of wisdom. We cannot evade the dilemma involved in joining.

The need to "belong" is a most basic human urge, and whether or not I feel a part of a group is always a preoccupation when I enter groups. I agree with the early theorists that group members naturally approach groups with unconscious expectations coming out of early experiences of mothering, those experiences that are our earliest experiences of belonging. I have been in groups where group members felt unusually vulnerable. When the leader failed to meet their unconscious needs for "good-enough" mothering, the group fell apart and the leader was the target of powerful expressions of outrage and abandonment from by group members. I observed over time that the leadership behavior, especially by a woman leader, that seems to trigger those reactions is behavior experienced by the group as abandoning or intrusive, sometimes both, the classic description of what Jungian theorists might call the archetypal Bad (or Terrible) Mother.

However, I disagree with Eishold that when group experiences touch my unconscious experiences of early mothering, I necessarily experience my sense of individuality and mature personhood to be at risk. The group relations theorists, including Eishold, are not describing conscious behavior in groups, but I believe that *their* unconscious assumptions profoundly influence the theory.

Certainly, joining a group of people I don't know can be uncomfortable. I wonder how I need to behave in order to fit in. If the group experience is stressful, my instinctive reaction is to move into my head and start thinking theoretically, fleeing into the world of ideas much as I fled into books as a child, distancing myself defensively from my need to belong to the group. However, I also know that everyone else in the group may be experiencing the same anxieties, whether I imagine them as arising out of earliest experiences of mothering or out of our shared human need for belonging. That knowledge gives me a powerful tool. I have found that being myself in a group and discovering that self to be acceptable to others is the way to a feeling of belonging in the group. I also know that being attentive to and respectful of others' contributions to the group discussion enhances the experience for all of us.

It's hard for an adult to know what an infant experiences or to say for certain where the difficult and fragmenting experiences we all have come from. Because we don't consciously remember our earliest experiences and infants can't tell us in mature ways what they experience, I wonder how much of the theory about infant psychology is grounded in real experience and how much is based in fantasies about infant experience, especially those fantasies based on our culture's dark assumptions about the mother-child relationship. The earliest group relations theorists operated without the information I described earlier that Stern and others had discovered as they observed infants in relationship with mothers. Because psychologists are rethinking fantasies about infant experience, perhaps it's time to rethink the early group relations theorists' ideas about what necessarily happens in shared group experiences.

Yes, group experiences can be unpleasant. That unpleasantness may originate with particular individuals in the group who behave in ways that I am suggesting arise out of the shared trauma of Western consciousness—or with the failure of the group's leadership to recognize that establishing an atmosphere of open, attentive respect is necessary to allow the group to be at its most creative. I always enter groups feeling vulnerable around my need for belonging, a need which may have been partially unmet in my earliest experiences of being mothered in the particular fashion that infants were mothered when I was an infant. I suspect my mother might have been influenced by child-rearing experts who insisted that hungry infants not be fed on demand if the demand is too frequent because they need to learn to wait, a view that was still prevalent when my son was born in the late '60s.

One weekend Tavistock group experience I attended a few years ago substantially modified the distant, enigmatic role of the consultant. The consultants were available and personally responsive, even though they commented on group behavior and remained apart from the group discussion. The group members were each given an opportunity to act as consultant for the group, allowing them to see the group experience from both sides. Even so, my experience of the group bound by the traditional limits of a Tavistock group was reminiscent of my earlier difficult experiences. I learned a lot about my own behavior in a group, even though it was years after I had finished my analysis and become an analyst. And, on the last day of the workshop, I experienced the shift in the group psychological energy that I have come to associate with a group becoming a community, a feeling of close connection, delight, and rapport, an experience of Eros.

In the paper published twenty years ago, I suggested that the practices of group relations theorists produced the dysfunctional group behavior that Bion and those following him assumed would always occur in a group. In my view, the distant, enigmatic behavior of traditional consultants to Tavistock groups and the lack of a designated leader for the group inevitably created what I thought of as the presence of the archetypal abandoning Bad Mother in the group unconscious, making the group feel threatening and inhospitable to its members and giving rise to off-task behaviors. The early Tavistock consultants were reliably producing the dysfunctional behavior their theory predisposed them to find, creating a self-fulfilling prophecy.

Some of the early group relations theorists assumed that needs for connection, nurturing, support, and a sense of belonging are childish. I quoted Margaret Rioch:

One of the major aims of the conferences is to contribute to people's ability to form serious work groups committed to the performance of clearly defined tasks. Whether or not members of such groups feel friendliness, warmth, closeness, competitiveness, or hostility to each other is of secondary importance. It is assumed that these and other feelings will occur from time to time, but that is not the issue.

On the contrary, I suggested, the feelings of the members in the group are precisely the issue. Rioch falls into the splitting consciousness of Marduk's world when she suggests that it is possible to separate the group's ability to accomplish a task from the group members' feelings of connection and rapport with the other people in the group. Sorenson describes a world in which members of a community performed all the tasks necessary for the group's physical survival in an ongoing condition of love and trust. There was no split between them.

I suggested that paying attention to the physical comfort of the participants and empowering them in a mutually respectful and collaborative way would enhance the possibility that creativity of the group would be released. In addition, my sense of the possibilities of group life went beyond the group relations theorists' hopes that the group could become a "serious work group." I suggested that under the right circumstances, a group could become a safe, creative community. I felt the assumptions in my paper were affirmed by my experience of the modified version of the traditional Tavistock group almost twenty years later.

Bion's powerful insight that the group exists, in unconscious imagination, as a psychic entity that can either be feared or joined might be taken one step further. The group is not just unconsciously *imagined* as one psychic entity; it *is* one psychic entity, the group-as-a-whole perspective the A.K. Rice Institute describes in the earlier quotation—a psychic entity which expresses its delights, challenges, and dilemmas through each of its members.

Each of us individually is a collective of the voices of those who have affected us during a lifetime, especially during childhood. I catch myself criticizing my grandson's haircut just as my grandmother might have or soothing a grandchild's misery in just the way that my mother did mine. I can be angry about something that can't be helped, just as my father sometimes was. Each of us is a sometimes fractious chorus of inner voices (yes, I want that, no, I don't; yes, I think that, no, I don't) and a group is just individual psyche on a larger scale. The process of taking a deep breath and holding conflicting inner perspectives, waiting for the small voice that is sometimes hard to hear, is critical to letting my creativity emerge. The process is no different in a group. The group, at its best, is more powerful and more creative than any one of the individuals in it.

COLLECTIVE WISDOM

There is a growing movement of organizational consultants and practitioners of a variety of disciplines writing about what happens in a group when it becomes a creative whole, more than the individual members making it up. Some of them describe the conditions which foster the emergence in the group of what they call "collective wisdom" or "collective intelligence." Collective wisdom is not a new idea. It underlies many of our theories about how democracies and markets work, as *The New Yorker* business columnist James Surowiecki describes in his book, *The Wisdom of Crowds*:

> Institutional structures such as democracies and markets rest substantially on the emergence of collective wisdom. Without a general tendency for groups of people to make reasonable appraisals and decisions, democracy would be doomed. The success of democracies, and for that matter markets, provides broad stroke support that at least some collective wisdom exists in the aggregate. Abundant anecdotal and small to large scale empirical examples also suggest the potential for a highly accurate collective forecast, a so called "wisdom of crowds."

Wikipedia has this to say about how the concept of collective wisdom has evolved:

> Thomas Jefferson referred to the concept of collective wisdom when he made his statement, "A Nation's best defense is an educated citizenry." And in effect, the ideal of a democracy is that government functions best when everyone participates. British philosopher Thomas Hobbes uses his *Leviathan* to illustrate how mankind's collective consciousness grows to create collective wisdom. Émile Durkheim argues in *The Elementary Forms of Religious Life*

(1912) that society by definition constitutes a higher intelligence because it transcends the individual over space and time, thereby achieving collective wisdom. 19th century Prussian physicist Gustav Fechner argued for a collective consciousness of mankind, and cited Durkheim as the most credible scholar in the field of "collective consciousness." Fechner also referred to the work of Jesuit Priest Pierre Teilhard de Chardin, whose concept of the noosphere was a precursor to the term collective intelligence. H.G. Wells's concept of "world brain," as described in his book of essays with the same title, has more recently been examined in depth by Pierre Lévy in his book, *The Universe-Machine: Creation, Cognition and Computer Culture.* Howard Bloom's treatise *The Global Brain: The Evolution of Mass Mind from the Big Bang to the 21st Century* examines similarities in organizational patterns in nature, human brain function, society, and the cosmos.

What seems new is a broader recognition that collective wisdom or collective intelligence is a powerful force that can be intentionally encouraged in a group. At the same time, the power released in a group is not always a force for good. Many discussions of collective intelligence seem to anticipate collective wisdom, not collective stupidity or worse. I have seen what happens when an angry group turns on its leader because the members feel abandoned or intruded upon. In two of those experiences, weekend retreats, leaders became ill during the night before the last scheduled group meeting, in both cases vomiting all night.

While intimations of the power of human collectivity began over a hundred years ago, it seems to me that a more widespread observation of both the creative potential and the apocalyptic implications of this phenomenon required a hundred more years of experience with mass communication, too often in the service of destruction and war rather than in the service of collective creativity. The most revolutionary development enabling the power of collective imagination has been the arrival of the internet.

In the fall of 2011, Clay Shirky, writer, teacher, and consultant on the social and economic effects of the internet, published *Here*

Comes Everybody: The Power of Organizing without Organizations.
He describes the transformative, paradigm-shifting moment of
human history in which we now live. Reading his book, I understood that the internet is more than an amazing communications
tool; it has made collective collaboration possible with amazing
speed and on a scale never before imagined. As Shirky notes:

> When we change the way we communicate, we change society. The
> tools that a society uses to create and maintain itself are as central
> to human life as a hive is to bee life. Though the hive is not part
> of any individual bee, it is part of the colony, both shaped by and
> shaping the lives of its inhabitants. The hive is a social device,
> a piece of bee information technology that provides a platform,
> literally, for the communication and coordination that keeps the
> colony viable. *Individual bees can't be understood separately from
> the colony or from their shared, co-created environment.* So it is
> with human networks; bees make hives, we make mobile phones.
> *[Emphasis added.]*

I participate in the internet and the internet shapes me. I can't
be understood separately from my shared, cocreated environment. When I step back from the technology that fills my life (my
computer, laptop, smartphone, and tablet) and think about my astonishing ability to have instantaneous communication with others in my life and the inexhaustible supply of information available
from all over the world, I realize that the predictions of an evolv-
ing "noosphere" by followers of Pierre Teilhard de Chardin, which
seemed so improbable to me only a couple of decades ago, have
come true. In just my lifetime.

Shirky argues that the evolution of human organizations and institutions into top-down hierarchical organizations was necessary
to manage human collaboration and production at an increasing
scale, all made possible by revolutionary communications technologies, starting with the printing press. The internet has radically changed everything, again, turning everyone who has access
to the internet through a computer, smartphone, or tablet into a
node in a global network of information exchange.

When email first became a mass communication tool, it made the traditional paths of communication faster, penetrating more deeply into my everyday life. Now, I am starting to see how the internet has also, more radically, made the evolutionary next steps in human organization both possible and inevitable.

The revolutionary potential of mass communication technology as it is experienced, apart from the content it contains, was first envisioned in the 1960s by Marshall McLuhan, who famously said that "The medium is the message." Somewhat less famously, he also said, "We shape our tools, and thereafter our tools shape us." How the internet has shaped us and our organizations is succinctly described by Shirky:

> For most of modern life, our strong talents and desires for group effort have been filtered through relatively rigid institutional structures because of the complexity of managing groups. . . . The old limits of what unmanaged and unpaid groups can do are no longer in operation; the difficulties that kept self-assembled groups from working together are shrinking, meaning that the number and kinds of things groups can get done without financial motivation or managerial oversight are growing. The current change, in one sentence, is this: *most of the barriers to group action have collapsed and without those barriers, we are free to explore new ways of gathering together and getting things done. [Emphasis added.]*

The history of technology teaches me one very important, if sobering, lesson. Technology is value-neutral, but human beings are not. The internet made possible the almost instantaneous organization by a group calling itself "Occupy Sandy" to assist many of those whose lives were devastated by Hurricane Sandy. The internet has also enabled the spread of international jihad and terrorism. These two arenas of shared human activity, collective compassion and collective violence, have been, until now, the monopoly of governmental, religious, and corporate institutions. Now I watch governments and other human institutions become increasingly helpless to manage the chaotic changes in our shared human and natural surroundings, many of which humans, intentionally or unintentionally, have brought about. For good or ill, humans now have a great deal more information a great deal faster about events in a shared world, along with an ability to participate in those events.

What human don't have is control. Shirky describes this loss of control and what he sees as the principle challenge of these technologies:

> We are being pushed rapidly down a route largely determined by the technological environment. We have a small degree of control over the spread of these tools, but that control does not extend to our being able to reverse, stop or even radically alter the direction we're moving in. Our [principal] challenge is not to decide where we want to go but rather to stay upright as we go there.

Shirky's thought about the challenge of staying upright as we travel toward a future over which we have no control reminds me of Leroy Little Bear's ideas about "surfing the flux." Shirky's book was published only ten days after the original Occupy Wall Street movement began in the heart of the financial district in New York City on September 17, 2011, almost exactly ten years after the attacks on September 11 devastated the Twin Towers and those streets. There has been a great deal of analysis and commentary about the beginning of OWS, as it came to be known, but many, including some of the protestors themselves, don't seem to have a new framework with which to understand how things in our world have so radically changed.

Much of the mainstream media declared Occupy Wall Street to be a failure. The mainstream media is imagining in the old, pre-internet terms about a movement. In the pre-internet world, a movement needed visible leaders and recognizable goals. It would have ongoing life, perhaps become institutionalized. But the lesson of Shirky's book is that we are now in a radically different world, and social change movements won't look the way they have traditionally looked. Now movements can be born when a sufficient number of people feel that it is time, and will be embodied in the ways that make the most sense to the organizers and the people in the movement, and will fade away when the time for that particular organized expression is over.

What makes a movement now is the collective creative energy of the times, as it is expressed by those who open to it and move with it. When the collective energy moves somewhere else, so do they. Increasingly, human institutions no longer mediate between movements of creative energy and the ordinary people of the world.

Whatever OWS was, it wasn't a failure. The demonstrations in the very heart of the global financial system catalyzed a world-wide discussion about income inequality. The phrases "the 99 percent" and "the 1 percent" instantly became rallying cries for those of us around the world who agreed with the protestors that twenty-first-century institutions and structures imperil democracy and the future of all of the species with which we share the planet.

Were the protestors "communists," "socialists," or "anarchists"? Those who resist changing the way things are put labels on the pro-testors, refusing to let them define their own reality. Sometimes the protestors put those labels on themselves. However, the on-going, moving energy that became the OWS movement in the fall of 2011 is defining itself by resisting all efforts to put it into boxes. Each protestor on the streets of the most powerful financial dis-trict in the world and each energetic offshoot of that paradigm-shifting event that OWS became defines what it means to them. OWS became an inspiration for countless others who have fol-lowed its example and are organizing to make significant changes in their communities, all over my country, and in the world.

As wrong as they were about what OWS was, the mainstream media may unintentionally have made a huge contribution to its impact when it covered OWS so extensively in its early days. Eventually, commentators in the mainstream media seemed to have realized what they had done and largely stopped covering the protests. Perhaps they just lost interest. But the progressive media continued covering OWS and its offshoots. Those who wish to participate in the on-the-ground organizing that has happened since OWS arose and manifested on the streets of New York City have access to ample information about what others are doing to bring about radical change from nontraditional media sources. Progressive websites and their email newsletters, Twitter, and Facebook are just a few of the most notable ways in which reporting and dialogue continue. The mainstream media no longer controls the public discourse.

Is there still an Occupy movement? At this point, I find it difficult to catalog the varieties of actions which have sprung up, some under the Occupy banner, some not. Many of these actions have little or no connection to the original protestors. The Occupy movement is not a movement in the ways I have been accustomed to thinking about movements, but it is still a movement, a tectonic shift in how the ordinary people of the world understand opportunities for organizing to create social, economic, and political change. As Shirky says in the paragraph I quoted above:

> The current change, in one sentence, is this: most of the barriers to group action have collapsed and without those barriers, we are free to explore new ways of gathering together and getting things done.

Where OWS is concerned, the medium is the message. How OWS arose, radically changed our collective conversations, persisted, and disappeared when its time was over is the message. Two years after the OWS movement began, Amy Goodman and Juan González of *Democracy Now!* interviewed Nathan Schneider, editor of the website Waging Nonviolence, author of *Thank You, Anarchy: Notes from the Occupy Apocalypse*, and one of a number of OWS organizers. I find it synchronistic that the word "apocalypse" surfaces in his book title. Schneider's book begins:

> For nearly two months in the fall of 2011, a square block of granite and honey locust trees in New York's Financial District, right between Wall Street and the World Trade Center, became a canvas for the image of another world.

Why did he choose to call OWS the "Occupy Apocalypse"?

It's a question I get a lot. The word in Greek meant "unveiling," right? It described a moment in which—in which something is revealed that changes our perception of everything. And I think that pretty accurately describes what happened with Occupy Wall Street, both for us as a society, in revealing the depth of income inequality, of the corruption of the political system, and also of the power of the militarized police state, but also for so many individuals who took part across the country. I have been privileged to meet so many people and to watch them as their lives were changed by this movement, as they became activated and haven't been able to go back to the way their lives were before.

Schneider was then asked to describe how he saw the "canvas for the image of another world" and he responded with two images of the reaction to OWS, the reaction in the heart of the financial system where the first OWS demonstration took place and the reaction among those inspired by the OWS demonstrations:

Well, to talk about that canvas itself, it's interesting to see the ways in which the movement is memorialized, kind of informally, in the Financial District. There's still a wall of barricades around the charging bull statue. There are still regularly barricades in Zuccotti Park. There are still barricades around Chase Manhattan Plaza, which was the original planned kind of decoy site for the occupation. It's amazing how the security state is still living in fear of this movement.

But at the same time, activists who were involved in it, many of them are spread out across the country in all kinds of networks that have formed through the course of this movement, putting their bodies in the way of the Keystone pipeline, calling attention to issues like a financial transaction tax, bringing housing activists together around the country to create a stronger movement. There are a number of campaigns that have been profoundly strengthened by networks formed in the Occupy movement.

It seems to me that those who resist change will be condemned by a profound failure of imagination and understanding to continue to fight the last war. They may have most of the financial resources of this country, even the world, on their side, but I believe they will lose. They may have bought and paid for all three branches of our national government, but I believe they will lose. Sooner or later, no matter how long or how destructively they wage war against the rest of us for the survival of their monopolistic power, they will lose. They will lose because they and their institutions no longer embody the ongoing, ever-moving energy of the world. They will use every resource and institution at their disposal to try to stop the rest of us from changing the way things are, but the creative energy of the world is moving on. The little furry mammals are eating the dinosaurs' eggs.

CREATIVITY IN GROUPS

Even if what arises in groups, communities, and societies is not always wise, I look to the writings of collective-wisdom theorists for ideas about how to foster group creativity rather than group destruction. In their writings, I recognize experiences I have had and that others have described. The descriptions of what can happen in a group at its best are remarkably similar. Only recently did I connect what Sorenson described as the relationship among the members of preconquest communities to the transcendent experiences people sometimes have in groups. I think of that transcendent experience as an experience of community.

I wonder if group experiences can help group members recognize and welcome something of their long-buried preconquest consciousness. Perhaps groups are a place where group members can learn how to hold two forms of consciousness simultaneously, the sense that each of us is both a separate self and a self-in-the-group. In groups, if I am attentive to my experience, I experience myself and the group at all times. Sometimes I focus on my separate self and sometimes on the group, seeing what is happening "inside" and what is happening "outside" in the group as always related, moving in and out of both forms of consciousness.

As Jungian analysts, my colleagues and I work with a similar dual focus on "inside" and "outside" in ourselves when we work in the analytic field created by the two individuals in it, as I described earlier in my experience with one of my first analytic patients. What analysts haven't often done is apply that understanding to life in groups. Such an integrative consciousness may be precisely what is being asked by these times. Marduk's separating consciousness says that group members think only with their minds and feel only with their hearts. A different understanding might allow group members to think with their hearts and feel with their minds.

It seems that those exploring experiences of collective wisdom often struggle as I do to find language for what happens in groups when they are at their finest. Even in the midst of a chaotic group process, there are times when something else enters the room, which suddenly becomes spacious. People breathe freely again. Their hearts open up. A feeling comes into the space that is hard to put into language. Suddenly, something much larger than the assembled group is present. A fractured and fragmenting collection of colliding egos becomes a deeply felt unity of everybody present and, paradoxically, a room full of unique separate selves. I feel, at those moments, that the group most needs me and everyone in it to be authentically and completely themselves and to speak the truth of our hearts into a space in which it is completely safe to do so.

Christopher Bache, professor of religious studies and consciousness researcher, describes his experience:

> Sometimes when I am simply doing my job covering the day's assignment, it's as if the floor suddenly falls away. The atmosphere in the room becomes supercharged, and everyone seems to congeal into a superunified state. My mind becomes unusually spacious and clear, and my students' eyes tell me that they have moved into a particularly receptive state. Our hearts seem to merge, and from this open field of compassion comes a slow stream of thoughts that I, as spokesperson for the group, unfold and work with.
>
> In these transient moments of heightened awareness, I sometimes have the acute sensation that there is only one mind present in the room. It is as if the walls that usually separate us have become gossamer curtains. Individual persons melt into a softly glowing field of energy, and this unified energy *thinks* and *feels* and hungers to speak. *[Emphasis in original.]*

I have come to believe, as Bache does, that however we talk about this "one mind" experience, it is always trying to happen in groups, although it rarely happens as powerfully as Bache describes here.

As the Latin phrase over Jung's door in Kusnacht says: *Vocatus atque non vocatus Deus aderit.* Whether we call them or not, the Gods will be present. This experience could be called community or collective wisdom or collective intelligence. When it enters the group, its members have a simultaneous experience of Eros, of love, and can move into spontaneous group creativity, finding imaginative ways to talk and think about the topic at hand, sharing half-formed thoughts and seemingly irrelevant images, and playing with them, all with a sense of communal delight and safety.

In the language of the Orphic creation myth, Eros hatches from the silvery egg in the womb of Darkness and sets the Universe in motion.

Certain phrases in Sorenson's paper leapt out at me when I re-read it as part of thinking about the potential for the emergence of collective wisdom in a group: his description of infant- and child-nurturing practices that spawn an intuitive group rapport and unite people without need for formal rules, the idea that the outstanding psychological condition of those communities is a heartfelt rapprochement based on integrated trust, and the core condition of an unabashed, open honesty. His description of pre-conquest communities as "simultaneously individualistic and collective" is a perfect description of my experience when something almost beyond language enters the room.

I am not suggesting that those experiences and what Sorenson describes are the same; I have no way of knowing. There is no Eden to which we in Western consciousness can return. But something presses on collective Western consciousness, insisting on admission. If we are not to require ongoing devastating personal and collective events to shatter us into transformation, the one-sided identification with the separate, isolated self needs to be reimagined. Sorenson's work provides rich material with which to begin that reimagining.

I don't want to suggest that groups can't fall hard into "collective stupidity," the bewildering and disorganizing chaos experienced as group members hurl opinions and judgments at each other. Still, experiences of collective stupidity can be as transformative as experiences of collective wisdom. At those times, powerful and bewildering feelings assault my sense of integrity as an individual self, separate from the group. Difficult experiences in groups send the same message that transcendent moments in groups send: I am never truly separate from others in a group.

Of course I can *feel* alone or separate in a group. But when I feel separate and alone in a group, I can understand that to be information about the group. Perhaps that feeling tells me that something that needs to be made conscious and worked through is preventing the group from coming together; perhaps others in the group are also feeling separate and alone. Perhaps I feel separate from the group because I am hesitant to say what I need to say about my experience of what's going on. The only way I know to feel more connected and present is to speak up honestly in a nonjudgmental way about my experience. Maybe it is only my experience. But the act of being present to and honest about my experience is an act of commitment to our shared life as a group.

When I realize that there is something I am compelled to say in a group that hasn't yet cohered as a community, I experience a kind of anxiety that I don't experience when I have only vague thoughts about what I could possibly say. That anxiety tells me that I need to speak up, but it also makes speaking up feel dangerous because I risk being rejected by the group. The larger the group, the more dangerous it feels. However, somebody, me or someone else, has to take a personal risk and honestly put something into the group, something it might reject, in order for it to begin to shift beyond being a collection of individuals worried about how they appear in the group and whether or not they belong.

I want to emphasize Sorenson's insight that coercion was not only completely absent from preconquest communities but also threatening to their continued existence. I experience coercion to be a fundamental quality of Western consciousness. Just as I try to argue my verbal opponents into oblivion when I am part of a group in a state of collective stupidity, so does my inner postconquest oppressor seek to intimidate me into rejecting all forms of thought, feeling, and awareness that do not conform to my culturally determined, idealized picture of myself. When a group is in a state of collective stupidity, group members often try to coerce other group members into seeing things their way. A group cannot be coerced into becoming a community.

In my experience, a split in the group that is the subject of a particular disagreement may be a proxy for a much deeper, though related, issue that needs to be worked with consciously. To understand the issue, I can only look for clues, for subtle, easy-to-miss hints. I can listen to marginalized and rejected voices speaking from the fringes of the group. I can notice what upsets me and arouses my defensiveness and judgment. I can listen to my visions and dreams.

That small, soft voice in my head, easy to override or dismiss, the casual thought passed over quickly by another group member or the whole group, the difficult member who challenges the certainties of the group and the lone quiet voice in the back of the room . . . these are the voices I most need to hear. And beyond listening for these voices, there is the hardest part, the part that goes beyond theory, beyond understanding, beyond everything I know and believe. That is the part where I admit defeat. I not only think it, I feel it. Then all my self-righteousness can give way to a deep and heartfelt humility, as I acknowledge the limits of my power, my brokenness and frailty, and the inevitability of error. It often takes enormous courage for somebody in the group to be the first to stand up and admit defeat or to say, from a vulnerable and open heart, the thing that the group most needs to hear. But the moment when the group falls into a humble, open place is sometimes the moment when something transcendent enters the room.

DREAMING ANOTHER WORLD

What do I imagine our twenty-first-century collective dream is telling us about the dreamer? I believe these events speak, first, to our culture's unconsciousness of the interrelationship and interconnection of everything on earth, indeed in the cosmos. I believe Sorenson is describing communities in which a profound experience of interconnection is woven into the fabric of an individual and community way of being. Even with Sorenson's precise and detailed descriptions of the communities in which he lived and worked, I have difficulty imagining what it might have felt like to live in those communities. Still, there have been times in groups when I have a momentary sense of what such a powerful sense of interconnection might have been like, when a sense of community emerges and I and everybody else in the room belong to something larger than any of us, larger even than the group assembled at that moment.

I imagine the apocalyptic events of our new century are speaking not just to the isolation and loneliness so pervasive in Euro-American society but also to the grandiosity of so much of our shared cultural understanding of who we are. Jungian analyst and author Jerome Bernstein says that because so many of us in Western culture cannot reign in our sense of omnipotence, we remain in danger of species extinction. That dangerously inflated collective sense of who we are in the world built the great towers that came crashing down on September 11, 2001. That dangerously inflated collective sense of who we are in the world failed to imagine that those architectural monuments to our outsized fantasies of American power could be attacked by airplanes and collapse in a terrifyingly short period of time, or that an apparently sturdy bridge in the heart of a major American city could fall down.

Percy Bysshe Shelley may have been imagining how history will remember us in his poem "Ozymandias," describing the writing on the pedestal of an enormous broken statue in a desert:

"My name is Ozymandias, king of kings:
Look on my works, ye Mighty, and despair!"
Nothing beside remains. Round the decay
Of that colossal wreck, boundless and bare
The lone and level sands stretch far away.

From that perspective, building the Twin Towers was no accident, nor was targeting them and bringing them down; these acts were psychologically inevitable, highly symbolic acts of humans who arrogated the power and righteousness of the Gods. The events of September 11, 2001, and of August 1, 2007, were human tragedy on archetypal scale, apocalyptic challenges to a dangerously inflated collective consciousness.

My experiences and those of writers exploring collective wisdom strongly suggest that dropping my defenses and embracing my vulnerability is paradoxically both a precondition for and the result of a collective experience of the wisdom of the group. In that sense, the September 11 catastrophe was an invitation to hold the almost unbearable feeling of vulnerability so many experienced, along with a deep and sorrowful connection to the traumatized New Yorkers, to the families of those who perished that day, and to a shocked and saddened world. It was a transcendent moment as those events plunged the global community into heartfelt empathy and a desire to support and assist those most stricken by the tragedy, a global irruption of Eros, of community, of love. It was tragic, but not surprising, that our government chose not to embrace that moment of Eros arising out of vulnerability and defeat as a collective experience of the creative energy of the universe but, instead, moved immediately into self-righteousness, victimhood, and aggression.

At that terrible moment, our nation had a president who could not face his own feelings of vulnerability, perhaps because they touched a deeply wounded place in him. On YouTube, I find a video of his blank reaction to the news of the attack on the Twin Towers as a group of schoolchildren read aloud, sitting in stunned silence for unbelievable minutes, unable to get up and leave the room. I cannot imagine how vulnerable and inadequate any leader of our nation might have felt at that moment. George W. Bush was the leader the nation had chosen for that moment in our collective lives, perfectly suited to rescue the nation from feelings of helplessness after an unimaginable assault, leading the US into two tragically unnecessary wars that allowed the nation to swagger defensively and throw around its military might.

Fears of collective vulnerability and the limits of human power persist. Instead of embracing those fears consciously, many engage in denial and repress their feelings in favor of fantasies of world-striding power, pushing their fears into their, and our, cultural unconscious, from which they inevitably return as the images of devastating technological and climate-induced collapse which appear in events, fantasies, stories, and movies involving the End of the World, our collective dreaming.

I believe the collapse of the I-35W bridge was a message to all of us about the essential interconnection of everyone and everything and about the way that the grief and vulnerability many of us felt in the wake of that tragic event opened us to an experience of community. It seems to me it would be better to go willingly to a humble understanding of human limits and vulnerability than to go on experiencing tragic apocalyptic events. I have told my story of where we are and where we have been to illuminate how a dangerously inflated Euro-American consciousness, operating from Marduk's arrogant splitting and disconnected perspective, may be creating a world that requires apocalyptic events to shock it into awakening.

If I can go consciously to a place of fear and vulnerability, on the other side of that fear will be a gift. The events I describe at the beginning of this book, and more that have happened since I first began to write it, have left many identified with Euro-American consciousness feeling vulnerable and afraid. Many of the people in the rest of the world know that vulnerability is an inescapable part of being human and go about their lives. Accepting that humans will always be vulnerable and embracing that understanding is a good place from which to dream the world that could be coming into being; the first step in moving toward an understanding that we are all in this together, that nobody knows what to do, and that each of us carries a vital and indispensable piece of what we need as a whole.

I will end by wondering if we, as individuals, might be having dreams and visions that belong to all of us in Western consciousness as much as they belong to us individually. Perhaps each of us has an obligation to bring those visions to the community, just as dreams and visions are brought into traditional indigenous communities for shared healing. In that spirit, I offer a vision from my own experience, a vision I experienced on the "vision quest" I mentioned earlier.

As I said then, I am uncomfortable now, remembering the way we all, leaders and participants alike, so easily appropriated the idea of that particular indigenous ceremony. Still, I wonder at the power of my experience of a Euro-American version of the ceremony of "crying for a vision," the English translation of the Lakota word *hanbleciye.*

I came to the experience in a state of unusual vulnerability. I had hit a wall in my analytic training and was facing the possibility that at the very end of a long process I would not graduate, the loss of a cherished dream. All of my usual strategies had failed, and I was up against the limits of my power and understanding. I felt helpless, powerless, and alone. Just as someone in a traditional indigenous community might, I was "crying for a vision."

In many ways, the entire experience was a vision. In a state of exceptional permeability, I often experienced a remarkable sense of interconnection with the beautiful, more-than-human surround and its creaturely inhabitants, who seemed as responsive and aware of me as I was of them, feeling at those moments that we were all moving together in a great dance of life. That experience came and went over several days. At the end of our time together, we were to go into the woods and spend thirty-six hours alone with no food or water.

Three of us silently paddled a canoe along the lakeshore, looking for a place to land. We followed a great blue heron which flew just ahead of us, waiting on the shore for us to catch up and then flying a little farther away. Eventually it flew off, and we landed the canoe as close as we could to the spot where the heron had last landed, moving off separately to choose our own places to wait. Near the end of my solitary hours in the woods, I was given a vision. Here it is, much as I wrote about it shortly after the event.

> Well after midnight of the second night I woke up. The almost-full moon had risen to a spot directly above my head. I was curled in my sleeping bag, on a carpet of needles and moss, between the boney roots of two tall pines, against the bottom of the small cliff which had supported my back during the daylight hours, inside a small circle of sticks where I had lived for almost two days. Suddenly, I realized that I was being lovingly watched: by the night sky, the stars, the dark shapes of trees . . . the moon. As I lay there, I was overwhelmed by a feeling that I was a tiny and helpless baby, yet utterly safe, utterly loved, held in the arms of the Mother. I relaxed into the limp body of the trusting infant and drifted back to sleep. A few hours later, the tender light above the trees directly across the lake to the East woke me up.

I have thought and written about that experience several times since it occurred so many years ago. That it returned as I wrote the paper which eventually became part of this chapter suggested that I look at it again. In a state of helplessness and vulnerability, of exceptional permeability, I fell into a visionary experience of absolute and unconditional trust and love. I believe that capacity for unconditional trust and love is the birthright of a child raised in a preconquest community. My visionary experience suggests to me that our inheritance of preconquest awareness is not lost forever, only forgotten. I believe it is still available to us if we can learn how to let down our defenses against the more-than-human surroundings and the groups and communities in which we are always immersed.

Something *is* ending, but it is not the End of the World. It is the end of one dream of the world and the beginning of another. We who live in these times have an opportunity to begin to shape the emergence of a very different world, a world that our children and grandchildren will also play a part in creating. The collective existential threats I have described, and more that I can hardly imagine, are and will be terrifying. Facing them together, at the limits of human power, may offer experiences of profound interconnection and interdependence, a renewed sense of community and hope. As Rebecca Solnit says in her book, *A Paradise Built in Hell: The Extraordinary Communities that Arise in Disaster*:

> Horrible in itself, disaster is sometimes a door back into paradise, the paradise . . . in which we are who we hope to be, do the work we desire, and are each our sister's and brother's keeper.

I imagine that in writing this book I am responding to something in the human and more-than-human collective that calls on each of us to be a part of what is emerging in these times. Not only does opening to my own creative energy allow me to make my unique contribution to a collective dream of another world, but also, I see increasing signs that we are dreaming an emerging world together.

I watched, with interest, the founding of the World Social Forum, an annual meeting of civil society organizations from around the world, beginning in 2001 in Brazil. "Another World is Possible" was chosen to be the slogan of the Forum at the first meeting, and that idea is reflected in the writings of many of those who are wondering where we are and where we might go as a global society. I drew on it when I was thinking about a title for this book. As I roam the internet, I bookmark articles and opinion pieces which, to me, embody a growing understanding of emerging possibility, just as I printed out articles from the *Minneapolis Star Tribune* after the collapse of the I-35w bridge.

International activist and writer Arundhati Roy said recently: "Another world is not only possible; she is on her way. On a quiet day I can hear her breathing." When I read Roy's statement, when I think about the many, many communities of activists working to create a just and sustainable world, solving challenging problems unique to the land and communities where they live, I hear "her" breathing, too. I hope there are moments in this book, my response to the demands of the always-moving energy of my own life, that encourage you to listen to the demands of the always-moving energy in your life, as the peoples of the earth wake up from a five-thousand-year-old dream and come together to dream another world.

ACKNOWLEDGMENTS

This book has been in process for twenty-five years, ever since I started thinking about the thesis required for graduation from my Jungian analytic training program. Over time, I have received valuable editorial input from the editors of the journals which published parts of it as it evolved from those early years. Most recently, the sage advice of Mary Logue and the book producers at Wise Ink Publishing, especially Patrick Maloney and Graham Warnken, have shaped an ungainly manuscript into the form you hold in your hands. And countless friends, colleagues and family members have given me their feedback. If it takes a village to raise a child, then it takes a community to write a book and I am eternally grateful for mine.

BIBLIOGRAPHY

David Abram. (1997) *The Spell of the Sensuous: Perception and Language in a More-Than-Human World.* Viking Books. New York City, NY

Adyashanti (Steven Gray). (2013) *The Way of Liberation: A Practical Guide to Spiritual Enlightenment.* Open Gate Sangha. Campbell, CA.

Jeanette Armstrong. (1995) *"Keepers of the Earth" in Ecopsychology: Restoring the Earth, Healing the Mind.* Theodore Roszak, Mary E. Gomes and Allen D Kanner, editors. Sierra Club Books. San Francisco, CA.

Christopher Bache. (2010) *Dark Night, Early Dawn: Steps to a Deep Ecology of Mind.* State University of New York Press. Albany, NY.

Ignacio Martín-Baró. (1996) *Writings For a Liberation Psychology.* Adrianne Aron, Shawn Corne, editors. Harvard University Press. Cambridge, MA.

Jerome Bernstein. (2005) *Living in the Borderland: The evolution of consciousness and the challenge of healing trauma.* Routledge. London.

Wilfred R. Bion. *Experiences in Groups.* (1991) Tavistock/Routledge. London and New York.

Yves Bonnefoy and Wendy Doniger, translators. (1991) *Mythologies, Vol. One.* Chicago, IL & London. University of Chicago Press.

Bronson, Matthew. "Lessons in the Old Language." Global Oneness Project. (website accessed 2018) San Francisco, CA.

Joseph Bruhac. (1991) *Native American Stories (Myths and Legends)*. Fulcrum Publishing. Golden, CO

Joseph Bruhac. (1996) *Roots of Survival: Native American Storytelling and the Sacred.* Fulcrum Publishing. Golden, CO.

Edward Edinger. (2002) *Archetype of the Apocalypse: Divine Vengeance, Terrorism, and the End of the World.* Open Court Publishing. Chicago, IL

Thomas Stearns Eliot. (1952) *The Complete Poems and Plays: 1909 – 1950.* Harcourt Brace. New York City, NY.

Betty Friedan. (1964) *The Feminine Mystique.* Dell Publishing. New York City, NY.

Tad Friend. (2010) *Cheerful Money: Me, My Family, and the Last Days of Wasp Splendor.* Back Bay Books. Little, Brown and Company. New York City, NY.

Robert Graves. (1955) *The Greek Myths, Vol. On.* Penguin Books, Inc. Baltimore, MD.

Carl Gustav Jung. (1959) Introduction to Toni Wolff's studies in Jungian psychology. *The Collected Works of C. G. Jung, Volume 10.* Princeton University Press. Princeton, NJ.

Carl G. Jung. (1971) *Man and his symbols.* Knopf Doubleday Publishing Group. New York City, NY. 5th printing.

Catherine Keller. (1986) *From a Broken Web: Separation, Sexism and Self.* Beacon Press. Boston, MA.

Kimmerer, Robin W. (2015) *Braiding Sweetgrass: Indigenous Wisdom, Scientific Knowledge and the Teachings of Plants.* Milkweed Editions. Minneapolis, MN.

Leroy Little Bear. Preface to David Bohm. (1996) *On creativity.* London & New York City. Routledge

Charles Long. (1963) *Alpha: The Myths of Creation.* Scholars Press. Atlanta, GA.

Michael Meade. (2008) *The World Behind the World: Living at the Ends of Time.* Green Fire Press. Seattle: WA.

Jean Baker Miller. (1976) *Toward a New Psychology of Women.* Beacon Press. Boston, MA.

Lao-Tzu and Stephen Mitchell trans. (1988) *Tao Te ching: A New English Version with Foreword and Notes by Stephen Mitchell.* Harper and Row. New York City, NY.

Medora Scoll Perlman. (1992) "Toward a theory of the Self in the group" in Murray Stein and John Hollwitz eds., *Psyche at Work: Workplace Applications of Jungian Analytical Psychology.* Chiron Publications. Wilmette, IL.

Nathan Schneider. (2013) *Thank You, Anarchy: Notes From the Occupy Apocalypse.* University of California Press. Oakland, CA.

Clay Shirky. (2009) *Here Comes Everybody: The Power of Organizing Without Organizations.* Penguin Books. New York City, NY.

Rebecca Solnit. (2009) *A Paradise Built in Hell: The Extraordinary Communities that Arise in Disaster.* Viking Press. New York City, NY.

Malidoma Patrice Somé. (1995) *Of Water and the Spirit: Ritual, Magic and Initiation in the Life of an African Shaman.* Arkana: A literary journal of mysteries and marginalized voices. New York City, NY.

Gary Snyder. (1974) *Turtle Island.* New York City, New York. New Directions Publishing Corporation.

E. Richard Sorenson. (1998) "Preconquest Consciousness", in *Tribal Epistemologies: Essays in the Philosophy of Anthropology.* Helmut Wautischer, ed. Ashgate. Brookfield VT., England.

Daniel N. Stern. (1985) *The Interpersonal World Of The Infant: A View from Psychoanalysis and Developmental Psychology.* Basic Books. New York City, NY.

James Surowiecki. (2005) *The Wisdom of Crowds.* Anchor Books. New York City, NY.

Mary Watkins and Helene Schulman. (2010) *Toward Psychologies of Liberation: Critical Theory and Practice in Psychology and the Human Sciences.* Palgrave McMillan. New York City, NY.